CELTIC GODDESSES

Warriors, Virgins and Mothers

Bronze model cult wagon from Strettweg, Austria, with central goddess figure holding up a large vessel. Seventh century BC.

CELTIC GODDESSES

Warriors, Virgins and Mothers

Miranda Green

British Museum Press

To my Mother
(*amoris causa*)

© 1995 Miranda Green

Published by British Museum Press
A division of The British Museum Company
Ltd
46 Bloomsbury Street, London WC1B 3QQ

A catalogue record for this book is available
from the British Library

Miranda Green has asserted her right to be
identified as the author of this work

ISBN 0 7141 2303

Designed by James Shurmer

Typeset by Create

Printed in Great Britain by Bath Press, Avon

Half title: Bronze figurine of the goddess
Sequana, spirit of the River Seine at its
source; first century AD. From the healing
spring of Fontes Sequanae near Dijon,
France.

Contents

Acknowledgements

I wish to thank the many individuals and institutions who
have helped me with this book. I am very grateful to the staff
of British Museum Press, particularly Carolyn Jones and
Teresa Francis, for all their skilful editorial work, and to
Charlotte Lippmann for picture research. Thanks are due to Dr
Alan Lane for his advice and to Drs Ray Howell and Tony Saul
for their support. I should like to express my gratitude to all
the museums who have supplied pictures; and to Walter
Brenneman, Jenny Brown, Roy Fry, Tristan Gray Hulse and
Paul Jenkins for their contributions to the illustrations. Finally
I am especially indebted to Stephen, Elisabeth, Antigone and
Oedipus for all their loving support.

Miranda Aldhouse Green
May 1995

Illustration acknowledgements

Miranda Aldhouse-Green 17, 25, 39, 48, 72, 92, 122, 126, 134;
Bath Museums Service 96, 97, 133; Courtesy of Bord Failte,
the Irish Tourist Board, Dublin 78, 83; Walter Brenneman
201; Jenny Brown 191; Cambridgeshire County Council,
photo Alison Taylor 113; Cardiff City Council 21;
Corinium Museum, Cirencester, photo C J Bowler, 37; County
Museum of Schleswig Holstein, Schloss Gottorp, Germany
159; Dijon, Musée d'Archeologique *half title*; Dorset County
Museum 181; English Heritage/Hadrian's Wall Museums 183,
Christopher Hill Photographic *front jacket* (*main picture*);
Tristan Gray Hulse 192, 193, 195; Paul Jenkins
(© Miranda Aldhouse-Green) 35 (below), 49, 61, 103, 163,
166, 174; Cliché La Cour d'Or, Musées de Metz 23, 129;
Photo Musée d'Alésia, Société des Sciences de Semur-en-
Auxois *front jacket, inset*; Cliché Musée Archéologique de
Châtillon-sur-Seine, photos Christian Labeaune 18, 81;
Musée Archéologique, Dijon 107; Musée de Bretagne,
Rennes, photos Jean-Claude Houssin 34, 35 (top);
Musée Archéologique, Clermont-Ferrand 16; Museum of
Antiquities, the University, Newcastle 100; Museum of
London, 86, 112; Betty Naggar (© Miranda Aldhouse-Green)
42, 59, 137; The National Museum, Copenhagen 89, 158, 164;
National Museums and Galleries of Wales 173; The National
Trust Photographic Library 75; Newport Museum and Art
Gallery, 65; Northern Ireland Tourist Board 76;
Reading Museum and Art Gallery, Silchester Collection 141;
Graham Reed 8; Rijksmuseum van Oudheden 177;
Spectrum Colour Library, 12; Steiermarkisches
Landesmuseum Joanneum, Graz, Abt. Bild-und Tonarchiv
frontispiece, 163, *back jacket*; Trustees of the British Museum
19, 152, 168, 184; The Trustees of the National Museums of
Scotland 197; University of Newcastle upon Tyne 144; Wales
Tourist Board 54

'I met a lady in the meads
Full beautiful – a faery's child
Her hair was long, her foot was light
And her eyes were wild.

I made a garland for her head,
And bracelets too, and fragrant zone;
She look'd at me as she did love,
And made sweet moan.

I set her on my pacing steed,
And nothing else saw all day long,
For sidelong would she bend and sing
A faery's song.

She found me roots of relish sweet,
And honey wild and manna dew,
And sure in language strange she said
I love thee true.

She took me to her elfin grot,
And there she wept and sigh'd full sore;
And there I shut her wild, wild eyes
With kisses four.

And there she lullèd me to sleep,
And there I dream'd – ah! woe betide!
The latest dream I ever dream'd
On the cold hill's side.

I saw pale kings and princes too,
Pale warriors, death-pale were they all:
Who cried – "La Belle Dame sans Merci
Hath thee in thrall!"'

(from *La Belle Dame Sans Merci*, John Keats)

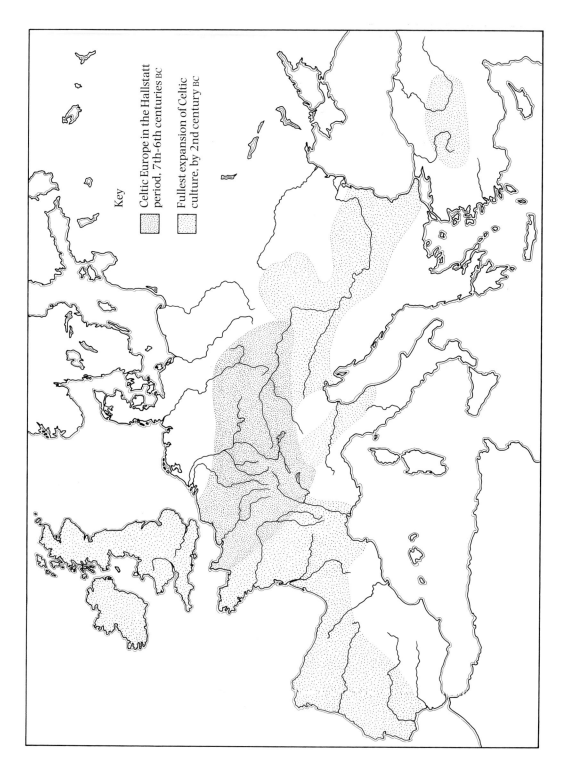

Key

Celtic Europe in the Hallstatt
period, 7th-6th centuries BC

Fullest expansion of Celtic
culture, by 2nd century BC

Prologue

A striking characteristic of Celtic religion – as presented both in archaeological evidence and in mythic literature – is the apparent closeness of the relationship between the sacred and the profane, the spiritual and the mundane, the supernatural and earthly worlds. The spirits surrounded humankind in all aspects of life and death; they dwelled in the landscape; and they presided over all human undertakings. This all-pervading sacred presence is a feature common to many polytheistic religious systems; another is the presence of spirits perceived as belonging to both genders. By contrast, many monotheistic religions – such as Judaism, Islam and Christianity – involve the perception of sacral power as exclusively masculine. Such systems also tend to be comparatively remote in terms of the relationship between divinity and the world of humans. Another difference between monotheistic and polytheistic religions is that, in the latter, the sanctity of the natural world is often crucial. Respect for animals and for the land is closely associated with the recognition that the supernatural is in control, and that individual spirits look after – and indeed may be personifications of – aspects of the living world. This is apparent in the evidence for religion in pagan Celtic Europe. As this book seeks to demonstrate, female spirits – goddesses – were central to Celtic perceptions of the divine world.

The World of the Celts

From about 500 BC chroniclers from the Mediterranean world wrote down their observations of a people living in Europe to the north of the Alps, whom they called Celts. Herodotus alludes to the origins of the Celts in the area of the Danube.[1] Other writers speak of migrations of Celts from their homelands in Central Europe during the fifth to the third centuries BC: they had spread south into the Po Valley by 400 BC, and attacked Rome in 387; in 279 a group of Celts plundered the great Greek sanctuary of Delphi, and in 278 a sub-group settled in Galatia. Archaeologists studying the material culture of temperate Europe have distinguished a certain homogeneity in the traditions of communities from Britain to eastern Europe from the period when iron was first adopted as a common metal in these regions, around 750–700 BC, until the Roman occupation effectively ended the prehistoric phase over much of the European continent. The names given by archaeologists to these traditions derive from important Iron Age sites: the Hallstatt phase is named after a great cemetery in Austria that is full of distinctive artefacts; the term La Tène is taken from the site of the same name on the shores of Lake Neuchâtel in Switzerland. Hallstatt covers roughly the eighth to the sixth centuries BC; La Tène from the fifth century BC to the Roman period.

From the third century BC the evidence of place-names and personal names (both in epigraphic and Classical literary sources) in a Celtic language endorse the great geographical spread of Celtic peoples indicated both by the testimony of the Graeco-Roman authors and by the archaeological evidence.

The map indicates the distribution of people speaking Celtic languages in Europe in about 200 BC. The main areas with which this book is concerned are Gaul and Britain. The geography of the latter is self-explanatory, but the definition of Gaul perhaps requires some precision. Gaul 'proper' is the region bounded by the English Channel and the Atlantic in the north and west and by the Rhine in the east. Gallia Cisalpina ('Gaul on this [the Italian] side of the Alps') was in the north of Italy around the Po Valley, and Gallia Narbonensis was in the south, around Marseille and the Lower Rhône Valley, bounded in the west by the Pyrenees. Narbonensis is special in that, although inhabited by Celts, it had been subjected to Classical influences since 600 BC, when the Greek colony was founded at Marseille. It should also be pointed out that not everyone living in Gaul was necessarily Celtic: there were Ligurians in the south-west; and some of the so-called Gallo-Belgic tribes in the north-east had a mixed Celto-Germanic culture.

Although the growth of the Celtic tradition across Europe was due partly to actual folk-movement, many regions probably became Celtic rather by the adoption of material culture (through trade or gift-exchange) and customs. For example, there is very little evidence for any kind of migration into Britain; yet by the time the Romans arrived in the first century AD, the Britons were thoroughly celticised, with a material culture which was broadly similar to that of their Gaulish neighbours. It is worth pointing out that nowhere do Classical writers refer to the Britons as Celts.

According to the ancient documentary sources, the power of the free Celts began to decline in the third century BC. The Celts in North Italy were trounced by the Romans at the Battle of Telamon in 225 BC and the Romans took over Gallia Cisalpina in the early second century. In Asia Minor the Galatians were subdued by the Pergamene kings and, from the second century BC, the Celts were coming under pressure from the Germans across the Rhine. In the late second century BC southern Gaul was conquered by the Romans, who turned it into 'The Province' (Provence), and in the middle of the first century Julius Caesar turned covetous eyes on the heartland of Gaul, finally subjugating the entire region by 50 BC. The emperors Augustus and Tiberius conquered much of the remainder of Celtic Europe. Claudius invaded Britain in AD 43 and by the later first century the armies of the Roman governor Gnaeus Julius Agricola reached the Caledonii of northern Scotland. The great battle of Mons Graupius, between Agricola and the Caledonian commander Calgacus in AD 84 effectively marked the end of the free Celtic world, with the exception of northern Scotland and

Ireland. Under the Romans the Celtic tradition in Europe inevitably changed, but it by no means disappeared. A new hybrid Romano-Celtic culture developed, which was a highly successful and dynamic blend of Celtic and Classical influence.

The western Roman Empire disintegrated in the fifth century AD and centralised power within Europe collapsed. The regions which had been under the domination of Rome were now subjected to a new Germanic culture which appears, from the archaeological evidence, largely to have replaced Celtic tradition in Central Europe, Gaul and much of Britain. After the collapse of Roman power the extreme west of Europe, particularly Ireland and Wales, which had been on the periphery of the Celtic world, became its focus. Only in these regions, together with Scotland, Cornwall, the Isle of Man and Brittany, did Celtic languages survive.

Finding the Goddesses

Information about the Celtic world of the supernatural comes from three sources: the testimony of the Classical authors, who observed, commented upon, but did not always understand their northern neighbours in Celtic Europe; archaeological evidence; and the earliest written myths of the Celtic west, which were compiled in the vernacular Celtic languages.

The evidence of the Graeco-Roman authors has the advantage of primacy, in that they were contemporary witnesses and chroniclers of the Celtic world who were writing, for the most part, in the first century BC and first century AD. However, these commentators came from a highly urbanised world, unlike that of the Celts, and were writing about a culture which was alien to them. If we use these sources, we have to bear in mind the bias, omission, purposeful or accidental distortion that may pervade them. Some writers may have had a specific agenda the primary purpose of which may not have been objective reporting. Prejudice – similar to that encountered today in the world of the tabloid newspaper – may have resulted in some deliberate sensationalism and stereotyping of so-called 'barbarians', creating archetypes of primitivism in order to emphasise the difference between the Celts and the 'civilised' world of the Mediterranean. The Classical writers make lengthy and detailed comments about Celtic ritual, including sacrifice and druidism, but say relatively little about goddesses and gods.

Archaeology – the study of the material culture of the past – arguably provides the main group of evidence that relates directly to the religion of the pagan Celtic period between 600 BC and the fifth century AD. By far the majority of the archaeological evidence for Celtic divinities dates from the period of the Roman occupation and comes from Gaul, the Rhineland and Britain. It consists mainly of iconography (images of divine beings) and epigraphy (inscriptions which allude to the goddesses by name). The Roman date of such evidence means that it is necessary to try and understand the Celtic and Classical influences that produced this pagan belief-system. Two points

11

concerning female imagery may be made here: one is that it may be difficult to judge whether a goddess or human is represented; the second is that the presence of a torc on an image ties it firmly to Celtic tradition.

The vernacular myths of the Celtic west describe a world which is essentially pre-Christian, a world redolent with the supernatural. The Irish mythic tradition is particularly rich, and presents us with an elaborate system of deities, semi-divine heroes of superhuman status, druids and druidesses, and a complex and ambiguous Otherworld. The over-arching problem of using Irish myths as evidence for pagan Celtic religion is that they were compiled in written form during the early medieval period and, what is more, their recording was the work of Christian redactors. It is unprovable whether these myths existed for centuries in oral form and were only committed to writing during the historical period of the eighth to twelfth centuries AD. Because of the chronological disparity between the pagan Celtic world presented by the contemporary testimony of archaeology and Classical literature on the one hand,

Bronze statue of Boudica on the Thames embankment, London; cast by T. Thornycroft in 1902. The warrior-queen is fancifully depicted, spear in hand, riding into battle against the Romans in a scythe-wheeled chariot, with her two daughters behind her.

and the vernacular myths on the other, any attempt to associate the two groups of evidence must only be made with extreme caution. Indeed, it is probably safer to treat them separately, even though both are relevant to the understanding of the pre-Christian west. A second reason for such a tentative approach is that the vernacular mythic tradition pertains only to Ireland and Wales. Whilst it may be possible to discern similarities between the Celtic world and Celtic religion described therein and that of continental Europe in the early first millennium AD (for example, the sanctity of water and the importance of the number three), there may also be profound differences.

It is the Irish mythic tradition which appears to contain the material that is of most use for a study of Celtic paganism. There are three main collections of Insular prose tales (throughout this book I use the term 'Insular' specifically to refer to Ireland): the Mythological Cycle, the Ulster Cycle and the Fionn Cycle. The first of these includes the 'Book of Invasions' (The *Leabhar Gabhála*) and the 'History of Places' (The *Dinnshenchas*), both compiled in the eleventh – twelfth century AD. The Book of Invasions probably had its origins in earlier works of monastic redactors writing a history of Ireland during the sixth and seventh centuries AD. The book chronicles a succession of mythical invasions of Ireland from before the Flood to the arrival of the Celts or Gaels. This is, in a sense, a myth of Creation, constructed to explain the presence of the Celts in Ireland. The most important of these 'invasions' was that of the Tuatha Dé Danann, the 'People of the Goddess Danu', a race of gods and goddesses. The *Dinnshenchas* is a topographical work but is nonetheless relevant to Celtic paganism since it links the names of places with mythical events or episodes.

The second collection of stories is the Ulster Cycle, of which the focal tale is the *Táin Bó Cuailnge*, the 'Cattle Raid of Cooley', which recounts the great conflict between the two most powerful Irish provinces of Ulster and Connacht. The Cycle is steeped in the supernatural, containing accounts of deities and heroes and describing an Ireland where the worlds of humans and divinities were closely interlinked. Here we encounter the powerful goddesses of Ireland: the Morrigán, Badbh, Macha, Medb and others. The earliest known form of the Táin dates to the twelfth century but its origin may be very much older: the language of the earliest form of the text is probably eighth century but some passages here also may be far earlier. Like the Mythological Cycle, it describes a pagan, pre-Christian world. Christianity was introduced to Ireland in the fifth century AD, although the land may have remained largely pagan for at least two centuries longer.

The third group of material is less relevant to the present enquiry than the first two, but has some important mythic content. This is the Fionn Cycle, another twelfth-century compilation: it contains the story of the superhuman war-leader Finn, and demonstrates a strong affinity between deities, humans and the natural world.

The earliest Welsh vernacular tradition contains traces of a rich mythology, but it is somewhat veiled in that far more influence from Christianity and from later story-motifs is present. The Welsh stories contain numerous references to God, and little allusion is made to pagan deities as such. The Welsh mythic tales have been so re-shaped by their redactors that their origins in myth are sometimes difficult to recognise. However, they present descriptions of a supernatural world which has little to do with the Christian tradition, and so these Welsh myths may well have their origins within the context of a pagan Britain. The Welsh mythic tradition is contained entirely within late compilations that belong mainly to the thirteenth and fourteenth centuries AD. Most relevant to our enquiry are the *Pedair Ceinc y Mabinogi* ('The Four Branches of the Mabinogi', commonly known as the Mabinogion), the Tale of Culhwch and Olwen, and a few other stories, such as Peredur. The earliest of these is probably the Tale of Culhwch and Olwen which, in its original form, may belong to the tenth century AD. The *Mabinogi* was a later redaction, whose origins may lie in the eleventh century. The Four Branches are preserved in two collections of texts, the *White Book of Rhydderch*, of about 1300, and the *Red Book of Hergest*, which dates to the fourteenth century. The Four Branches consist of four independent but related tales, which chronicle the activities and events associated with ruling families in Dyfed, Harlech and Gwynedd. Each of the stories is named after a focal member of these families: Pwyll; Branwen; Manawydan; and Math. Despite their late redaction, both the *Mabinogi* and Culhwch and Olwen must relate to a much earlier tradition, since they are full of references to supernatural beings, such as Rhiannon, Brân, Modron and Mabon, whose qualities suggest that they are disguised deities. Moreover, there is a Welsh Otherworld, Annwn, which bears no resemblance to a Christian heaven or hell, but which relates very closely to the Otherworld of Insular myth.

The goddesses and gods who appear in the earliest Irish and Welsh written tradition are given personalities and, sometimes, clear functions. But their separateness from the pantheon of pagan Celtic Europe (as presented to us in archaeological and Classical literary evidence) is emphasised not just by discrepancies in chronology but also by the absence, in the vernacular myths, of any references to a cohesive religious system, ritual practices or worship. This may be the result of Christian chroniclers, seeking to sanitise the pagan traditions of the Celtic west by demoting the divine beings to the status of demons and heroes and to neutralise the pre-Christian system by, in a sense, trivialising the divine.

All these categories of evidence have flaws, problems and limitations. However, they combine to present us with a rich tapestry of Celtic paganism, a kaleidoscope of shifting but richly-coloured images in which sacred beings are presented in their multi-faceted forms. This book follows the fortunes of the goddesses, who were clearly fundamental to the belief-systems of the ancient Celts and whose roles were at least as prominent as those of their male counterparts. The pages which follow demonstrate that, in fact, they may have dominated the religion of the Celtic world.

1 Women in Celtic Society

The chapters which follow demonstrate the prominence and popularity of female divinities in Celtic Europe, and raise the inevitable question as to what extent the high status of the goddesses reflects the position of women in Celtic society. This chapter addresses two fundamental issues: whether there is, on the one hand, any correlation between the presence of powerful goddesses in a religious system and the status of women within the society to which that system belongs; and, on the other, whether there is any specific evidence which points to attitudes of society towards Celtic women in later prehistory and the early historic period.

Some modern feminists have argued that the presence of powerful female figures in a given mythic tradition implies a strong social and political position for the women in that secular society. Such a correlation is basically unsound in two ways: first, there is little evidence that the divine and human worlds are reflections one of the other in terms of gender; second, even if there is evidence for a few powerful female leaders within a particular culture, that need not correlate with the position of women in general. The religious life of Athens in the fifth century BC was focused upon the all-important eponymous goddess Athene, yet Athenian women had no societal status beyond the sphere of ritual activity,[1] and did not even enjoy citizenship. We can see how, in our own day, the leadership of Margaret Thatcher for more than a decade has done little for the status of women in Britain.

Both Ehrenberg and Márkus[2] stress the danger of making close links between the rules of Celtic society on the one hand and of myth and divinity on the other. Márkus rightly argues that the case for high-status women in Celtic society rests largely upon the mythic tradition of early Ireland, yet close scrutiny conveys a very different message. The treatment of women in Celtic myths is in fact remarkably homogeneous: they are, in general, portrayed as unstable, a challenge to men's honour-code and indeed highly dependent upon their menfolk. Medb herself is given a thoroughly bad press in the Ulster Cycle and is by no means a positive role-model for high-ranking women in Insular society.[3] She is cruel, jealous, capricious and promiscuous and she gains much of her power, for example over Cú Chulainn, by means of sorcery. Although Celtic goddesses of war do appear in the myths, in reality warfare appears to have been male-dominated.

As we have seen, evidence for the status of Celtic women comes from three main sources: the early historical, non-mythic literature of Ireland and Wales; the observations of Classical writers; and Iron Age archaeological – mainly sepulchral –

evidence. In addition, there is abundant epigraphical evidence for women with Celtic names and thus, arguably, of Celtic origin in Roman Gaul and Britain, but this is more difficult to assess since these women were, to a large extent, romanised and their status affected by Roman law and custom.[4]

The evidence of Iron Age tombs in Europe suggests that some women enjoyed a high social status in the later first millennium BC. Females were interred with great ceremony and accompanied by rich grave-goods in the late sixth and early fifth centuries BC in southern Germany and eastern Gaul. The funerary ritual included interment of the body within a wooden mortuary chamber, beneath a great mound. The grave-goods included feasting-utensils and sumptuous jewellery, with some material imported from as far away as the Mediterranean world. The lady at Vix in Burgundy, who died at the end of the sixth century BC, was buried with an enormous bronze *krater* or wine-mixing vessel of Corinthian or Etruscan make.[5] At Hohmichele

(*Left*) Wooden figurine of a veiled woman, wearing a torc; early first century AD. From the healing spring-shrine of Chamalières, Puy-de-Dôme, France. The statuette may depict a pilgrim, priestess or goddess.

(*Right*) Stone statuette of a young person, clad in a heavy Gaulish coat (*sagum*) and holding a set of pan-pipes. The base is inscribed 'Deae Ianuariae' ('to the goddess Ianuaria'). From the Romano-Celtic healing spring-sanctuary of Beire-le-Châtel, Burgundy.

in Germany a huge funeral mound contained the body of a woman in the main chamber but in one of two secondary chambers lay a man and a woman placed side by side. At Klein Aspergle, also in South Germany, a woman decorated with gold and silver finery was accompanied by rich goods imported from Etruria.[6] It could be argued that such graves need not be indicative of female status but may, rather, be symbolic of the displayed wealth of the community or of the deceased's husband. Nonetheless, it seems significant that there is often no comparably rich male grave in the vicinity. The association of some of these tombs with seats of power suggests that the burials may represent chieftains: the Vix grave lies in close proximity to the stronghold of Mont Lassois; and Hohmichele is clearly linked with the Heuneberg nearby.[7] The fourth century BC lady buried with rich sepulchral goods at Reinheim by the River Blies in Germany exemplifies the persistence of this tradition.[8] In Britain, too, comparatively rich Iron Age female graves are not unknown: the group of three chariot-burials from the fourth-second century BC site of Wetwang in Yorkshire consists of a central grave, the earliest and the largest containing the skeleton of a woman with a mirror and a bronze box (the presence of which implies a certain status), flanked by apparent warrior burials.[9]

Large bronze *krater* (wine-mixing vessel) of Greek make; end of sixth century BC. From the 'princess's' tomb at Vix, Burgundy. The vessel was transported over the Alps from either Etruria or Corinth.

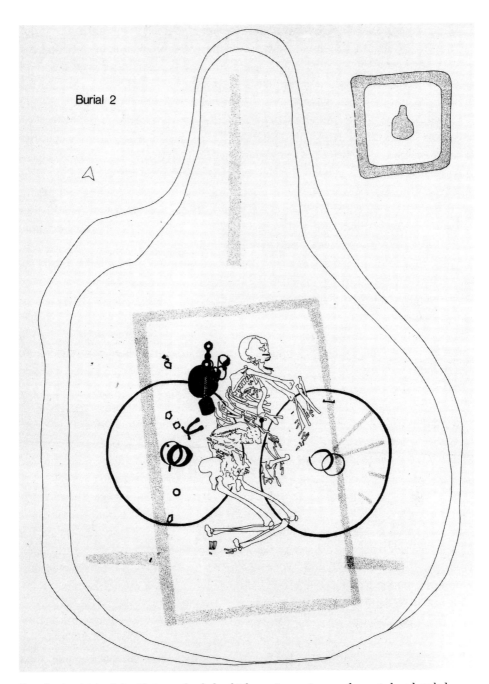

Burial 2

Female chariot-burial with two-wheeled vehicle, an iron mirror, a decorated and sealed bronze box and other grave-goods; third century BC. Wetwang Slack, Yorkshire. The comparative wealth of the tomb suggests that the deceased was probably of relatively high status.

The tomb-evidence for women of high rank during the early Iron Age is borne out by the later evidence from Classical writers of the first century BC to first century AD, who speak both of the existence of female rulers and of the relative prominence of women in Celtic as opposed to Roman society. The most important clues to the presence of powerful Celtic women come from Britain in the middle of the first century AD. Tacitus speaks of Cartimandua, who ruled the great northern hegemony of the Brigantes for about twelve years, and comments that she owed her position and influence to her high birth.[10] Cartimandua was a client-ruler who entered into a collaborative relationship with the Roman government whereby she kept her tribe quiet and Rome protected her position. Cartimandua was married to one Venutius but deserted him for his armour-bearer Vellocatus, using Roman power to keep her erstwhile husband under control. But her greatest notoriety comes from her betrayal of the British freedom-fighter Caratacus who sought sanctuary with her from Roman retribution, only to be handed over in chains. Cartimandua's activities demonstrate that it was possible for British women to hold supreme power within a tribe, to own property, lead armies, change marriage-partners at will, and to enter into negotiations and treaties with Rome, receiving its support despite its intolerant attitude to female emancipation.[11] That Cartimandua was not the only Brigantian woman of high status is implied by Tacitus' comment,[12] put into the mouth of the Caledonian commander Calgacus, that a group of Brigantian soldiers led by a woman stormed Roman installations sometime between AD 71 and 83.

The Icenian female commander, Boudica, who was roughly contemporary with Cartimandua and who led a huge uprising against the Roman government of Britain in AD 60, is well known from her commentators Tacitus and Dio Cassius.[13] Boudica herself is discussed in some detail in Chapter 2, which examines the theme of war and the goddesses. Here it is sufficient to note that, like Cartimandua, Boudica is indicative of the presence of British women with high political profiles although, unlike the northern queen, Boudica seized power for herself, illegally in Roman eyes, after the death of her husband, the client-king Prasutagus. An interesting aspect of the Boudica episode concerns the speeches put into the mouths of both the British leader and her adversary, the Roman governor Suetonius Paulinus, by the Classical historians. Even taking account of dramatic licence and literary 'purple passages', these speeches must surely have some validity and a basis in reality. They display a fundamental difference between attitudes to women in Celtic and Roman society. Suetonius Paulinus clearly has a derisory and incredulous attitude to the notion of British females participating in warfare ('in their ranks there are more women than fighting men'), whilst Boudica's own speech implies that the Britons were by no means

(*Right*) Marble statue of Boudica and her daughters. Carved by J. Howard Thomas in 1913–15 and set up in Cardiff. The group was inspired by the description of the Icenian warrior-queen by Classical writers such as Tacitus and Dio Cassius.

unused to female leaders in battle.[14] Interestingly, Tacitus repeats this elsewhere: 'for the Britons make no distinction of sex in their leaders',[15] which strengthens the statement's validity. Dio makes it clear that the Romans were particularly incensed by Boudica's victories because she was female.[16]

The difference between the position of women in Celtic and Mediterranean societies during the later first millennium BC is reflected by a number of Greek and Roman writers. According to Plutarch, writing in the second century AD about Gaulish women in around 400 BC, they participated actively in public affairs as mediators.[17] The association between women and war, which is so well illustrated by the examples of Cartimandua and Boudica, is alluded to many times by such writers as Diodorus[18] and Ammianus,[19] who describe the bravery and ferocity of Gaulish women. Caesar points out the relative freedom of women in Gaul and Britain, in terms of marriage and property: they could choose their own husbands, to some extent. But Caesar also records instances of arranged marriages: the Aeduan noble Dumnorix arranged a union between his mother and a member of the Bituriges.[20] Caesar also refers to the custom of joint dowry-provision in Gaulish marriages.[21] Both partners contributed to a joint property-account which was kept throughout the marriage; on the death of one, the survivor (husband or wife) took possession of the whole plus any profits. That women could own and inherit property under British tribal law is indicated by Prasutagus' legacy to his daughters, who could clearly be his legitimate heirs.

Both Caesar and Dio Cassius allude to a kind of polyandry in Britain: Caesar refers to groups of ten or twelve men, usually kinsmen, who shared wives, but all the children of a particular woman were deemed to belong to the man who first co-habited with her.[22] According to Dio, the Caledonii of Scotland displayed their extreme barbarism by holding their women in common, all the children being reared communally.[23] Dio has been accused of ignorance and of barbarian stereotyping,[24] but this need not be the case. Not only does Caesar mention similar customs, but such communal living is also not unknown among present-day traditional societies. Despite this apparent sexual liberalism, however, Caesar points out that in Gaul, at least, husbands had powers of life and death over their wives and children.[25]

It is clear from the comments of Classical observers that Celtic women in Gaul and Britain, unlike their Greek sisters, were not shut away from public life. They played more of a part in society and in theory they could, in Britain at least, rise to the highest power. But it is difficult to gauge how usual it was to have Celtic female commanders and rulers. Caesar mentions many Gaulish leaders by name but women are not among them. On the other hand, there are hints that British women were more prominent: very few leading Britons are referred to by name in the sources, so it may not be significant that Boudica and Cartimandua are the only female political leaders named. But it is also possible that Classical chroniclers either exaggerated or made much of the social prominence of Iron Age women in the deliberate image-projection

Inscribed tombstone of a female doctor; first century AD. Metz, France.
The stone is important in its rare testimony to the presence of professional
women in Romano-Celtic Gaul.

of a primitive stereotype: thus, the presence of female rulers may have been equated with primitiveness. Strabo makes an obscure comment, that in Gaul, 'as in many barbarian societies', the female roles were the reverse of those associated with Roman women.[26] We need to pose the question not only of how widespread was women's participation in various aspects of public life but also over what timespan. Classical authors tend to present a timeless picture, whereas in fact Celtic societies were dynamic and must have undergone changes through time. The situation in the first century AD may have been very different from that of the fourth century BC, but most of the Graeco-Roman commentators were recording occurrences no earlier than the first century BC.

Whatever the precise nature of the role of women in pre-Roman Celtic society, the large quantity of Classical literary allusion to the relatively prominent public participation of women indicates a genuine difference between Europe north and south of the Alps. However, it was probably the case that, in general, men retained most of the real power, albeit with some exceptions.

As I mentioned at the beginning of this chapter, the status of Celtic women in the Roman provinces is difficult to evaluate because of the presence of romanising influences. Lindsay Allason-Jones[27] alludes to the continued importance of British women's tribal identity, which was sometimes recorded on Romano-British tombstones. Whilst change to the Roman *paterfamilias* system (whereby women came under the complete jurisdiction of the male head of the household) extended to some women in Britain, this seems by no means to have always been the case: curse-tablets from Bath and elsewhere indicate that British women under Roman occupation owned property and engaged in business.[28] Pelletier[29] has demonstrated that this was also the case in Gaul, where there is evidence that Celtic ladies followed many professions, from wine-seller to doctor and from butcher to chemist. This ability to follow their own careers must have had a profound effect upon the status of Celtic women and their independence from male kin.

Documents of early historical date from Ireland and Wales, excluding the myths, give some indication of the social and political status of women from about the sixth century AD onwards. These texts include lives of saints and law-tracts. They constitute the earliest written testimony for the organisation of Celtic society in the West and it may well be that they reflect not only contemporary practice but also earlier tradition. It is inconceivable that the law-texts express completely new ideas, but must rather have built upon some pre-existing structure belonging to the pre-literate past.

Whilst the Insular myths present a picture of powerful and autonomous women, such as Medh, this state of affairs is not reflected in the secular law-texts. It is possible to place these legal documents into a chronological sequence, which show a progression towards greater legal status for women. In the earliest laws women appear to have had no independent legal position and very little power of any kind.[30] Indeed, both the Irish and Welsh texts make it very clear that Celtic society in the early historical period was essentially androcentric. Women's legal status is defined in the law-texts in terms of their relationship to male relatives, and the Irish and Welsh laws both suggest that women were subject to men. There is little allusion in the laws to women taking a prominent position in public life, although some eighth-century Insular (Irish) queens are mentioned in the Irish Annals.[31] The most important Irish women were the abbesses of prominent monasteries, such as Brigit of Kildare.

The Irish and Welsh laws are particularly illuminating on the position of women with regard to property and marriage. Women could own and control property, although there were restrictions on their ability to control inherited land. Marriage seems often to have been the result of arrangements between families, but only male kin were involved in negotiations. Monogamy was the rule, although concubinage was practised, particularly in Ireland. Women possessed clear rights within marriage, including equal claim on jointly-held marriage-goods. There is, indeed, a striking similarity between descriptions of matrimonial dowries and wedding-presents in the accounts of Classical writers and the early historical law-texts. Both speak of the

Stone images of worshippers, a female on the right; Romano-Celtic period. From the sanctuary of Forêt d'Halatte, Oise, France. The shrine produced several simple stone carvings, including human heads, people and animals.

contribution of wealth by both partners and their kin and the pooled property accumulated at the time of and after the wedding. Separation, divorce and remarriage were relatively easy, with comparatively generous settlements for divorced women. Virginity was considered obligatory for girls embarking on their first marriage and, in recognition of its high value, the bridegroom paid his bride or her family a 'maiden-price'. This was, trustingly, given before the wedding-night!

The influence of organised Christianity in the Celtic west brought about certain changes in attitudes to women. One effect was to tighten up the marriage-contract so that divorce became more difficult. But the most important contribution of Christianity to Celtic women was the choice it gave them to renounce their secular role as dependent daughter, wife and mother and to become holy women, who chose celibacy and a monastic life and who thus shook themselves free of dominance by male kin, whether father or husband. Even so, these holy women were perceived to be betrothed to God and so still retained a subordinate relationship to a male figure. Nuns could become powerful leaders of religious houses and thus acquired a ruling status which sometimes involved the control of great wealth and lands. The impact of the Church upon women is exemplified by the *Cáin Adomnáin*, the 'Law of Adomnán', a document which dates to the late seventh century AD. Adomnán was the ninth abbot of Iona between AD 679 and 704, who wrote his *Cáin* in order to promote a greater respect and protection for Celtic women. Allusion is made to their exploitation in war, abuse, rape, insult and abandonment. Adomnán wished his own monastery to play a substantial part in the enhancement of women's status within society[32] by setting down guidelines as to their treatment and position within their communities. The very existence of such a tract demonstrates the low esteem in which Irish women were held in the late 7th century AD, although the document may have a propaganda element designed to persuade women to espouse the new faith.

The evidence for the status of Celtic women examined in this chapter is disparate in nature and belongs to a wide temporal and geographical spectrum. The sepulchral information from Iron Age Europe between the sixth and fourth centuries BC implies the presence of some high-ranking females. The ladies of Vix, Reinheim and Hohmichele must have occupied a high political, social or religious position within their communities. Greek and Roman writers comment on a Celtic society in which women seem certainly to have achieved a relatively high public profile and, by the first century AD, Britain at least possessed some independent female leaders. The earliest mythic literature of Ireland and Wales alludes to a number of important women but, although goddesses figure prominently in these myths, the females who are not portrayed as specifically divine (such as Deirdre and Rhiannon) are generally dominated by men. The one major exception to this rule is Medb, but it is clear that she is in fact a goddess of sovereignty – even if, in the *Táin*, she is depicted in a somewhat unflattering light.[33]

The early Insular historical annals and the law-texts of both Ireland and Wales suggest that, in general, though they had some property- and marriage-rights, women were nonetheless a subject group. There is no hint in these secular documents of powerful females like the lady of Vix, Boudica or Medb. The independence and raised status of women in the post-Roman Celtic west seems to have been enhanced by Christian ethics. This was partly due to deliberate Church policy but also because holy women in charge of wealthy monastic foundations generated prosperity. Margaret Ehrenberg[34] has argued convincingly that the status of females in traditional societies is linked, at least in part, to their ability to contribute economically to their communities or kinship-groups.

In concluding this chapter, we may return to the main question posed at the beginning, namely whether any significant correlation can be made between the prominence of Celtic goddesses and the status of women in Celtic society. Broadly speaking, such links are insecure: the presence of evidence for goddesses provided by archaeology and mythic literature need have no specific bearing on the position of women themselves. However, it may be more than coincidence that in a society where female deities seem to have been perceived as particularly powerful, both in terms of pagan material evidence and early myth, there is also evidence for a relatively high status for women, which compares favourably with that enjoyed by their counterparts in the Mediterranean world.

2 Goddesses of War

Here we are concerned with the identification of Celtic goddesses with warfare. The evidence for such divinities consists mainly of iconography and references in the Irish vernacular mythic tradition. In addition, there are allusions to a British war-goddess in Classical literature, and this same source paints a – possibly significant – picture of a strong link between Celtic women and war. This last phenomenon is interesting, although it may not help us identify an actual warrior-goddess. Margaret Ehrenberg has suggested[1] that the recurrent Classical literary references to women at war in Gaul and Britain reflects Mediterranean attitudes to war and conquest, and a deliberate Roman stereotyping of the Celtic enemy as a barbarian. To them, only a primitive society would entertain the idea of involving women as participants in battle and even as warrior-rulers. So we need to try and get behind the façade of Roman prejudice, and the image of an archetypal barbarian society that may have been projected by Graeco-Roman observers of Celtic custom on to the reality of Celtic warfare. But there is another aspect of the link between women and war, which brings us closer to the concept of divinity: that is the association between war and ritual. We know from such writers as Arrian[2] that hunting among the Celts was an activity closely related to ritual. The same may have been true of warfare. If this was the case, then the presence of women on the battlefield could have been partly because the presence of representatives of the whole tribe was sometimes symbolically important in order for a battle to be successful. Tacitus' reference to the black-robed women of Anglesey, who cursed and threatened the invading Roman forces of AD 60,[3] may indicate female religious officiants who acted with the druids in attempting to harness the powers of the supernatural against the enemy. We need now to examine the relationship, if any, between the warlike image of Celtic women and the concept of a war-goddess.

Women and Warfare

A whole troop of foreigners would not be able to withstand a single Gaul if he called his wife to his assistance who is usually very strong and with blue eyes; especially when, swelling her neck, gnashing her teeth, and brandishing her sallow arms of enormous size, she begins to strike blows mingled with kicks, as if they were so many missiles sent from the string of a catapult.[4]

Thus the late Roman writer Ammianus comments on the Gaulish viragos who so unnerved the Roman forces sent against Gallic armies 400 years previously. Here it is the sheer size, ferocity and appearance of these ladies that he wishes to draw attention to, as well as their very presence on the battlefield. Ammianus comments on their white skin and piercing blue eyes, features which Graeco-Roman observers also comment upon with reference to Celtic men. He implies that these women were more ferocious than their husbands. The image of huge females, necks bulging with rage and teeth champing, brings to mind descriptions of the heroes of Irish mythic tradition such as Cú Chulainn, who became temporarily insane in battle, going into 'warp-spasm' when he was so possessed by the lust for blood that he could no longer distinguish friend from foe.[5] Diodorus Siculus[6] makes a similar comment to that of Ammianus, observing that Gaulish women were as large, fierce, strong and brave as their men. Strabo[7] remarks that Gaulish women combined the qualities of mother-hood with forcefulness. This is interesting because we will see later that the goddesses of Irish myth exhibit exactly the same combination of roles: fertility and warfare.

Certain Classical writers depict Celtic women as being involved in the thick of battle; others describe their role as that of onlookers. Ammianus' comment implies active participation in conflict, and this is endorsed by a reference in Plutarch's *Life of Marius*:[8] here he mentions the behaviour of women belonging to the tribe of the Ambrones, an apparently Celtic tribe, though associated with the Teutonic Cimbri, in the region of Aix-en-Provence. In a battle between this tribe and the forces of the great late-Republican war-leader Marius, the women of the Ambrones took an active role in battle; when their menfolk retreated before the Roman onslaught, these women wielded their weapons against both the Romans as enemies and their own men as traitors.[9]

Tacitus discusses the customs of the German tribes, in his *Germania*. Some of these people were ethnically close to the Celts and, though in general their society seems to have been less developed, had many customs in common with them. German women seem to have had a degree of equality with men, and were closely associated with warfare. Thus, when two people married, each partner gave the other gifts which included arms; apparently the women were by no means excluded from the so-called 'manly pursuits' of warfare and hunting.[10]

The role of Celtic and German women actually on the battlefield was usually that of supporters, who were ranged in carts or platforms at the rear of the army or some other vantage-point, yelling curses and insults at the enemy and encouragement to their own forces – almost in the manner of modern cheer-leaders at an American football game. Tacitus and Caesar both remark on this and also say that, although the women were essentially spectators, they were sometimes killed or wounded in the fighting nonetheless. Caesar[11] speaks of Gaulish women standing behind their own lines on a barrier of wagons. In his *Histories*,[12] Tacitus describes how, in the rebellion of Civilis and his Batavians (from the Rhine Delta) against the Romans in AD 69–70, the native war-leader positioned his mother, his sisters and the wives and children of his men behind his army in order to spur and shame the soldiers into fighting all the more savagely: the men gave their war-cries and the women shrieked in concert. This situation occurred also in Britain during the rebellion of Boudica,[13] when British women were placed on carts at the edge of the battlefield, where they would have a good view but be out of the direct line of fire. Clearly, according to Roman observers, Celtic women were often associated with warfare, even if in a passive role as vociferous spectators.

There may have been a genuine perception that their presence made their men fight harder and better, since honour, pride and shame were involved. But there may also have been a practical reason for the positioning of women and children in the sight of their own armies: for protection. At least there they would not be in danger of rape, slaughter or capture by enemy-groups raiding homesteads under the cover of of battle. There may also have been a quasi-religious purpose for their presence if, as seems likely, warfare possessed an element of ritual. This is certainly implied by such customs as going into battle naked or wearing only a torc, the ritualistic boasting and challenges to single combat, the importance of symbols of beasts and other talismanic emblems on weapons, shields and helmets, and the display-element in the use of horses and chariots.[14]

An examination of the earliest vernacular literature from Ireland and Wales also reveals some evidence for a link between women and war. Whilst there is little early historical material which relates to the active participation of women on the battle-field, the late seventh century Irish law-text, the *Cáin Adomnáin*, (mentioned in Chapter 1) has some interest. One concern of the Iona abbot Adomnán was to legislate against the forcible use of women in fighting.[15] It is difficult to know how to interpret this document and how far women were, in practice, involved in battle. The *Cáin* may, in part, be a vehicle for Christian propaganda but it is hard to imagine that the need for women to be protected from the perils of warfare was purely fictitious.

The majority of the early vernacular sources pertain to myth, and it is extremely difficult to assess the reality of the position of women as it is reflected in this mythic tradition. Women-warriors appear in abundance, particularly in the Irish literature, sometimes as goddesses, sometimes as rulers or trainers. But even where they are present apparently as humans, it may be that there is a supernatural element in their identity. The warrior-females present in Irish myth may have been very closely tied to the supernatural and perhaps emanated from the imagination through the medium of religion rather than being based upon genuine women.[16]

Before we examine the battle-goddesses, it is worth looking for a moment at some of the mythological evidence for the association between females and war. In the Ulster Cycle tale 'The Birth of Conchobar' Ness, mother of the future king of Ulster, took up arms as a young girl and went to war herself after the massacre of her guardians. She wrought havoc and terror among her enemies and gave up fighting only when she married.[17] In both Welsh and Irish myth, women were often responsible for arming and training war-heroes. The Fourth Branch of the *Mabinogi* tells the story of Arianrhod and her son Lleu, whom she refused both a name and weapons unless she consented to give him a name herself and to arm him. In the early Welsh tale of Peredur, the young hero received a horse, arms and training from a witch with whom he resided for three weeks in order to gain skills in riding and handling weapons.[18] In the Irish Fionn Cycle, the warrior-champion Finn was reared as a child by two warrior-women who initiated him in warfare and hunting.[19] The Ulster Cycle records the training given by the female war-teacher Scáthach, who was responsible for the martial education of both Cú Chulainn – arguably the most famous of the mythical warrior-heroes – and of Naoise, lover of Deirdre. So great were Scáthach's skills that Cú Chulainn could slay a hundred of his enemies at once, single-handed, and though the Scottish king sent Naoise into the thick of battle time and time again, he always emerged unscathed.[20] But there is evidence that the warrior-women were not ordinary ladies but had supernatural affinities: the witch-trainer of Peredur possessed prophetic powers and so did Scáthach. Her name means 'Shadowy One', and it is clear from the trials which Cú Chulainn had to undergo before he reached her domain that it lay in the Otherworld.[21] It may even be that in these myths, the fact that heroes were taught or presented with arms by women reflects their own superhuman status.

Boudica and Andraste

'We British are used to women commanders in war.'[22]

This may well have been the case: we certainly know of at least two prominent female rulers who commanded their own armies, Queen Cartimandua of the Brigantes and Queen Boudica of the Iceni. Cartimandua was a tribal ruler in her own right[23] but, although Boudica only enjoyed the lower status of consort, it is Boudica who has maintained her fame through the history of Britain, as a passionate nationalist and rebel against the Establishment. Boudica is interesting in the present context for two reasons: first, she was a historical female war-leader, documented both by Tacitus in the first century AD and Dio Cassius[24] at the end of the second century; and, second, because Boudica is closely associated with Andraste, the only native Celtic war-goddess whose name we are given by more or less contemporary Graeco-Roman commentators.

Boudica's name is derived from the Celtic word for victory, 'bouda'.[25] She was the wife of Prasutagus, tribal ruler of the Iceni in Norfolk, a client-king of the Roman government. Client-kings entered into a special and personal treaty of alliance with the Emperor, whereby the king kept his sovereignty and territory and gained Rome's patronage but guaranteed, in return, to keep his land peaceful. The death of Prasutagus meant the automatic dissolution of the client–king relationship, which was then up for re-assessment. In fact Prasutagus left a will naming the Emperor and his two daughters as his co-heirs,[26] presumably in the hope that Nero would not seize everything. It is interesting that Boudica was not named as heir to Prasutagus' possessions. Whilst Nero's financial representative, the procurator Decianus Catus, was within his rights to make an inventory of Prasutagus' assets prior to their appropriation for the Emperor, there is no doubt that Catus carried out his mission with unbelievable insensitivity, behaviour that was to place the entire province of Britain in serious jeopardy. Boudica proclaimed herself ruler of the Iceni and challenged the imperial authority; she was flogged, her daughters raped and Icenian property confiscated. The Iceni took up arms, together with the Trinovantes, who were disaffected because of taxes, misappropriation of their territory in and around their capital and the presence of the expensive and blatantly provocative temple of Claudius in their city of Camulodunum (Colchester). Boudica amassed a huge army, sacking the Roman cities of Camulodunum itself, London and Verulamium (Saint Albans) before being finally defeated by the Roman governor Suetonius Paulinus, who had to interrupt his annihilation of the druidic groves on Anglesey in order to put down the uprising. There is archaeological evidence for the destruction of the three Roman towns.[27]

Dio Cassius[28] speaks at some length of the native British war-goddess Andraste, who was venerated by Boudica and the Iceni. Her name, which is philologically related to that of the Gaulish goddess Andarta, may mean 'unconquerable'. Andraste and the unspeakable rites carried out in her honour are described by Dio in connection with the massacre of Roman women by Boudica at London (see below) where, in her sacred grove, the Britons performed sacrifices, feasted and gave way to the abandoned excesses which were associated with the Maenads of Dionysus' cult in Greece. Dio says that Andraste was the Icenians' name for Victory, and that the goddess enjoyed their especial reverence. This is perhaps significant since that is also the interpretation of Boudica's name. He records that, before setting out on campaign, Boudica performed a rite involving the release of a live hare while invoking Andraste.[29] The symbolism of the hare, in this context, is not immediately apparent. It may represent the hunt, the hare acting as a symbol of the Romans pursued by the victorious Britons. With its nocturnal foraging habits, the hare could also have represented darkness and thus death and destruction. After the sack of London, Boudica's female prisoners were sacrificed in Andraste's grove, their breasts cut off and stuffed in their mouths, before being impaled vertically on great skewers. This grotesque retribution is surely a parody of the rape of Boudica's daughters and symbolises the deliberate violation of the Roman state. What befell the male prisoners is not recorded: it may be that the

Roman women were singled out as appropriate sacrifices by a female war-leader to a female divinity. Tacitus makes the significant comment that the rebels exacted vengeance in advance for what they knew would be their fate once the Romans overcame them.[30] But the treatment of the women is not just the savagery of war. The propitiation of the goddess appears to have demanded blood-sacrifices of especial ferocity, while the slaughter of the women seems to have been part of a specific rite associated with a goddess of battle.[31] What is interesting is the close link between Boudica and Andraste: in a sense, they appear to have represented two aspects of the same identity, one of which resided in the world of the supernatural, the other as an earthly war-leader.

The Iconography of the War-Goddess

In Iron Age and Romano-Celtic Europe, certain images of goddesses display a close association with warfare, and are sometimes indicative of a direct role as warriors. Pots from the seventh-century BC graves at Sopron-Varhély in Hungary bear incised decoration in the form of goddesses associated with warriors on horseback.[32] The Strettweg bronze model cult-wagon from an Austrian grave, which dates to the same period, bears images of a goddess associated with stags and soldiers or hunters, some on foot, some mounted.[33] The tomb itself was that of a cremated warrior, his remains interred with a spear, three horse-bits and an axe. The Strettweg goddess is normally interpreted as a divine huntress, but we know that war and hunting were closely associated in the European Iron Age and that warriors used the hunt as battle-practice.[34]

To the late Iron Age belongs a fragmentary bronze figure of a goddess whose warrior-role is unequivocal. She comes from Dinéault in Brittany and she is depicted wearing a helmet the crest of which is in the form of a goose, its neck outstretched in aggression.[35] Celtic Iron Age warriors are portrayed on the Gundestrup Cauldron (fully discussed in Chapter 8) wearing helmet-crests in the form of birds or animals, and the ancient author Diodorus Siculus refers to this custom among the Celts, explaining that it increased the stature of the wearer and made him appear more threatening.[36] The goose-crest worn by the Breton goddess is particularly appropriate since, because of its nature, the goose was a symbol of aggression, alertness and guardianship. The graves of certain Iron Age soldiers in the former Czechoslovakia contained goose-bones,[37] probably in recognition of this symbolism; and the Celto-Germanic god Mars Thincsus, venerated at Housesteads on Hadrian's Wall in the Roman period, was associated with goose-imagery.[38]

Perhaps the most evocative pre-Roman Iron Age images of war-goddesses are those on coins, some of which depict female warriors who are probably best interpreted as divine. Certain Gaulish coins bear images of a running woman brandishing weapons

Bronze statuette of a war-goddess; first century BC. From Dinéault near Rennes, Brittany. The goddess wears a goose-crested helmet: the goose was a potent Celtic symbol of war, aggression and guardianship.

in both hands. Issues struck by the north-western Gaulish tribes, the Redones and Turones, depict naked female riders or charioteers waving weapons, branches, torcs or shields in a gesture of furious excitement; one such coin portrays a female, perhaps a goddess, wearing a torc and carrying a spear.[39] Are we seeing the portrayal of reality or the supernatural? Are these women earthly warriors (with all the implications for gender-roles in society) or are they goddesses? One clue to the answer may lie in the observation that the horse pulling the chariot or carrying the horsewoman is often human-headed, a monstrous type which surely reflects its supernatural status. The chariot-driving image is reminiscent of the divine lady represented on the Gundestrup Cauldron accompanied by two stylised wheels.[40]

Gold coins minted by the Redones, a Breton tribe living in the Rennes area; first century BC. One coin (*above*) depicts a horsewoman brandishing a victory-wreath and a shield; the other image (*right*) is that of a female charioteer driving a human-headed horse.

35

In the Romano-Celtic period, war-goddesses occur only under the guise of the Roman Minerva, who wears a helmet, gorgon-decorated cuirass and carries a spear. The tribal goddess Brigantia, who ruled over the great northern federation of the Brigantes, appears on a relief at Birrens in southern Scotland, and is equated with Victory and Minerva.[41] An interesting, though very worn, relief from Lemington (Gloucestershire) in the Chedworth Roman Villa museum depicts a goddess with a halo of hair, wearing a long robe and carrying a spear in her right hand. Beneath the image is an inscription *'Dea Regina'* ('the Queen Goddess').[42] If she is a war-goddess, then her title shows an iconographic and epigraphic link between sovereignty and battle, a connection which is very marked in the Irish mythic literature (see below). But several goddesses appear to be associated with war-symbolism, probably transmuted under the *pax romana* into the concept of protection and guardianship rather than warfare *per se*. The horse-goddess Epona, though her role was that of a peaceful, beneficent deity, was nonetheless venerated as a protector of soldiers and their mounts not only in such areas as Burgundy but also by cavalrymen stationed on the Rhine frontier. Epona may have been popular precisely because the free Celtic knights or *equites* were the Gaulish aristocratic elite. Epona's role away from military areas seems to have been associated with domestic prosperity and fertility, but such wellbeing can only come about if tribal lands are protected and frontiers made stable, so there may have been a link between warfare, guardianship, fertility and prosperity, symbolised by the goddess Epona. It may even be that the war-goddess of the Celtic coins was transmuted in the Roman period to become the peaceful Epona who, nonetheless, retained her symbolism of protection and defence.[43]

The role of the goddess as one who brought prosperity and fertility linked with guardianship may be suggested by certain images of the British mother goddesses (see Chapter 5): a stone at Kingscote (Gloucestershire) depicts a lady seated on a throne-like chair, holding bread and fruit, accompanied by a mounted god,[44] probably a warrior. In the same tribal region of the Dobunni, one of the many depictions of the mother-goddess at Cirencester consists of an image of a seated woman accompanied by three *genii cucullati*, of whom two bear swords.[45] The *cucullati* are hooded, dwarf-like gods, often associated with fertility and the mother-goddess in western Britain, and are probably beings subservient to the great mother, enhancing her symbolism of plenty.[46] On this relief, the *cucullati* are defending the goddess and her beneficence, or they may represent a martial aspect of the goddess herself. In their triple form, the mothers were worshipped by soldiers of the Roman army both in Britain and the Rhineland: an example of this military association is the great temple-precinct to the *Matronae Vacallinehae* at Pesch in Germany, whose dedicants were almost entirely army personnel.[47] It is possible that the three Lamiae venerated at the North British Roman fort of Benwell were triple war-goddesses: the ninth-century AD Irish writer Cormac refers to the Insular battle-fury, the Badbh, as Lamia.[48]

Stone relief of a seated goddess accompanied by three *genii cucullati* (hooded spirits), two of whom carry swords; second-third century AD. From Cirencester, Glos.

In Gaulish cult-art a recurring image is that of the divine couple or the sacred marriage (discussed further in Chapter 6). One aspect of this group of divinities is relevant to the present discussion since, on occasions, the goddess is accompanied by a warrior-god. The female deity does not bear arms herself but her companion is depicted with weapons. Most of the carvings of such couples occur in Burgundy: three come from Alesia and, in each case, the symbolism of the goddess appears to display her role as a provider of plenty and of regional prosperity. She bears such emblems of abundance as cornucopias, offering-dishes and bread or fruit; her partner carries a spear or sheathed sword. Similar symbolism appears on a stone at Autun.[49]

The Burgundian healing sanctuary of Mavilly was the cult centre of a native version of Mars, whose curative role as a fighter against disease was one of his most important functions in the Romano-Celtic world. On one carved stone the god is depicted wearing chain-mail and a torc and carrying a spear and a shield of late La Tène type (a specifically Celtic form). His companion is a goddess whose close affinity with her consort is indicated by the intimate manner in which she rests her hand on his shield.[50] The presence of the ram-horned snake – a symbol of rebirth and fertility – beside the god endorses his role as a beneficent healer. The Remi of Reims worshipped a similar divine couple: a worn stone from the town depicts a goddess and a male consort with a spear and a goat (a creature which, in Classical religion, symbolised fecundity).[51] Among the Triboci at Oberbetschdorf, near Strasbourg, a pair of deities was venerated who may have been associated with the protection of the vine-harvest: the god carries a lance and a shield, while she holds a pot, which may represent wine. The accompanying inscription dedicates the image to Mars.[52]

The iconographical association between a fertility goddess and a warrior-god is interesting, especially in view of the presence of Irish myths associated with certain divine females whose main role was that of the personification of the land and of sovereignty (see below and Chapter 4). Medb of Connacht is a prime example: like all sovereignty-goddesses, she took successive mortal kings as consorts, a ritual union which ratified their rule and brought prosperity to their territory. It is possible that a similar tradition is reflected in the pagan iconography of warrior-couples: the goddess disseminated plenty and the bounty of the earth, of which she is perhaps the divine manifestation; her consort may be both man and god, defender of the land and of the goddess herself. The goblet-bearing goddess at Oberbetschdorf may even reflect a specific concept of sacral kingship present in Irish myth, in which Eriu, the eponymous goddess of Ireland, offered a goblet of red liquor to her mortal consort to signify his right to the kingship. The depictions at Kingscote and Cirencester may equally reflect the mythical union of the goddess of fertility with the tribal god.

Stone carving of a divine couple. From the Romano-Gaulish town of Alesia (Alise-Sainte-Reine), Burgundy. The goddess carries a cornucopia, symbol of abundance; her male companion bears a spear, as a symbol of protection, but otherwise appears as a peaceful consort.

War, Fertility and Sovereignty in Irish Myth

The Insular mythic tradition presents us with a very direct relationship between goddesses, sovereignty and warfare, which is hinted at in the iconography. There is an apparent paradox in the nature and roles of these Irish deities, in that warfare and fertility are closely aligned. But this seeming contradiction may reflect a profound and dualistic thought-process involving giving and taking, birth and death, and the opening and closing of life, much as modern Christianity presents the cyclical image of 'dust to dust'. The link between fertility and war is clearly present in some pagan iconography of North Britain, where simple stone images of Roman date, found at such sites as Maryport (Cumbria), depict a naked, ithyphallic and horned warrior-god. Indeed, both war and the sexual act could be perceived as associated with aggression, and the sexual penetration of the female could be seen as analogous to the penetration of spear or sword into flesh. In the Baringo region of Kenya, spears are symbolic of young manhood and sexual prowess. In addition, war and hunting were closely linked in Iron Age society, and the quest for the female conjures up images of the hunt. Some of the hunters depicted in the Iron Age rock-art of Camonica Valley in North Italy are ithyphallic, again suggesting a link between virility, aggression and hunting.[53]

Many of the Irish goddesses were destructive and promiscuous. They personified territory, its sovereignty and its fertility, and their warlike nature may, in part, arise from the need to defend the land so that it could flourish. Medb was a queen-goddess of Connacht, a mythical figure who was given a spurious historicity in the early literature. Her activities are chronicled in the Ulster Cycle, where she emerges as the great Connacht leader of the conflict with the neighbouring province of Ulster. Medb's name is philologically related to mead and this may be significant both in terms of warfare and sovereignty: it could be that the drinking of liquor gave warriors a fighting temperament, but we should also recall the function of drink as a symbol of the union of the sovereignty-goddess with the mortal ruler. Medb is a good example of a divine female who is both ruler-goddess and battle-queen. She fought on the battlefield, controlled an army, and she brought her own troops with her when she married Ailill. Medb rode her chariot around the field of battle, encouraging her soldiers, inducing quarrels, bribing warriors (even using her own daughter Finnebair) to take up arms against friends and relatives as well as against the Ulstermen.[54] Thus Medb was not simply fighting for the supremacy of Connacht: she gloried in war, bloodshed and destruction for their own sake; she was the essence of death. She was sexually active, mating with nine kings, and allowing no man to rule at the royal court of Tara unless he slept with her.

Two other goddesses, apart from Medb, show a similar link between war, fertility and sovereignty. Macha is a complex entity, with three differing but interrelated manifestations, embodying concepts of war, rulership and fecundity. She established the Ulster royal seat of Emhain Macha; she was closely associated with horses, competing against the king's steeds in a race and winning, though at terrible cost to herself (see p. 77).

The other relevant goddess is the Morrigán, one of the battle-furies discussed below. She was the great warrior, but again she was associated with fertility and sovereignty. The Morrigán was a goddess of victory and prophecy but she was also promiscuous, mating with a number of gods and heroes and attempting to seduce Cú Chulainn on several occasions. Her role as goddess of sovereignty and fecundity is demonstrated most clearly in an episode in the *Dinnshenchas* (History of Places), a twelfth-century compilation which links topography and myth: the Morrigán had sexual intercourse with the Dagdha, the great tribal god, whilst she stood astride a stream.

He [the Dagdha] beheld the woman in Unius in Corann, washing herself, with one of her two feet at Allod Echae, to the south of the water, and the other at Loscuinn, to the north of the water. Nine loosened tresses were on her head. The Dagdha conversed with her, and they made a union. 'The Bed of the Couple' is the name of the place thenceforward. The woman that is here mentioned is the Morrigu.[24]

This is an act of sovereignty which caused the land to prosper: there is a clear sexual connotation in this water-imagery, but there is also liminal symbolism in that, besides being a life-force, the river was a boundary between worlds and a point of contact between the upper world of humans and the supernatural Otherworld.

The character of these goddesses is complex and apparently ambiguous. What is clear is that fertility and destruction are equally important and are interdependent. The symbolism may be explicable in terms of an association between the darkness of death with that of the earth and the womb. Thus the apparent absence of life when the seed lies germinating in the dark soil may have been perceived as analogous to the death of warriors on the battlefield and their rebirth in the happy Otherworld.

The Battle-Furies

> Badbh and Macha, rich the store
> Morrigán who dispenses confusion
> Compassers of death by the sword
> Noble daughters of Errimas.

Thus the Irish battle-goddesses are described in a verse from the Book of Invasions.[55] The war-goddesses of the early Irish myths were very closely interlinked with one another: they had many characteristics in common and they were, to an extent, interchangeable. The most important of these beings are the Morrigán, Badbh, Macha and Nemhain. They were simultaneously one goddess and three: the entity of the

Morrigán may be tripled or Badbh, Nemhain and Morrigán may be combined to become the triadic Morrígna. The goddesses combined destruction, sexuality and prophecy. They were prognosticators of doom, and one powerful image created in the myths was that of the 'Washer at the Ford': when a hero is about to meet his death, one of these battle-furies may be seen at a stream, washing his weapons and armour in a liminal act which anticipates his removal from the world of humans and his transference to the Otherworld.

These war-goddesses did not physically join in combat; their method was psychological. Their appearance was enough to unman the bravest warrior, and their howls of menace could freeze the blood and cause soldiers to throw away their weapons and flee the battlefield. Their presence during a campaign could encourage those whom they supported and they were harbingers of death for those they did not. The problem is that it was impossible to be sure to whom they would give the victory. One method of inducing terror used by all these furies is that of shape-shifting: they frequently appeared among opposing armies as crows or ravens, sinister black carrion birds of death. They could also change their image from that of a mature woman to a beautiful young girl or to a hideous old hag. Thus they showed their power over time, and the all-embracing nature of their role as divine females.

Nemhain was the fury about whom least has been documented in the myths. Her name, which means 'frenzy', symbolises her role in inciting warriors to the insane

Bronze ravens from a hoard of religious bronzes found at Felmingham Hall, Norfolk. About twenty-three objects had been placed in a pot, together with a coin of AD 260. In Celtic symbolism, ravens represented war and destruction.

savagery born of fear; she created panic and, when she shrieked at the Connacht army facing the Ulster hero Cú Chulainn, a hundred soldiers dropped dead with fright during the night.[56] That Macha belongs with this group of 'weird sisters' is indicated by the ninth-century commentator Cormac, who glosses the name of Macha thus: 'Macha, that is a crow; or it is one of the three Morrígna, Mesrad Machae, Macha's mast, that is the heads of men after their slaughter.'[57] The horrific image here painted is that of the crow-goddess hovering, harpy-like, on the battlefield waiting for her dues, the severed heads of the slain.

The name of the Badbh carries connotations of rage, fury and violence, a fitting title for a war-spirit. She is very closely linked with the Morrígán, and their identities seem often to have been interchanged. The Badbh is frequently referred to as 'Badbh Catha', the Battle Crow. A Romano-Celtic inscribed dedication to a goddess called Cath-obodua, found in Haute Savoie, may be the same divinity. Badbh represented battle, destruction, chaos and death, and her appearance as a crow prophesied disaster. There is an Irish mythic tale known as 'Da Derga's Hostel' in which the Badbh played a prominent role. She appeared at the hostel or *bruidhen* where King Conaire was staying, awaiting his pre-ordained death (see p. 71). In fact, the encounter between Conaire and the Badbh seems to have taken place in the Otherworld, or at least at its threshold. The Badbh is represented as a hideous, black, crow-like hag in triple form, bleeding and with a rope round her neck: she was a harbinger of doom but her image was that of a human sacrifice. Here the manifestation of the goddess of destruction as hag and carrion-crow merged one into the other. The Badbh stood at the entrance to the *bruidhen*, perched on one leg and using one hand, in a well-known magical formula of the supernatural. She answered Conaire's request for her to reveal her identity in a series of meaningless riddles, again signifying her Otherworld status. The crow-goddess was not alone but was accompanied by a man with one hand, one eye and one leg, conforming, once more, to a magical image, and he carried a roast pig on his back which, appallingly, was still squealing. The Lord of the Otherworld is frequently presented in myth with a pig on his shoulder, and these animals represented the ever-renewing meat-resource that was so characteristic of the Otherworld feast, in which a pig was slaughtered, cooked and consumed only to regenerate endlessly.[58]

It is the Morrígán herself whose nature and character is the most fully developed of the Irish battle-goddesses, both in the Ulster Cycle and in the Mythological Cycle. Her name 'Phantom Queen' betrays her association with death and the shadowy world of the supernatural. She was a goddess of victory for whichever army she chose to support, and she was fickle and capricious in her allegiances. She was a prophet of either death or victory; an instigator of war; she interfered with combat; changed her shape; and she was closely associated with destruction, fertility and sovereignty. At the Second Battle of Magh Tuiredh, an episode in the Book of Invasions in which the divine race of Ireland, the Tuatha Dé Danann, confronted the indigenous demons of the island, the Fomorians, the Morrigán promised aid to the Tuatha Dé Danann, but it was psychological, magical help she offered, not physical support. After the battle she celebrated the victory as a bard or poet, but she also prophesied the end of the world.[59] Both battle and prophecy took place at Samhain, the winter festival of 31 October and 1 November, a liminal, dangerous occasion when time and space were suspended, and the barriers between the supernatural and earthly worlds were temporarily dissolved, so that the spirits could interfere with human affairs and mortals could enter the realms of the dead. In the Ulster Cycle, on the eve of the final battle between Ulster and Connacht, the Morrigán stirred up both armies, standing between them and making mischief by promising victory to both sides. She deceived the Connachtmen in that it was always her intention that Ulster should prevail.

The most important feature of the Morrigán in the Ulster Cycle was her relationship with the great hero Cú Chulainn, the champion of the Ulstermen and himself of superhuman status. This relationship was an ambivalent one: if Cú Chulainn did her bidding, she favoured him, but any contrary independence on his part brought out the Morrigán's destructive temperament. On one occasion, when Cú Chulainn was preparing himself for battle, she appeared to him as a beautiful young seductress. He spurned her impatiently, telling her that he had more important things on his mind than sex and, in her fury, she pitted herself against him in the form of an eel, a wolf and a hornless heifer. These creatures betray the Morrigán's Otherworldliness: the wolf was greyish-red, the colours of the Cwn Annwn, the hounds of the Welsh Otherworld; the heifer was white and red-eared, and again this combination belonged to beasts of the supernatural realms, both in Wales and Ireland. At each shape-change, the Morrigán attacked Cú Chulainn while he fought a human opponent, Loch, at a ford, and she incapacitated him each time so that Loch could wound him. But he was equal to her assault; he could injure her and, indeed, temporarily blinded her. Both Cú Chulainn and the Morrigán were badly hurt and he was overcome by exhaustion. Then she appeared to him in the guise of an old woman milking a cow with three teats,[60] another manifestation of the supernatural. He blessed her and she gave him milk to restore him; only then was she healed of her battle-wounds.[61]

In another important episode concerning Cú Chulainn, the Morrigán and the Badbh appear to have been interchangeable, different versions of the story using one name or the other. The hero was lying asleep one night when he heard a fearful shriek and rushed, naked, outside, his wife following with his weapons and his clothes. He encountered the battle-fury in the image of a red woman, with red eyebrows and a red cloak, riding in a chariot to which was attached a single red horse with one leg, the chariot-pole passing through its body and secured to its forehead with a peg. Next to the vehicle walked a man holding a fork of hazel, driving a cow. Cú Chulainn challenged the appropriation of this animal, since he was guardian over all the cattle of Ulster. The couple responded in riddles (just as does the Badbh to Conaire); Cú Chulainn leapt in rage upon the chariot but the apparition disappeared save for the fury herself who remained, in the form of a crow.[62] The colour red is highly significant, in that it marked the vision as emanating from the Otherworld.

On the morning of Cú Chulainn's death, the Morrigán was able to foretell what would befall him, so she tried to prevent him from going into battle by breaking his chariot-shaft, but in vain. When he died, she (or the Badbh) perched on his shoulder in the form of a crow or raven, and thus signified to his enemies that he was indeed dead and could be safely approached. Her attitude to him remained ambivalent even at his death. The relationship was a curious one: she continually tried to manipulate him in combat and, though his power was nearly as great as hers, in a sense she did succeed in controlling him.[63] The Morrigán was a spirit of destruction and Cú Chulainn was the arch-destroyer, a fighting-machine (equivalent to the 'Terminator' of modern film) that defeated the forces of Connacht virtually single-handed. Where death was, there was Cú Chulainn, and the goddess-crow was present, too, to feed on the results of the slaughter.

That the Morrigán was not only a goddess of war and death but also of fertility was indicated by her recurring association with cattle. She used her prophetic powers to warn the great Donn of Cuailnge (the Brown Bull of Ulster) of his danger, perching on his shoulder as a crow and whispering in his ear. In one tale, the 'Echtra Nerai', the Morrigán is presented as being responsible for the *Táin* (the 'Cattle Raid of Cooley') by stealing an Otherworld cow belonging to one Nera and transferring it to the earthly world. The cow was pregnant by the Donn and the calf born of the union challenged the Findbennach (the White-horned Bull of Connacht). When he failed under the onslaught of Ailill's bull, the calf bellowed for his father to come to the rescue. The Morrigán possessed a herd of magical cows which she guarded jealously. An episode in the *Dinnshenchas* described how, when the bull of a mortal girl, Odras, mated with one of the goddess's herd, the Morrigan cast a spell upon her, turning her into a pool of water. The act was in vengeance for the tainting of Otherworld stock with that of mortals, an unacceptable mingling of the earthly and the supernatural.[64]

The different facets of the Morrigán's character are closely interlinked. She was a spirit of war, death, prophecy, sexuality and fertility. Her role was ambiguous: she was a guardian against chaos, hence her championing of the Tuatha Dé Danann against the demonic Fomorians. But she was also a cause of chaos, especially in the Ulster Cycle.[65] In the episode where she had sex with the Dagdha, she was a goddess of sovereignty, fertility and liminality. Even here the Morrigán's role was complex: the Dagdha came upon her while she carried out the task of the 'Washer at the Ford', a prophetic act which spelled out the imminent destruction of the warriors whose weapons and armour she bathed: thus life, sexuality, prophecy and death are all represented in a single vignette.

45

3 The Divine Female in Welsh Myth

The early Welsh vernacular literature shows evidence of a complex series of myths which relate to a tradition when a polytheistic system was in place. But when we compare this medieval Welsh literature to that of early Ireland, it is clear that the Welsh material has suffered far greater influence from later stories. The Christian God is referred to on numerous occasions, and there is a curious mix of Christianity and paganism. Nevertheless, the supernatural world dominates these tales: the presence of superhuman women and men, enchanted animals, shape-shifters, magical heads and cauldrons of regeneration, all make it possible to refer to this early Welsh written tradition as myth. In addition, we may perceive fundamental mythic features associated with death and rebirth: the Otherworld is an important theme in the Welsh tradition. Occasionally we catch glimpses of a profound mythic system, even a cosmogony, with stories that hint at ancient legends of creation and supernatural explanations of natural phenomena, such as the cultivation of cereals, or the introduction of pigs into Wales. The most recognisable Welsh mythology, in which goddesses and gods are demonstrably present, is contained within 'The Four Branches of the *Mabinogi*', the Tale of Culhwch and Olwen, and a few other works, notably 'The Spoils of Annwn' and the Book of Taliesin. The Welsh mythology is recognisably present, even though it has been overlain by later influences so that it is less easy to identify than similar elements in the comparable Irish material. Nonetheless, the superhuman, heroic, status of many characters may refer back to a series of pagan deities who were, perhaps deliberately, demoted to a less positive, fairy-like status by story-tellers seeking to 'launder' the Welsh tradition for Christian consumption.

The women who feature prominently in the Welsh myths have certain characteristics in common: they often appear to be passive creatures, beings to whom things happen rather than initiators of events. But their power lies in their role as facilitators or enablers; they are catalysts, stimuli whose very existence causes momentous occurrences which are crucial to the development of the myths themselves. So, while the females in Welsh stories may appear shadowy, insubstantial and ineffectual, we may perhaps regard them as archetypes, whose specific characters may not be as important as their symbolic roles.

Rhiannon

The story of Rhiannon appears at its most fully developed in the First Branch of the *Mabinogi*, where we are introduced to her as the wife of Pwyll, lord of Dyfed. Rhiannon recurs in the Third Branch, this time married (after Pwyll's death) to another powerful hero, Manawydan. But there is a link between the First and Third Branches: in the Second Branch there is a brief allusion to the magical singing birds of Rhiannon, a theme which reappears outside the Four Branches in the Tale of Culhwch and Olwen (see pp. 66–7). Throughout the *Mabinogi*, the supernatural status of Rhiannon is very evident.

It will be useful briefly to outline the tale of Rhiannon before considering her identity and function as a mythical being. In the First Branch, Rhiannon appeared to Pwyll as he sat on the Gorsedd Arberth, a magical meeting-place near his court of Narberth. Pwyll saw a beautiful woman in dazzling gold, riding past him on a white horse. He bade one of his men to follow her but, however fast he rode, he could not catch up with her, even though her horse was apparently moving quite slowly. The next day the mysterious woman appeared again and Pwyll sent his swiftest horseman after her, but to no avail. On the third day, in desperation, Pwyll called to the lady and she immediately reined in her horse to speak to him, telling him that she had indeed sought him out to marry him, in preference to her affianced suitor, Gwawl. The two made plans to marry in a year and a day and Rhiannon asked Pwyll to come then to the court of her father, Hefeydd the Old. There Pwyll encountered Gwawl but won Rhiannon by means of her trickery.

The second major episode concerning Rhiannon in the First Branch is the conception, birth and loss of her son. When she arrived at Pwyll's court, she gave lavish presents to all the nobles, and thus gained the reputation of being a bountiful queen. But when, after three years, she had not conceived, Pwyll's men turned against Rhiannon, castigating her for her barrenness and exhorting Pwyll to put her away. Her husband demurred and soon afterwards, Rhiannon conceived and, in due course, produced a baby boy. But on the night he was born, the women appointed to guard the infant woke in terror at dawn to find the child missing. In their fear they put the blame on Rhiannon, killing a puppy and smearing its blood on her face and hands as she lay asleep, to make it look as though she had murdered and eaten her own son. Rhiannon was judged guilty of infanticide but the punishment imposed on her by Pwyll was a curious one. She had to spend seven years seated near a horse-block outside the gate of Llys Arberth, telling her story to anyone who came by and offering to carry visitors up to the court on her back, like a beast of burden.

The baby turned up far away at the stable of one Teyrnon, who had been the victim of a series of curious events: each year, on May eve, his best mare gave birth to a superb foal, which mysteriously disappeared. On this occasion, Teyrnon decided to keep

Stone relief of the Celtic horse-goddess Epona with her mare and foal. From Meursault, Burgundy. The horse-symbolism associated with the goddess, who was venerated in the Roman period all over Europe, has led to her identification with the Welsh mythic heroine Rhiannon.

watch: the mare gave birth and, as she did so, a great claw reached through the stable-window to seize the foal. But Teyrnon was ready and struck off the claw. Hearing a great scream and commotion, he rushed outside but could see nothing in the darkness. When he returned, lying on the threshold of the stable was a baby boy, wrapped in a silken shawl and thus clearly of gentle birth. Teyrnon and his wife fostered the child, noting his superhuman rate of growth and development. The boy showed a great affinity with horses and, when he was four years old, Teyrnon gave him the colt that he had saved the night the child arrived. At about this time Teyrnon began to note their foster-son's close resemblance to Pwyll and, knowing the story of the royal child's disappearance, realised that their foster-son must belong to Pwyll and Rhiannon. The boy was taken to the court and named Pryderi ('worry') by Rhiannon as a memento of her troubles.

In the Third Branch, Rhiannon remarried after Pwyll's death. Her new husband, Manawydan, was a craftsman and a magician. The focus of this story was the enchantment of Dyfed, whereby the countryside turned into a wasteland and everything in Dyfed disappeared save for Manawydan, Rhiannon, Pryderi and his wife Cigfa. One important episode in the tale concerns Rhiannon: after many vicissitudes and sojourns in England, the four returned to Dyfed and the two men went hunting. Their hounds encountered an enormous boar, white and shining, which lured the dogs into a strange *caer* (fort or castle). Despite Manawydan's warning, Pryderi followed his dogs into the *caer* and saw a beautiful golden bowl which he touched. As he did so, he fell under a spell: he could neither move nor speak and his fingers were stuck to the bowl. On hearing of her son's plight, Rhiannon went to find him and suffered the same enchantment.

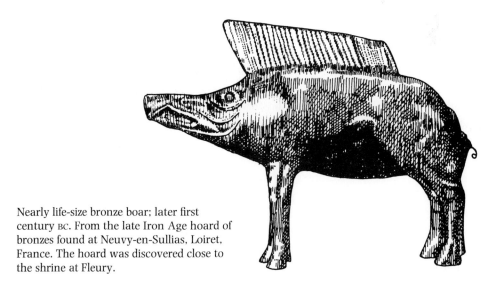

Nearly life-size bronze boar; later first century BC. From the late Iron Age hoard of bronzes found at Neuvy-en-Sullias, Loiret, France. The hoard was discovered close to the shrine at Fleury.

At the climax of the tale Manawydan, bereft of his hunting-dogs, was forced to turn to agriculture. He planted three fields of wheat but, just as they were ripe for harvesting, the first two fields were destroyed during the night. Manawydan kept watch over his surviving field and witnessed the extraordinary sight of his corn being attacked by an army of mice. The creatures were all too fast for him but for one, a pregnant mouse which was slower than the rest. Manawydan now embarked upon the bizarre process of hanging the captured mouse on Gorsedd Arberth, despite the fact that he was petitioned not to do it by a clerk and a priest, the first strangers Manawydan had seen in Dyfed since its enchantment. Finally a bishop arrived to intervene: it turned out that he was one Llwyd, a magician, who confessed that he was the source of Dyfed's enchantment, explaining that this was done in revenge for the trickery of Pwyll and Rhiannon against Gwawl, Rhiannon's original suitor. Dyfed was now restored and the mouse, Llwyd's metamorphosed wife, was redeemed.[1]

The supernatural, mythic nature of Rhiannon herself is suggested both by her own character and by her conformation to archetypes of myth. Rhiannon's name is important: it is usually accepted as a modern derivative of the ancient name or title Rigantona ('Great Queen'), and a pagan Celtic goddess Rigantona may have been given a human identity as Rhiannon, queen of Dyfed. But there have also been suggestions that the name Rhiannon may also be derived from two Welsh words *rhiain* meaning maiden and Annwn, the Welsh Otherworld. The idea of Rhiannon as a goddess of the Otherworld is a theme to which we shall return.[2]

The most important aspect of Rhiannon's identity is that which associates her with horse-symbolism, and many scholars have equated Rhiannon with the Celtic European horse-goddess Epona. The horse-symbolism surrounding Rhiannon is intense and repeated: the initial encounter with Pwyll, when she appeared riding a great white horse that could not be outpaced, contains a supernatural dimension. The close bond that existed between Rhiannon's son and Teyrnon's foal shows that the horse-link had been transmitted from mother to son. Pryderi's close affinity with horses, especially with the foal born at the same time as himself, conforms to a mythic theme associated with Celtic heroes: we may cite a parallel example in the myth of Cú Chulainn, who had a birth-death link with two foals, which became his chariot-horses. Rhiannon's penance reinforces her essential horse-symbolism: it involved her in the behaviour of a horse, sitting by a horse-block ready to carry people on her back. Finally, in the Third Branch, the horse-symbolism was reasserted: at the end of the story, when Dyfed was restored, Manawydan asked Llwyd to describe the nature of Rhiannon's and Pryderi's bondage under the enchantment of the golden bowl. He replied thus: 'Rhiannon would have the collars of the asses, after they had been carrying hay, about her neck.'[3]

The link between Rhiannon, her son and horses must come about because of Rhiannon's identity as a horse-goddess.[4] It may even be that she was a goddess of sovereignty, as in Ireland, where the female deity of the land married the mortal king in order to promote and maintain the prosperity of the territory. An Ulster myth recounted by Giraldus Cambrensis contains details of a royal initiation ceremony in which the new king simulated a union with a white mare, which was then sacrificed, carved and boiled. The king and his retinue ate the meat and he washed in the broth, drinking it directly from the bath. This completed his inauguration and his authority was assured.[5] It is possible that Pwyll's union with Rhiannon is part of a similar mythic tradition. There is an ancient Greek legend recounted by Agesilaos: a mysogynist named Stellos copulated with a mare, the result of the union being a beautiful baby girl who was given the name Epona by the mare herself.[6] This confusion between human and animal identity is close to the shape-shifting that is so strong an element in Celtic myth. Both Epona and Rhiannon may have been both woman and horse.

The possible link between Rhiannon and sovereignty may relate to her role as a mother-goddess. There are suggestions of this in her character: when she arrived at Pwyll's court as his bride, she established herself as a generous queen, a source of largesse, like Epona herself (see Chapter 8). She was the mother of Pryderi, a powerful hero who carried forward the line of Pwyll. Indeed, there is a suggestion that Rhiannon may have been one of the three ancestresses of Britain alluded to at the beginning of the Second Branch, of whom Branwen is another[7] (see p. 55). It may be significant that it was Rhiannon who named her son, not Pwyll. This tradition of mothers naming their male offspring recurs in the Fourth Branch, when Arianrhod refused to give her son a name, thus denying him his first rite of passage. Rhiannon's role as a goddess of sovereignty, similar to those of Irish myth, could manifest itself in a particular theme which is common to European myth, namely that of the sorrowing mother and the lost child. Caitlin Matthews[8] compares the fate of Rhiannon and her stolen son with such Classical legends as that of Demeter, the Greek corn-goddess, who lost her daughter Persephone to the Underworld powers. In addition, the fact that Rhiannon chose Pwyll (rather than the other way round) appears to parallel the Irish tradition whereby the goddess of sovereignty selected her mortal mate.

The theme of the 'wronged wife' is another common thread which runs through many myths, and one which we meet in the tale of Branwen. Both Rhiannon and Branwen (the heroine of the Second Branch) were foreign queens, brought to their husband's courts from a different region or country.[9] At first Rhiannon was popular because of her generosity, but her barrenness either turned Pwyll's people against her or was used as an excuse to get rid of her, because of jealousy or xenophobia. In fact, if Rhiannon was some kind of goddess of sovereignty, her apparent lack of ability to produce an heir would have had serious consequences for the prosperity of Dyfed, since she would have conferred her sterile status on to her husband and thence to the land itself.

Rhiannon was falsely accused of killing her son, who was in fact stolen away under supernatural circumstances. What is interesting here is that the watchwomen not only framed her for the child's supposed murder, but for eating him as well, hence the smearing of the puppy's blood on the face of the sleeping queen. So the 'crime' was doubly monstrous and unnatural. But Proinsias Mac Cana[10] makes the point that Rhiannon's penance was totally inappropriate to her supposed offence. Surely such an dreadful act would incur banishment at the very least. Instead, Rhiannon was given a grotesque punishment which only makes sense if she were tied to a particular function, that of a horse-goddess.

The supernatural status of Rhiannon manifests itself in other ways: she first met Pwyll when he was at the Gorsedd Arberth, a magical, perhaps liminal, place where the Otherworld imposed its strange values on the world of humans. Any person within the Gorsedd either suffered wounding or encountered a wondrous spectacle or event: for Pwyll, it was his first sight of Rhiannon. This, in itself, made her special. There are strong indications of a link between Rhiannon and the Otherworld. It is even sometimes suggested that she was the daughter of a king of Annwn and that her suitor, Gwawl, also belonged to this shadowy realm.[11] Certainly, if Rhiannon's name can be interpreted as 'Maid of Annwn', then her affiliations are very clear. Another possible link between Rhiannon and the Otherworld is her white horse: animals which were white, or white and red, often belonged to the Otherworld, both in Wales and in Ireland. Rhiannon's connection with the Otherworld is present also in her marriage to Pwyll, who had the title 'Head of Annwn', from his sojourn there for a year in place of Arawn. But if Rhiannon was a goddess of Annwn, then her own enchantment in the Tale of Manawydan seems curious: she and Pryderi both fell under the spell of the enchanted bowl; their loss of speech symbolises death and, by implication, their presence in the Otherworld. Thus Rhiannon was subject to the same deprivation as any human who encountered Otherworld forces. Loss of the power of speech occurs in the Tale of Branwen, when dead warriors were resurrected by their immersion and cooking in the Irish Cauldron of Rebirth, but could no longer speak because they were really still dead and belonged to the supernatural world. But perhaps the strongest indication of the Otherworld status of Rhiannon is the allusion, made in the Tale of Branwen and in the Tale of Culhwch and Olwen, to the three magical singing birds of Rhiannon. In the Tale of Branwen, these birds had power to heal and soothe, causing men to forget their sorrows.[12] The birds could be clearly heard even though they were almost too far away across the sea to be seen: this phenomenon betrays their supernatural character.[13] The fatally-wounded Brân prophesied the birds' presence to his men: 'In Harlech you will be feasting seven years and the birds of Rhiannon singing to you.'[14] There is a sense in which Brân's warriors were perhaps already in the Otherworld: their feast may have been an Otherworld banquet. Certainly, magical singing and healing birds were part of the Irish Happy Otherworld. Clíodna was a goddess of that world, who possessed three brightly-coloured birds: they uttered such a sweet song that the sick were lulled into a healing sleep.[15] In the Tale of Culhwch and Olwen, the acquisition of Rhiannon's birds was one of the 'insuperable' tasks imposed upon Culhwch by Olwen's father Ysbaddaden before he would be allowed to marry her: '... there is that thou wilt not get. The birds of Rhiannon, they that wake the dead and lull the living to sleep ...'[16]

Rhiannon was of high status compared to many of the 'women' in Welsh myth: she enjoyed much greater prestige than, say, Branwen, who appeared as a passive pawn in a man's world. But Rhiannon was far from passive: from the time she met Pwyll and announced her intention to marry him, she is presented as an initiator, one who controlled events. She was able to prophesy the downfall of Gwawl; she, unlike Manawydan, had the courage (or temerity) to brave the supernatural forces to try and rescue Pryderi from the enchanted *caer* in the Tale of Manawydan. As well as being an initiator, Rhiannon was, in addition, a catalyst, someone whose presence or behaviour triggered momentous events: thus it could be argued that Rhiannon's jilting of Gwawl led to the supernatural theft of the infant Pryderi, and to the devastation of Dyfed, which Llwyd laid waste directly because of Gwawl's displacement.

Rhiannon's status is interesting: she was as much of a 'hero' as Pwyll, Pryderi or Brân. She and Pwyll appear to have been equal in love, but Jean Markale makes the point that motherhood reduced her rights, power and rank.[17] The equality of their marriage is interesting in that it may reflect early medieval Welsh law, which was liberal towards women in this respect. Celtic sexual equality may be evidenced, too, in the iconography of pagan Celtic Europe, where divine couples are depicted as of equal size, despite the natural size difference between men and women, which is deliberately not represented.[18]

Rhiannon's character is full of mystery, contradiction and paradox, features which attend many mythical heroes. She may have been a goddess of fertility, although she had difficulty in conceiving a child; she was, by implication, a goddess of the Otherworld, although she suffered from its power; she was an initiator but was powerless to prevent the abduction of her son; her link with horses appears to indicate that she was a horse-goddess, although the extent of her actual conflation with a mare is unclear. The monstrous allegation of child-eating appears to arise from nothing, except to emphasise her role as a 'calumniated wife', unless it is to stress her Otherworldly origins in a realm where human values did not apply. Rhiannon was extremely powerful. She could cause the land to be prosperous, but she was also instrumental in transforming Dyfed into a desert. The paradox of life and death, fertility and barrenness, is precisely the kind of ambiguity that we find in the characters of such Irish goddesses as the Morrigán, Medb and Macha.

Branwen

The Second Branch of the Mabinogi is named after its main female character, Branwen. The story is concerned with the fortunes of the royal family ap Llyr of Harlech and a disastrous war between Wales and Ireland. The patronym ap Llyr means 'Son of the Sea', and this first points us to the disguised divinity of the family. Branwen's two most prominent brothers were Manawydan and Brân the Blessed (Bendigeidfran), who was superhuman in size and moral stature. A brief description of the main events in the Tale of Branwen demonstrates the centrality of Branwen herself even though, at first glance, she seems to be a passive victim. Matholwch, king of Ireland, travelled to Harlech to seek the hand of Branwen in marriage. Brân agreed and the betrothal took place. But another brother, Efnisien, was angered by the union and grossly insulted Matholwch by savagely mutilating the horses of the Irish delegation. Matholwch was apparently appeased by the generous compensatory gifts heaped upon him by Brân, and was especially mollified by the most precious present of all, a cauldron (originally from an Irish lake) that could resurrect the dead. Branwen and Matholwch sailed for Ireland and all seemed well for a while. The royal couple produced a son, Gwern. But the Irish court began to murmur against Efnisien's insult to their king and turned Matholwch against his queen. Branwen was banished to the

The late-thirteenth-century castle at Harlech, Gwynedd. Harlech is mentioned in the Second Branch of the *Mabinogi* as the seat of the family of Llyr, members of which included Branwen and her brother Brân.

kitchen as a cook and was humiliated by being boxed on the ears by the butcher every day after he had finished cutting up meat. Matholwch took care that all communication between Ireland and Britain was cut off, so that Brân would not hear of Branwen's fate, but she reared and trained a young starling to speak and to recognise her brother, and sent it off to Harlech with a message tied to its feet.

Brân's discovery of his sister's plight caused him to mobilise his forces for war on Ireland. Matholwch's look-outs saw a weird sight which looked like a mountain amid a forest approaching Ireland on the sea. This was Brân's navy and Brân himself, too large for a ship, wading through the water. Matholwch sued for peace and the noblemen of Wales and Ireland gathered in a house, specially built so that it would hold the vast Brân, to witness the conferral of the Irish kingship upon Gwern. But some of the Irishmen were armed and hidden in flour-bags and they were crushed to death by Efnisien, who also seized Gwern and thrust him into the fire. Branwen was restrained by Brân from casting herself after her child, and there ensued a full-scale war between the two countries. Brân's forces won but it was a Pyrrhic victory: only seven of his warriors survived and he himself was fatally wounded. He instructed his men to cut off his head, which remained alive and uncorrupted for many years, until it was finally buried, on Brân's instructions, in London, its face turned towards the east so that no invader would ever penetrate British soil. After the great battle, Branwen herself sailed to Aber Alaw on Anglesey, where she died of shame, broken-hearted that she should be the cause of the ruin of two great nations.[19]

We need to look for signs that Branwen was other than a passive figure in myth to see if anything in the story points to her divine or supernatural status. Her first claim to this rank lies in the undeniably god-like being of her brother Brân. But early on in the story, Branwen is described as one of the three ancestresses or matriarchs of the Island of Britain.[20] This is a curious epithet, since she died without an heir. It may be that the title 'ancestress' or 'matriarch' relates to an earlier, lost, tradition where Branwen's divine status was more fully revealed. There is no trace of Branwen anywhere in the surviving early literature, apart from the Second Branch of the *Mabinogi*,[21] and we might speculate whether she existed as a character prior to the compilation of the Tale of Branwen. The name does survive in the name of a North Welsh mountain-peak, Cadair Fronwen (Branwen's Seat) but this name could itself be derived from the *Mabinogi* and need not precede it. Once in the *White Book of Rhydderch* Branwen's name appears as Bronwen, possibly an earlier version of her name, which was altered to Branwen perhaps because of her brother Brân's name. Proinsias Mac Cana is of the view that the Bronwen form could imply the one-time existence of an earlier tradition, and it may be significant that the name Bronwen occurs on one of the two occasions in the *Mabinogi* where she is called an ancestress.[22] Who were the other two ancestresses mentioned? Candidates could include Rhiannon of Dyfed, who bore Pryderi, and Arianrhod of Gwynedd, who gave birth to Lleu, both heroes of divine rank.

We need to examine the apparent passivity of Branwen's role. Like Rhiannon, Branwen is portrayed as the archetypal suffering or 'calumniated' wife and again, like Rhiannon, she was a foreign bride, whose husband's followers turned against her, even though she was bountiful. Both Branwen and Rhiannon were falsely condemned and punished, and both penances were bizarre and humiliating. Indeed, there may be greater similarities between the punishments inflicted on the two queens than is immediately apparent. Rhiannon was treated like a horse and, since Branwen suffered blows from the butcher after he had been chopping carcasses, is there not a sense in which she, too, was being treated like an animal? Mac Cana emphasises Branwen's passive role, comparing her unfavourably with the Irish Deirdre (see Chapter 6), who suffered but had a fully-developed and dominant personality.[23] Rhiannon, too, appears to have had more character and more control over her own destiny.[24] Mac Cana says of Branwen, 'Branwen herself is a shadowy, wilting figure of whom it might be said with some truth that she never comes to life until she comes to die.'[25] But I think this view can, to an extent, be challenged. Like Rhiannon, Branwen was an enabler, a catalyst, whose existence caused things to happen: in the case of Branwen, it was war. But, in addition, there are episodes in the Tale of Branwen which demonstrate her active, independent role. For example, the episode of the starling shows initiative and also some supernatural skills in bridging the gulf of communication between human and animal. Later on, when Matholwch and Brân were wavering between war and reconciliation, Branwen's counsel was powerful and influential in persuading the two to come together at Gwern's feast.[26] Indeed, the meeting of the Irish and Welsh nobles was called the Assembly of Branwen and Matholwch, as if she had the primary rank. Only Branwen was able to decipher the apparent mystery of the forest and the mountain on the sea that represented the invasion of her brother and his ships.[27]

Emphasis is sometimes put upon the Irish influences in the Tale of Branwen, which could have come about either through borrowing or, more likely, from a commonality of mythic tradition between Ireland and Wales. Most striking, in this respect, is the Cauldron of Regeneration, which does not only closely resemble those of early Insular myth but is itself described as of Irish origin. Branwen herself has links with Irish female 'heroes': there is a similarity, for instance, between the deaths of Branwen and Finnebair, daughter of Medb, the queen-goddess of Connacht. Both died of broken hearts because they had caused disaster for so many men.[28] But the link with Irish myth may be even greater, in that there is some reason to see Branwen as a goddess of sovereignty. Her marriage to Matholwch was clearly of prime importance to him and, like Rhiannon and Pwyll, Branwen may have been confirming Matholwch's kingship by her union with him, though she could not, as Matthews suggests[29] be conferring kingship upon him since he was already Ireland's king. If Cadair Fronwen is named after Branwen and is an early name, this may imply that Branwen was perceived as a personification of territory, like the Irish goddesses of sovereignty. Branwen's description as ancestress or matriarch seems to support her role as a mother-goddess. Finally in this context, Branwen's image as a provider of plenty is perhaps significant. Like Rhiannon, when she entered her new realm as Matholwch's wife, she established herself as a generous, bountiful figure, a source of new wealth and prosperity: 'Not one great man or noble lady would come to visit Branwen to whom she gave not a brooch or a ring or a treasured royal jewel.'[30]

Arianrhod: Virgin and Mother

The Fourth Branch of the *Mabinogi*, the Tale of Math, is concerned with the descendants of Dôn, a probable ancestor- or mother-goddess. Math was lord of Gwynedd: a peculiarity of his rule was that, unless at war, he had to have his feet resting in the lap of a virgin, a phenomenon examined below. The mythical figure of Arianrhod comes into the story because when Goewin, Math's virgin-footholder, was raped, Arianrhod (Math's niece) applied for the job. But as Arianrhod undertook the chastity-test, stepping over Math's magical wand, she gave birth to two infant-boys, one Dylan who slipped away into the sea and another, whom Arianrhod's brother Gwydion took under his protection. The main focus of the Tale of Math consists of the three curses imposed by Arianrhod upon this second son: he would never be named unless his mother decided to name him; he would never bear arms, unless his mother agreed to equip him; he would never possess a human wife. Thus Arianrhod effectively denied her son the three essential rites of passage towards manhood. Gwydion's trickery caused the boy to be named inadvertently by his mother: Lleu Llaw Gyffes, the 'Bright One of the Skilful Hand'. In the same way, Gwydion tricked his sister into arming Lleu. But the only way Lleu could marry was for Gwydion and his fellow magician, Math, to conjure up for him a wife made of flowers, Blodeuwedd.[31]

Before we discuss Blodeuwedd further, it is worthwhile to explore the nature and status of Arianrhod in mythic terms. She was clearly a powerful figure to be able to impose such terrible bonds on her son. She resembles Rhiannon and other Celtic supernatural women, in that it was she who had the right to name him, or not. Arianrhod provides a good example of the paradox that is so prominent in Welsh myth: she was apparently a maiden and a mother able, like the Virgin Mary, to conceive and bear a son of divine status, while still a virgin. Lleu himself was likewise surrounded by paradox, not only in his 'immaculate conception' but also in the 'impossibility' of his death. He could only be killed in very particular and seemingly contradictory circumstances: for instance, he could not be slain by night or day, neither in nor out of doors, and only by a spear made when work was forbidden. In fact, it was only a woman's betrayal, that of Blodeuwedd, that could destroy him (see below). If we examine the virginity theme of Arianrhod, we can see that it is not straightforward. Math's magical staff, over which Arianrhod had to step as proof of her virginity, could be, in some sense, a phallic symbol with which a maiden had to avoid contact. Jean Markale argues that the Welsh word used for Arianrhod's apparent virginity, *morwyn*, has more than one meaning. To a man, the term may have had the very precise connotation of virginity, a thing which was highly-prized according to Welsh medieval law-texts. But to Arianrhod herself, *morwyn* may simply have meant a free, unattached young girl, unbeholden to any man's patronage. Thus Arianrhod and Math may have misunderstood each other.[32] An interesting point here is that, although in the version of the *Mabinogi* which has come down to us, it was Math's footholder Goewin whose virginity he so closely guarded, a late 15th-century allusion to the Tale of Math names Arianrhod, not Goewin, as the original virgin footholder. It has been suggested[33] that the two poets involved in the compilation of this text may have been quoting an earlier and more authentic version of Lleu's conception than appears in the extant text.

Arianrhod is important in terms of her role in the succession of the divine family of Dôn. It was vital that Lleu was preserved and that the rites of passage due to a man were not denied him. Thus the powerful magic of Math and Gwydion was brought to bear on the curses inflicted by Arianrhod on Lleu. Interestingly, one of the Welsh Triads names Arianrhod as one of three fair maidens,[34] an accolade similar to that applied to Branwen. The implication may be that Arianrhod, like Branwen, was a ancestor-goddess, perhaps forming a triad with Branwen and Rhiannon.[35]

Two related questions need to be posed: first, who was Lleu's father and second, why was Arianrhod so hostile to her son? The behaviour of the magician Gwydion is crucial to both questions: he intervened to save Lleu at his birth, took him under his protection, brought him up as his own child, and imposed his own powerful magic to break Arianrhod's curses. The obvious conclusion is that Lleu's uncle was also his father and that Lleu's birth was the result of an incestuous relationship between brother and sister. The horror of this unnatural union and its consequences may have turned Arianrhod's natural mother-love into a disgusted hatred and a desire for Lleu's destruction. This is the only reasonable explanation for Arianrhod's unremitting malevolence towards Lleu. The situation may be even more significant in that, in Irish myth, birth as a result of incest could be a sign of divinity.

Certain features point to the divine status of Arianrhod. She may, as suggested earlier, have been an ancestor-goddess, like Modron in the Tale of Culhwch and Olwen, and Branwen and Rhiannon. Her son Lleu was almost certainly divine, a cognate with the Irish god of light, Lugh. Lleu's name was 'Bright One', which seems to denote his function as a celestial god and, when he was finally struck a mortal blow (see p. 60), he did not perish but flew, in eagle-form, to the top of a great oak. Both the eagle and oak were symbolic of the Roman sky-god Jupiter, who was worshipped all over Europe in his Celtic form during the early first millennium AD.[36] If Lleu was divine, then it is probable that his mother was a goddess. Indeed her name, which means 'Silver Wheel', may likewise point to her function as a sky-deity, perhaps a moon-goddess. Finally, the three bonds imposed by Arianrhod on Lleu have important symbolism, apart from the clear denial of the boy's development and maturity. The naming of Lleu comes about when Arianrhod witnesses his skilful killing of a wren, a seemingly senseless act, except that wren-killing itself may have had a symbolic meaning: there is an Irish folk-custom in which the killing of wrens symbolised the death of the old year in winter and the rebirth of the new spring season.[37] If this has any relevance to the Welsh tradition, it may mean that hidden in the story is a seasonal myth of re-creation and fertility, which only works if the mother-goddess Arianrhod initially denied Lleu a name until he earned it by his own skill.

The second curse, that which denied Lleu arms, may imply that Lleu had to earn his right to weapons and that the magic of Gwydion was essential to bring about this supernatural event. In the myth of the Ulster hero Cú Chulainn, the champion had the greatest difficulty acquiring weapons which did not break at his touch. This 'difficulty' in gaining arms may belong to a common Hiberno-Welsh tradition, whereby the overcoming of the problem imbued the warrior-hero with sanctity and prowess.

Small bronze eagle, symbol of the sky-god, from the Romano-Celtic temple at Woodeaton, Oxfordshire. In the Fourth Branch of the Mabinogi, Arianrhod's son Lleu was transformed into an eagle after his betrayal by his wife Blodeuwedd and his mortal wounding by her lover Gronw.

The final curse, the denial of a human wife, may point to Lleu's own divinity and the need for his mate to be 'special'. It is even possible to argue that Lleu's divinity is only finally proved by his transmutation into the eagle, emblem of the sky-god. Perhaps it was necessary, in terms of his status, for him to go through the ordeal of death and rebirth in bird-form, before being rescued and re-transformed by his creator-protector Gwydion.

Blodeuwedd the Betrayer

The existence of Blodeuwedd, the other important woman-goddess in the Tale of Math, is closely linked with the behaviour and actions of Arianrhod, since it was because of her that Blodeuwedd was created.

Lleu's protector Gwydion was concerned to overcome the 'wife-denial' curse of Arianrhod. So he conspired with Math to create Blodeuwedd, a 'Flower-Woman' made from the blossom of the oak, meadowsweet and broom, wild flowers each of which blooms at a different time of the year, in different habitats. Flowers have been defined as being '... from nature at its most fully evolved.'[38] But, although Blodeuwedd was beautiful, she was supremely unsatisfactory as a human being. Because she was not born of a normal sexual union, she was unstable and, because she was Gwydion's creation and not human, she was rootless, treacherous and without moral values. Gwydion's magic may have been able to fashion the body of a woman but it could not give her a soul. In a sense, she remained as a being of the Otherworld and did not belong on earth. Blodeuwedd has a parallel in the creation-myth of Adam and Eve, in which a wife was specially made for Adam by God. It could be argued that Eve was as unstable as Blodeuwedd and for the same reason, but her existence was essential for the creation-myth to be developed. It was because Blodeuwedd was fashioned by magical means that she could cause Lleu's downfall.

Blodeuwedd was faithless and took a lover, Gronw. The lovers conspired to destroy her husband. Because Lleu could only be slain under extremely difficult circumstances, Blodeuwedd questioned him closely as to the manner in which he was vulnerable. She even persuaded the unsuspecting (and remarkably gullible) Lleu to simulate the position in which he could be killed. As he did so, Gronw leapt from his hiding-place and inflicted a mortal spear-wound upon his rival. Lleu demonstrated his godlike immortality by his immediate transformation into an eagle. Vengeance finally overtook the lovers: Gronw was slain by the restored Lleu, but Blodeuwedd could not be killed because she was the magical creation of Gwydion and belonged to the Otherworld. Instead, she was condemned by her creator to live in owl-form, shunned by all other birds and forced to exist by hunting at night.[39]

The story of Blodeuwedd contains many symbolic features which confirm her supernatural, perhaps divine, status. Her immortality is significant; and it may be that her link with the Underworld is confirmed by her transformation to a night-predator. Blodeuwedd has an Irish cognate, Blathnait, whose name also means 'Flower'. Blathnait, too, was treacherous, and betrayed the hero Cú Roi for love of Cú Chulainn. It is possible that the story of Blathnait was well-known in medieval Wales, and could well have influenced the Blodeuwedd myth,[40] if the two stories did not arise from a common pool of tradition. It is interesting that the paradoxical 'death' of Lleu came about because of the woman closest to him, his wife; it was only by the betrayal of a female that his 'difficult' death could be accomplished. But Lleu's supernatural power was stronger than Blodeuwedd's: both shape-shifted to bird-form but he was a daytime creature and survived (having regained human form), whilst she, as a night-owl, remained within her animal-enchantment for ever.

If we pose the question as to why Blodeuwedd behaved as she did, the answer may not simply lie in her creation as an amoral, rootless being. It appears that, although she was specifically conjured up as a wife for Lleu, she rejected her passive role and, like Frankenstein's monster, took on an independent entity, eschewing her chosen mate and selecting one of her own choice. Perhaps – and the same may be true of Arianrhod – Blodeuwedd's behaviour reflects a female attempt to rebel against masculine domination. The Tale of Math is about the family of Dôn, who was apparently an ancestor/mother-goddess. But the real power in the story rested with men and the myth may, in addition to its character as a creation-story, symbolise a battle for power between the gods and the goddesses. Both Arianrhod and Blodeuwedd tried very hard to end the male line of the house of Dôn. We are not told whether Lleu had issue of his own after his 'death' and 'rebirth', or whether the two women ultimately succeeded in their endeavour.

Bronze handle-mount in the form of an owl, from the Brå Cauldron, Denmark; third century BC. The flower woman Blodeuwedd was turned into an owl as a punishment for her treachery.

The question as to whether or not Blodeuwedd was a true goddess is a difficult one. She was the creation of Gwydion and Math, who were certainly of supernatural status. She was immortal, though she could be severely punished by being meta-morphosed just as, earlier in the Tale of Math, Gwydion was himself so punished for facilitating the rape of Goewin and fomenting war between Gwynedd and Dyfed (see below). Blodeuwedd belonged firmly in the realms of the Otherworld, a force for evil because of her unnatural creation. But she was the wife of a god and was thus treated as an equal in the divine house of Math.

Virginity, Sexuality and Sovereignty in Welsh Myth

One of the most curious elements of the Tale of Math concerns the lord of Gwynedd himself: '... Math son of Mathonwy would not be alive, except while his feet were in the lap of a virgin, unless it were the disturbance of war which prevented him'.[41] This statement raises some fascinating and complex issues: the virginity of the footholder was crucial; so was the close contact between Math and the body of the girl; a state of war temporarily cancelled the need for this contact between king and virgin. Goewin was the footholder in post when the story begins. Math's nephew Gilfaethwy lusted after her and Gwydion, his brother, contrived a war between Gwynedd and Dyfed to ensure Math's absence. When the king returned, Goewin had been raped and his footholder was thus unable to continue her duties. Math's fury caused the three-year punishment of the brothers, who were transformed annually into successive pairs of animals. Goewin herself was not simply discarded, but was clearly a person of some importance: she spoke out against her violation, thus triggering the penance of Gwydion and Gilfaethwy; and she was offered marriage by Math so, by implication, becoming queen of Gwynedd.[42] The symbolism of the footholder is complex: we know, from the Laws of Hywel Dda, of a tradition whereby a medieval Welsh king had a *troediawc*, a footholder who was male and acted as a royal bodyservant. This individual was employed to hold the king's feet from the time he sat down to eat until he went to bed. During this time, his royal duties were suspended and, in a sense, he temporarily ceased to be king. It was now that the *troediawc* wielded his power: clemency and freedom could be demanded of him by criminals since, while he held the king's feet, mercy gained ascendancy over royal justice.[43]

It would appear that the conception of the virgin-footholder in the Tale of Math may be associated in some way with the historical court-position as outlined in the law-texts. But there are important differences between the myth and the reality of medieval court-tradition. Goewin's femininity and her untouched virginity were essential and must have carried important symbolism associated with that state. A maiden was perhaps perceived as a powerful source of fertility, precisely because her sexuality was particularly intense, being undiluted, undissipated and thus entire.[44]

Virginity is traditionally highly prized in many, especially patriarchal, societies: this may not simply be because the paternity of the heir is all-important, but because purity and fertile power were seen to be concentrated in a maiden. The Welsh laws make specific mention of the importance of the virgin-state of a bride before her first marriage. The power of virginity is stressed in early Welsh myth: a good example, which corresponds to the value put upon Goewin's position, lies in *Preiddeu Annwn* ('The Spoils of Annwn'), a thirteenth-century poem ascribed to Taliesin, which describes the cauldron of Annwn, the subject of Arthur's quest. This vessel could only be heated by the breath of nine virgins.[45] Thus the fertile potency of the great cauldron of plenty and regeneration was activated by the sexual intensity of the virgin.

Goewin's position perhaps implies that she, in a sense, represented a goddess of sovereignty, a personification of the fertile land itself. If that is the case, then it is significant that Math's feet only had to be in contact with her during peace-time. There may be a suggestion implicit in the myth that war itself generates a life-force and, if that is accepted, then the same link between sexuality, fertility, territory and war which is evident in the personae of the Irish goddesses is present in the Welsh mythic tradition.

Sheet-gold bowl with chased and repoussé decoration, bearing images of deer, the sun and moon; sixth century BC. From Zürich, Switzerland. In the Mabinogi, Rhiannon and Pryderi were enchanted by a golden bowl or cauldron, a symbol of the Celtic Otherworld.

It has been suggested[46] that Goewin represents the goddess of sovereignty through whose power Math ruled, and that the rape of Goewin may symbolise disaster, leading to war and the devastation of the land. It may even be that Goewin's violation may be paralleled to the fall from grace of Adam and Eve and all the tribulations of humankind that followed their expulsion from Eden. Math's relationship with Goewin may have symbolised a mythic time when the relationship between humans and the land was passive and non-laborious, when people could be nourished simply by resting their feet on the earth, and enjoyed immortality. The rape of Goewin and the loss of her innocence may thus represent a catastrophic upheaval, whereby humankind had to cultivate the land in order to survive, and to endure hardship, war and death. Whether or not the detail of the myth has been interpreted correctly, it is clear from the text of Math that the virgin footholder must symbolise a crucial power-source tapped by the king, so that he and Gwynedd itself could flourish. In a very real sense, the female principle was paramount in the Tale of Math; Goewin was more important than Math himself. It is worth noting, in this respect, that Gwydion, Gilfaethwy and Arianrhod were identified as the children of Dôn, who was probably a divine Mother, perhaps a founder-goddess, just as the Irish Danu was the ancestor-goddess of the Tuatha Dé Danann in the Mythological Cycle.

Modron

In the Tale of Culhwch and Olwen, a story affiliated to the *Mabinogi*, though outside the Four Branches, we are introduced to the hunter-god Mabon, who is described as the son of his mother Modron. In Welsh and Irish myth, divine heroes were frequently named as sons of their mothers rather than of their fathers: allusion has just been made to the family of Dôn; and we saw earlier that both Rhiannon and Arianrhod were the parents who named their sons Pryderi and Lleu. In Ireland, King Conchobar of Ulster was described as the son of his mother Ness; the great hero Cú Chulainn was known as the son of Dechtire, his mother.

Strictly speaking, 'Mabon' and 'Modron' are titles rather than names and the symbolism of these terms is important in understanding their role in myth. Mabon means 'son' or 'young man', the archetypal divine youth who is found in many mythic traditions. The Irish god Oenghus was called mac Oc, the 'young son', and this may be linked to the circumstances of his birth: he was born as the result of a clandestine union between the deities Daghda and Boann, who sought to keep his conception secret by causing the sun to halt in the sky for nine months, so that Oonghus was both conceived and born on the same day.[47] The character of Mabon was rather similar: he was eternally young, because of events associated with his birth: he was stolen from Modron when three days old and disappeared for many years, the presumption being that he sojourned as a captive in the Otherworld until rescued by Culhwch and Arthur from Gloucester Castle, as an adult. But Mabon is a paradox: he was the youngest of souls but he was also described as the oldest; he was the first-born of creation, of Modron, whose name means simply 'mother' or 'divine mother'. The inescapable conclusion is that Modron is a mother-goddess or, even, *the* great mother-goddess. The word Modron is cognate with Matrona, the word for mother-goddess inscribed on many Romano-Celtic altars to the Mothers in Gaul and the Rhineland during the early first millennium AD. The name of the River Marne is also derived from Matrona.

That Mabon and Modron belong to a mythological tradition which is very early and of pre-Christian origin is suggested by the incontestable link between Mabon and Maponus, a pagan Celtic hunter-god known in northern Britain at, for example, Chesterholm and Corbridge, but also venerated in Gaul, at the healing spring-sanctuary of Chamalières.[48] Maponus was linked with Apollo, a hunter-healer in Celtic, as in Graeco-Roman, religion; and in iconography, Apollo is always depicted as a divine youth. That Modron may also have belonged to an early pagan tradition is

Small stone image of a mother-goddess, found deep in a well at the Roman town of Caerwent, tribal capital of the Silures.

suggested by a Romano-British stone at Ribchester which is dedicated to Maponus (Mabon) and bears the images of two goddesses, one or both of whom may represent Modron.

In the Tale of Culhwch and Olwen, Modron is presented as a shadowy figure whose character is undeveloped. But her name carries her symbolism as a mother-goddess, and her son Mabon played a crucial role in the quest for Olwen, which is the focus of the story. Modron may have been closely associated, or even equated, with other Welsh goddesses: her fate resembles that of Rhiannon, who also lost her hero-son as a newborn infant; Branwen, too, lost her son Gwern while he was still very young and Branwen is described as a matriarch or ancestress. Modron conforms to the mythic archetype of mother and lost child which may symbolise creation and loss, life and death, spring growth and winter barrenness.

The identity of the pagan goddess Modron may have been transmuted in early Christian tradition to that of the female saint Modrun, who was the patron of Trawsfynydd in Merionethshire and of other churches in Cornwall and Brittany. It is, perhaps, significant that Modrun's iconography appears to refer to the myth of Modron: she is represented as a woman fleeing, with a small child in her arms.[49]

Olwen, the Giant's Daughter

The Tale of Culhwch and Olwen is primarily a quest-tale.[50] The story is focused upon Culhwch's search for Olwen, a woman whom he had never seen but with whom he had fallen in love. Culhwch's father Cilydd remarried after the death of his first wife Goleudydd. The new stepmother had a daughter of her own whom she wished Culhwch to marry, but he demurred on the grounds of his youth. Cilydd's wife was angry and laid a curse on Culhwch to the effect that he would not marry anyone but Olwen. This was a spell similar to that imposed by Arianrhod upon Lleu. In fact Culhwch's stepmother was condemning him never to marry, since the attainment of Olwen was well-nigh impossible.

Culhwch went from his father's house at Cilydd's suggestion. He was to visit his cousin Arthur, the object being to get his hair cut. This odd allusion must simply refer to a rite of passage from youth to manhood, and may also be an obscure reference to the Celtic custom of fosterage between noble families. The description of Culhwch's departure from his father's house clearly indicates his heroic status: his appearance was that of a young god. His supernatural rank is demonstrated by an episode which took place at the gates of Arthur's court. The gate-keeper refused Culhwch entry because he arrived unannounced, and Culhwch replied by threatening to give three shouts which would make all the women of Arthur's realm barren. This must mean that Culhwch possessed the power to ensure or deny fertility; the implication is that he could cause a land to flourish or to become a wasteland.

The quest for Olwen began and Culhwch enlisted the help of Arthur and his men. After a year, they found Olwen: she was a lady of divine presence, dressed in flame-red silk and adorned with pearls and rubies and, perhaps significantly, she wore a heavy gold torc, a symbol of high status and, in some instances, divinity in pagan Celtic iconography.[51] Olwen explained that her father was Ysbaddaden, Chief Giant, and that he would never permit her to marry because her wedding would mean his own death. Nevertheless, Culhwch approached Ysbaddaden, who first tried to kill him and his companions and then imposed a number of 'impossible' tasks, very similar to the Labours of Hercules, which he had to perform successfully before he could take Olwen as his wife. Culhwch, hero-like, overcame all difficulties and the union of the couple took place.

Olwen is an insubstantial figure, whose character and personality are never developed. In many ways, she had an essentially passive role, like Branwen. Olwen was an enabler, a catalyst. She was the cause of momentous events. She appears weak because, having sworn not to disobey her father, she never took the initiative nor did she help Culhwch in any active way. Her name 'White Track' may link her with Blodeuwedd; she was given this title because white clovers sprang up behind her as she walked.[52]

The character of Olwen's father Ysbaddaden is fascinating and complex: he appeared as a monstrous, Titan-like figure; indeed he closely resembles Balor, the demonic Fomorian leader of the Irish Mythological Cycle. Balor had one enormous and evil eye, which had to be propped open with ropes and pulleys.[53] Ysbaddaden's eyelids were kept open with forks. Olwen was clearly only able to marry at the cost of her father's life. This raises significant questions, because Olwen's union with another man apparently meant that her father's power would drain away from him, presumably to that other man. It may be that here, heavily disguised and overlain, are the remains of a myth of sovereignty, in which potency and prosperity were in Olwen's gift, to be transferred from one man to another. In Irish myth the queen-goddess Medb cohabited with several mortals, on whom the union conferred legitimate kingship. Maybe Olwen had the same function.

Another important parallel between the Welsh and Irish tradition concerns the 'triangle' of Olwen, Ysbaddaden and Culhwch. A common theme in Irish myth is a triangle of love and jealousy, involving rivalry between an elderly suitor and a young lover over a beautiful girl. This pattern is exemplified by the stories of Diarmaid–Gráinne–Finn and Naoise–Deirdre–Conchobar. In the Welsh version, the father Ysbaddaden took the place of the old suitor, but the symbolism may be similar: the young girl was a vehicle for the transference of power from old to young in what is, perhaps, a seasonal myth of death and rebirth.

Crones and Cauldrons

Two stories in Welsh myth demonstrate a close link between supernatural women and the concept of the Cauldron of Regeneration. In the Tale of Branwen, Brân's greatest conciliatory gift to Matholwch, after Efnisien's insult, was a cauldron of Irish origin which could bring the dead to life. Matholwch told Brân the story of the cauldron: he was out hunting one day near the Llyn y Peir (the Lake of the Cauldron) when he saw a huge and hideous man, with a shock of unkempt red hair, emerging from the water with the cauldron on his back. This figure was followed out of the lake by an equally monstrous woman who was twice his size. Her companion described to Matholwch how, every six weeks, this woman conceived and gave birth to a fully-grown and fully-armed warrior. Her name was Cymidei Cymeinfoll,[54] which literally means 'bloated with war'. She was seemingly both a regenerator and a war-goddess, like many of the Irish female spirits. Just as the cauldron itself could resurrect dead soldiers, so she could create them: in a sense, she was the personification of the cauldron. That the couple was of divine rank is indicated by their immortality: Matholwch recounted to Brân how he built an iron house to incarcerate the pair, and set fire to it: the cauldron-bearers emerged unscathed from their white-hot prison.

The link between magical cauldron and goddess is present in a myth preserved in the Book of Taliesin, a thirteenth-century manuscript[55] which is named after the great Welsh satire-poet of the 6th century AD. The story of Taliesin is the description of a mythical or euhemerised historical figure wherein the birth of the poet was associated with magical circumstances. The story concerns a supernatural female, Ceridwen, who is described as a witch or sorceress. She was the keeper of the Cauldron of Inspiration and Knowledge. Ceridwen had two children, a daughter Crearwy ('Light', 'Beautiful') and a son Afagddu ('Dark', 'Ugly'). To compensate for her son's disadvantages, his mother brewed a cauldron of magical liquid intended to make Afagddu completely wise. The potion had to boil for a year and Ceridwen instructed a young lad, Gwion, to watch over the vessel. But as he stood guard, three drops of the liquid splashed onto his hand and he instinctively licked his scalded finger. Ceridwen was furious: all the knowledge brewed for Afagddu had gone instead to Gwion and, as the boy fled from the sorceress, the cauldron burst. Ceridwen chased Gwion, causing both herself and her quarry to change form as they ran: she was transformed first into a greyhound, then an otter, then a hawk, while Gwion was her prey, hunted as a hare, a fish and a bird. Finally, Ceridwen metamorphosed to the form of a hen and changed Gwion into a grain of corn, which she swallowed. Nine months later the boy was reborn; Ceridwen's vengeful hand was stayed by his extreme beauty and, instead of killing him, she set him adrift in a coracle. He was recovered from the water by Elphin, a nobleman at the court of King Maelgwn; he was named Taliesin ('Radiant Brow') and became the greatest poet and satirist in the land. He had the gift of prophecy, and foretold the death of the king. Maelgwn is attested historically and, according to the *Annales Cambriae*, died in AD 547. Taliesin was perceived by his peers as the genuine incarnation of druidism.[56]

In order to understand the supernatural nature of Ceridwen, we need to examine not only the nature and behaviour of the cauldron-keeper herself but also to bear in mind the character of Taliesin and the symbolism of the cauldron. When he arrived at Maelgwn's court, Taliesin announced that he possessed all knowledge and was present at the creation/birth of Mabon. This implies that he was immortal and even older than Mabon, who was described as the oldest being in the world. The acquisition of knowledge by Gwion/Taliesin has strong links with the Irish myth of Finn, who gained wisdom from licking his burnt finger that had touched the roasting flesh of the Salmon of Knowledge.[57] Finn was, like Gwion, associated with powerful females, being brought up by a druidess. The character of Taliesin, his antiquity and his divinatory powers, as described in his story, indicate that a divine or superhuman origin was ascribed to the poet.

Ceridwen is described as the 'Old One', a Hag of Creation, a witch. She was the keeper of the Cauldron of Knowledge and only she could concoct the magic potion it contained. Her crone-like image is akin to the hags of Irish myth, who were goddesses of sovereignty and who could shape-change into beautiful young girls or into animals. Ceridwen was both creator and initiator: her pursuit of Gwion may be interpreted not simply as angry vengeance but, at a deeper level, as an initiation ritual designed to hone Gwion to a primeval, original life-state. This first-state was represented by a single grain of corn to which Gwion was finally transformed, which may have symbolised the clarity and simplicity of true knowledge or wisdom. Ceridwen's ability to metamorphose herself and others is indicative of her supernatural, perhaps divine, status. Most important of all was the cauldron itself, which is described as a vessel of knowledge but which was clearly also the cauldron of rebirth that appears in the Tale of Branwen and in Irish myth. In a sense, Ceridwen was the cauldron: she swallowed Gwion and caused him to be reborn; the symbolism of the grain of corn eaten by the hen could be seen as an allegory of the seed buried in the womb of earth for regeneration. It is pertinent that Ceridwen dwelt in the area of Bala covered by the Lake of Tegid[58]: the Irish cauldron described in the Tale of Branwen also came from a lake; and there is abundant archaeological evidence for the ritual deposition of cauldrons in lakes and marshes during the last millennium BC.[59]

At the very least, Ceridwen had a supernatural role as cauldron-keeper, spell-maker and shape-shifter. But she was almost certainly a goddess, a prophet and a creator. The dualism of her role as a divinity associated with life, death and regeneration is symbolised by her children, Crearwy and Afagddu, who perhaps represented day and night, light and dark and perhaps also the sky and underworld, summer and winter.

4 Sovereignty, Sexuality and the Otherworld in Irish Myth

The Myth of Sovereignty

Women were not sovereigns, but sovereignty itself was conceived of as female.[1]

The idea of sovereignty personified as a divine female is an extremely persistent tradition in early Irish myth. She was the goddess of the land, the spirit or essence of Ireland itself, and on her depended the fortunes, fertility and prosperity of her territory. The myth of female sovereignty is particularly fascinating because of its dynamism and its complexity. The myth was not static but mutable; and the nature of the goddess embraced not only guardianship of the land but also promiscuous sexuality, fertility, physical force and death, none of which is mutually exclusive. There is some evidence that the notion of a goddess whose main concern was the prosperity of the land was not confined to Ireland. The many images of goddesses and divine couples in Gaulish and British iconography (see Chapter 7) suggest that the concept of the divine female as the personification of plenty and the earth's abundance was central to pagan Celtic religion.[2]

Great play has been made of the prominence of the goddess in Insular tradition and it has been argued – falsely in my opinion – that this, together with the presence of autonomous queen-rulers in the myths, implies that women had high status in early Celtic society. It has to be remembered that we are dealing with myth; in early historical Ireland, the rulers were generally kings, not queens. It seems clear that the mythic female ruler Medb of Connacht, whose exploits are chronicled in the Ulster Cycle, was a humanised goddess, endowed with a spurious historicity by hostile Christian redactors, who could thereby point with horror at her promiscuity.[3]

The relationship of female to male supremacy in the mythic tradition is worth exploring because it changed through time. In the earlier myths, the goddess of sovereignty occupied a primal position, but in later tradition the king had primacy. In the early texts of, for example, the *Táin*, the goddesses appear as independent deities, but in later versions some of these same females are presented as wives of male spirits, and this suggests a new androcentrism which altered the status of the goddesses.[4] It is significant that where Irish mythic women possessed real power, this is frequently presented as being a bad thing: thus deities such as the Morrígan, queen-goddesses such as Medb and heroic mortals such as Deirdre, are all represented as destroyers, bringers of sorrow and disharmony.

The goddess of sovereignty as personification of the land was responsible for its fertility, and this role was symbolised by her apparent sexual promiscuity and polyandry. But her marriage with several successive mortal rulers was not the result of unbridled sexual appetite but of the need to choose the best consort for the well-being of Ireland. This is discussed below in the section on sacral kingship. The symbolism of sexuality and fertility is interesting and complex. Christine Raudvere[5] has made the point that in Norse myth, sexual prowess and the ability to shape-shift were frequently linked. This seems also to be true for Ireland: the Morrigán, for instance, could transform herself into bird-form, and she exhibited sexual energy in her relationships with the Ulster hero Cú Chulainn and the Daghda, a tribal father-god of the Mythological Cycle. In common with Norse shape-shifters, the Morrigán had power both to aid and to harm humans. The fertility-symbolism of the sovereignty-goddess could also manifest itself in the relationship between her and cattle.[6] Both the Morrigán and Medb were closely associated with these animals and both owned herds (see Chapter 8). The close link between the goddess and the fertile land is also indicated by references to the Paps of Anu and the Morrigán as Irish place-names.

The sexual imagery of the goddess can also be less obvious: in the story of Da Derga's Hostel (see p. 73), the doomed King Conaire refused entry to a crone, who was the Badbh in her guise as sovereignty goddess, because he was under a *geis* or taboo whereby he could not receive the company of a single woman after sunset.[7] So, even if the woman was an ancient hag, there appears to have been the peril of contamination of male by female, a sexual danger which may – like the myth of Samson and Delilah – be associated with male weakness brought about by women. The converse of this may in fact be present in the Welsh Tale of Math (see Chapter 3). The concentrated, undissipated sexual energy of the virgin may be another manifestation of female sovereignty.

The Irish goddess of sovereignty is frequently presented as a triad, and this triplism recurs in the trifunctionality of some individual members of these triads. The three tutelary goddesses Eriu, Banbha and Fódla of the Book of Invasions were apparently virtually identical eponymous personifications of Ireland, but the war-triad, the Morrigán, Badbh and Macha, is more complex. Indeed, there is an asymmetry in this group in that both the Morrigán and Macha were trifunctional (sovereign-ruler, war-goddess, promoter of fertility) but Badbh was only concerned with battle.[8] The names of the goddesses encapsulate their symbolism: Morrigán can mean 'great', 'terrifying' or 'phantom queen', the concept of rulership being crucial; Badbh means 'battle-crow'; Macha's name is generally thought of as meaning 'field' or 'plain', which refers directly to the land. It may be that triadism itself was associated with sovereignty: the sanctity of three, to be discussed below in connection with the Celtic mother-goddesses (see Chapter 5) may also be linked with the divine females of the Irish sovereignty myths.

The concepts of war and death appear, on the face of things, to have little to do with

Small clay group of three goddesses, each with a lapful of fruit, grain or coins, from Bonn, Germany; first or second century AD. The central female is young, her two companions are older, with typically Rhenish headdresses.

life, fertility and the land, yet these apparently polarised concerns were both under the tutelage of the Irish sovereignty-goddesses. In fact war and land need not be opposed images: at a basic level, war may be necessary to protect territory, so battle and guardianship are linked. The earth can only be successfully cultivated within the context of peace, because it requires constant attention, and thus the protection of boundaries is essential for prosperity. At another level, war and sexuality are both expressions of physical force, and both battle and sexual infidelity can result in or cause chaos and disorder. At a more subtle and obscure level, there is a sense in which warfare and bloodshed may be perceived as promoting fertility, just as the divine hunt reinforced the link between life, death and rebirth.[9]

Blood and carnage on the battlefield fertilised and replenished the earth. The close connection between destruction and the land is exemplified by a description of Macha's harvest of human heads.[10] The sovereignty-goddess could foretell the death of kings and heroes since, in a sense, she was responsible for it. King Conaire died in Da Derga's hostel because the goddess had withdrawn her favour; the Morrigán in her guise as the 'Washer at the Ford', washing the weapons of heroes who were about to die, had a similar function. As a war-goddess, she possessed the power of life and death and, like the Roman Fates, she could cut the life-thread whenever she chose.

The identity of this Insular sovereignty-goddess is clearly extremely complex. Juliette Wood suggests[11] that its composite nature may have been constructed of different layers through time, beginning perhaps with an early fertility/mother-goddess strand, with war and the political ruler-dimensions being added later. An alternative construct involves the presence of an all-embracing single goddess-figure for whom sovereignty was just one of many aspects.[12] One important point about the concept of sovereignty is that, although it was personified as a female deity, there is a sense in which it involved a gender cross-over; the idea of the sovereign was so crucial that it could not be perceived as exclusively male or female but inclusive of both, a total entity. The sovereignty persona had also to be 'extraordinary, excessive, dangerous':[13] certainly such Irish spirits as Medb and the Morrigán answered to all three.

The Sovereign Goddess and Sacral Kingship

Central to the Irish sovereignty-myth was the sacred marriage, the ritual union of the goddess of the land, spirit of Ireland itself, with the mortal king. This metaphor of a marriage between the king and the land was retained within Irish tradition at least until the seventeenth century. The idea is that the king entered into a sacred partnership with his kingdom, and that the union both legitimised his rule and gave him sovereignty, and caused the land to prosper.[14] The goddess would only enter this union if the king-elect were suitable and, even after the marriage, she could reject a weak ruler in favour of another who would be better for Ireland's well-being. This sacral marriage was important for successful government; the goddess was both spouse and validator of rulers. The *locus* for the sacral marriage-ceremony was the court of Tara.[15] The apparent promiscuity of Medb was in fact the action of a goddess seeking out the best mortals to marry, for the sake of Ireland.

The focus of the marriage itself was the sacred goblet of red liquor (presumably wine) which was handed to the king by the goddess. The eponymous goddess Eriu, after whom Erin (Ireland) is named, gave her mate a golden cup of wine, interpreted by some as symbolic of the sun.[16] An eleventh-century tale called *Baile in Scáil* ('The Phantom's Frenzy') describes a goddess who gave a drink to each successive king of Ireland. Her name was Flaith Erenn (the 'Sovereignty of Erin').[17] What is significant here is that in this version of the sovereignty myth, the goddess was instructed by a male, the king/god Lug, to give the cup to a series of surrogate kings.[18] So there had been a shift of supremacy from female to male, which corresponds to our earlier discussion of the mutability of the myth. The symbolism of liquid as a marriage-gift between goddess and king pervades many of these mythical stories. Conaire was an 'unjust king' and his parsimony was exemplified by his refusal to allow the goddess (disguised as a hag) into Da Derga's hostel. As a punishment, the druids inflicted on him a great thirst which he could not assuage and of which he died; the manner of his death appears to symbolise the withdrawal of the sacred cup of liquor by the goddess, and with it his right to rule.[19]

The relationship between Conaire and the hag is worthy of scrutiny: the act of union between the king and the sovereignty-goddess involved the transformation of the goddess from an ancient hag to a young and beautiful girl, as the marriage is consummated (see below). The fact that, for Conaire, the goddess remained in her hag-form indicates that his reign had not been validated.

The origins of the sacral marriage myth probably lie in the religious system of communities whose livelihood was essentially agricultural, and so the myth would have reflected the belief that the fertility of the earth required an input from humans in order to reach its full cultivable potential. A successful harvest needed the combined energy of the earth (perceived as female) and of human beings (perceived as male).[20] This notion of wild nature on the one hand, and human society on the other, is similar, in some respects, to the ancient Greek philosophical conceptions of *nomos* (law and order) and *physis* (untamed nature) which, in that context, caused conflict and disharmony. For Insular Celts, the union of natural and human forces became easily adapted and personified as a sacred marriage between land and king.

The idea of a partnership between male and female to enhance the earth's abundance may be represented not only in Insular myths of sacral kingship but also in the iconography of Romano-Celtic Gaul and Britain. Here, the symbolism of these images (see Chapter 6) suggests that the goddess was an unvarying entity whose primary concern was fertility, whilst her male companion could be depicted in various guises, including that of a warrior. It may also be significant that, in this iconography, the male deity often holds a cup of wine. It is too speculative to make definite links between these two systems, but it is at least possible that a common tradition of divine union was present in Europe as well as Ireland.[21] The earliest documentary Irish evidence for pagan myth must relate, in part, to a pre-Christian past, even though it survives only in redactions of Christian writers from the seventh century onwards. There is evidence that much of Europe shared religious traditions during the early first millennium AD, and both Europe and Ireland may well have participated in a common system, even though iconography for the period in Ireland is absent.

The final question to ask concerning the union of the sovereignty-goddess and the king in Insular tradition is whether there is any historical basis for the concept of a sacred marriage. It seems clear that in the early historical Ireland of the first millennium AD, kings ruled independently. It is also the case that the male rulers who are linked in the early sources with sovereignty-goddesses are not historically authenticated kings. Thus, the notion of sacral kingship, validated by a goddess of the land, belongs entirely to myth. Historical and mythical traditions became intertwined because storytellers deliberately transferred the mythic idea of the sanctified king to a historical context, so that genuine rulers received a spurious sacred legitimacy.[22]

Small stone relief of a goddess with a spear and bucket; second or third century AD. From Lemington, near Chedworth, Gloucestershire. The base bears dedication to goddess Riigina ('Queen'). Her two emblems suggest that she was responsible for protection and plenty.

Macha and the Morrigán

Macha and the Morrigán were trifunctional goddesses who appear in both the Ulster and the Mythological Cycles. Each possessed a sovereignty-dimension. Macha's name ('plain' or 'field') immediately links her with territory. Her triplistic role embraced prophecy, fertility and rulership. In the Book of Invasions, Macha is presented as the wife of Nemed, leader of the third mythic invasion of Ireland. In this myth she had two significant roles: she prophesied the destruction brought about by the Táin Bó Cuailnge, which all but annihilated Ireland; and she was a clearer of plains, thus physically claiming land. In this, she fulfilled two elements of the goddess of sovereignty: prophecy and territory. In another story, an origin-tale of the founding of the royal site of Emhain Macha, Macha was a warrior-ruler, claimant for the kingship but challenged by men who denied the right of women to rule. Again, her sovereignty-status is clear: the male challengers were the five sons of Dithorba whom she defeated by visiting them in the guise of a leper, while they sat feasting after a hunt. Despite her repellent appearance, each man desired to sleep with her and, as each union took place, Macha overcame and enslaved them, forcing them to build the royal stronghold

Navan Fort, Co. Armagh, N. Ireland. The site has been identified with the royal Ulster stronghold of Emhain Macha, founded (in Irish myth) by the goddess Macha. The circular timber structure was built in 95/94 BC, burnt down and covered with a stone cairn.

which was named after her. Macha's ability to shape-shift to the form of a hideous leper bears a strong resemblance to the transformation of the sovereignty-goddess to hag-form (see below). Instead of the union between deity and mortal endowing the man with kingship, this encounter led to his subjugation.

The fertility-aspect of Macha's sovereignty-role is demonstrated by an Ulster Cycle myth in which she was the divine bride of the Ulsterman Crunnchu. Macha's husband boasted that his wife was so swift that she could outrun the king's horses, and he pledged that she would compete in the horse-race at the next great Ulster Assembly. Even though Macha was nine months pregnant, she was forced to run; she won but died giving birth to twins. As she expired, she cursed the Ulstermen with the *ces noiden*, a weakness-curse which caused them to become as helpless as a woman in childbirth, for five days and four nights (the normal duration of menstruation) whenever their strength was most needed.

Macha's role is complex but interlinked: she was a warrior, ruler, prophet, matriarch, guardian and benefactress of the land, careful of Ireland's well-being but vengeful if wronged at the hands of mortals. In some stories she is presented, like Medb, as a human queen who had supernatural qualities, although she could die. But she was clearly a goddess associated with sovereignty in all its aspects. Some scholars see the downfall of Macha in the various stories as akin to 'crushing the serpent', the overthrowing by men of female domination.[23]

Like Macha, the Morrigán was a triplistic being: she was first and foremost a goddess of war and destruction, but she was also strongly linked with fertility and with rulership. Her very name includes the word 'rigan' meaning 'queen'. The Morrigán's most prominent image is that of a battle-fury (this dimension is fully explored in Chapter 2). Allied to her role as a destroyer was that of a prophet of doom: she was a 'Washer at the Ford' and, like the Norse Valkyries, she was a selector of the slain. But the Morrigán's prophetic role could be more positive: she warned the Donn (the Brown Bull) of Cúailnge of his danger from Medb and the forces of Connacht (see pp. 79–81), and she advised the Daghda, a god of the Tuatha Dé Danann, where their enemies, the demonic Fomorians, would land and attack.

The sovereignty-aspect of the Morrigán's identity is reflected above all in her vigorous sexuality. We saw in Chapter 2 that she had intercourse with the Daghda while straddling a stream, a powerful image of the life-force.

Rivers and fords have powerful liminal symbolism: the Morrigán was, in a sense, poised between two worlds (that of humans and that of the spirits). The Morrigán's sexual voracity revealed itself, too, in her association with the Ulster hero Cú Chulainn, with whom she seemed to enjoy a love-hate relationship. She tried to seduce him and, as we saw in Chapter 2, was savage in her reprisals when spurned. But her link with both Cú Chulainn and the Daghda demonstrates her sovereignty-role, as does her connection with cattle. Cú Chulainn was the essence of Ulster and

Bronze sculpture of the
dead Cú Chulainn,
with the raven-goddess
of death on his
shoulder. The Ulster
hero bound himself to
a tree so that he would
remain upright, and
preserve his honour,
even in death. The
statue was cast in
1916 by Oliver
Shepherd, and stands
in the main Post Office
in Dublin.

its fortunes, and she helped him against the forces of Connacht; the Daghda was a fertility-god, lord of the tribe and its prosperity, and she helped him against the Fomorian threat to Ireland, promising to kill Indech, the son of the Fomorian king: 'and would deprive him of the blood of his heart and the kidneys of his valour'.[25]

Like other sovereignty-figures, the Morrigán was a multi-functional and many-layered character. War, death, prophecy, guardianship, sexuality, fertility and ruler-ship were all inextricably intertwined in this complex divinity, whose relationship to humans appears to have been capricious and changing, but who was strongly committed to the fortunes of Ireland.[26]

Medb of Connacht

The treatment of one sovereignty-goddess, Medb, is especially worth examining because she has been endowed with a spurious historicity and humanity in the myths. She is presented not as a goddess but as a warrior-ruler of the province of Connacht, and has clearly undergone a humanisation-process whereby the goddess became a queen. As Máire Herbert puts it, Medb is the 'realisation in human terms of the goddess of sovereignty'.[27] Medb is frequently cited as an example of high female status in Celtic Ireland, but this argument falls apart if one strips away the layer of humanity from her identity. Medb's image is that of a rich, independent, powerful ruler, owner of substantial property, including land and cattle, controller of Connacht's army and battle-commander in the campaigns against Ulster. Patricia Kelly[28] sees Medb's role in the *Táin* as crucial. She was the chief instigator of the war between Ulster and Connacht; she ruled the army; she was the dominant partner in her many marriages. Unlike the other war-goddesses, Medb could – because of her mortality – participate actively on the battlefield, whilst the Badbh and the Morrigán waged war by fear. It was because of the humanisation process that Medb has been painted in such negative colours by Christian redactors with an androcentric perspective, who saw her as an unnatural human woman, unacceptably promiscuous and a destroyer, rather than as a spirit, a figment of the pagan Celtic imagination.

Medb fulfils all the criteria of a goddess of sovereignty. She was a ruler, sexually vigorous and a warrior, with the death-dimension already seen in Macha and the Morrigán. The most important aspect of her sovereignty-image is that of the goddess who conferred prosperity on the land by mating with the king in a sacred marriage which sanctified his rule. Her name, 'She who intoxicates', is probably significant at least partly in terms of the goddess' conferral on her mate of the wine-cup as a symbol of her support, which was so central to the sovereignty-myth. She was the 'goddess who slept with many kings.'[29] It is interesting, in the context of human or divine status, that all Medb's husbands belong to the mythic past; none is from the historical king-lists. Medb's choice of sexual partners was dictated by what was best for Ireland: she would not allow any mortal king to rule at the royal court of Tara unless he first had sex with her, thus validating his kingship. Her sexual activity (she had nine consorts) is explicable in terms of her role as goddess of the fertility of the land, which means that an unsuitable king had to be abandoned in favour of one who would promote Ireland's prosperity. In all the unions, Medb was the dominant partner, and the decision over who ruled in Connacht rested with her willingness to confer sovereignty upon him.

Medb's first husband was the Ulster champion Fergus who, significantly, was himself a fertility-god. When Fergus relinquished the kingship of Ulster, Medb mated with his successor, Conchobar. But she quickly deserted him, partly because she did not wish to confer sovereignty upon him and by doing so unite the whole of Ireland. In his attempt to gain the sacral kingship, Conchobar then raped her, and this outrage caused all the kings of Ireland to unite against him in the Battle of the Boyne. Subsequently Medb married Ailill, and gave as her reasons his fearlessness and generosity (which matched her own) and that he was without jealousy (unlike her). This last is important because Medb needed to be sexually active and take many partners for the sake of Ireland,[30] but there is irony in that, when Ailill was unfaithful, she killed him. The sexuality which is so important a part of Medb's image was apparent even on the battlefield. There is an episode in the *Táin* where the queen, at the heart of the fray, needed urgently to urinate; she was also menstruating at the time. Her urine was so copious that it carved a great furrow in the earth. Medb's plight is ridiculed by the storyteller, but this may hide the essential sexual imagery present in the allusion to her body-fluids, which is paralleled by the episode of the Morrigán's union with the Dagdha at the river.

This Insular link between goddesses, sexual activity and water may all be part of the same tradition in which divine females were frequently associated with springs, wells and rivers. In pagan Celtic religion, as expressed in iconography and epigraphy, there were numerous female river-spirits including Matrona ('Mother') of the Marne and Sequana, the personification of the Seine at its source. Many of the great healing-spring sanctuaries were presided over by goddesses (see Chapter 5).

Like other sovereignty-goddesses, Medb had her dark side, as a wielder of death. She could shape-shift from girl to hag-form and thus presented her dualism as a symbol of young life or dying old age. She was not only a destroyer in battle but she also brought about the death of many kings and heroes, including those of Fergus, Ailill and Cú Chulainn, whose downfall she achieved by magic. Her relationship with Cú Chulainn was ambivalent: she was his enemy, but he spared her life in the final battle of the *Táin*,[31] an episode which may represent Cú Chulainn's rejection of her right to warrior-status on the grounds of her sex. But despite her supernatural identity, Medb was also mortal, just about, and it may be this ambiguity which gave rise to the myth of her incongruous, bizarre death: she was slain by a sling-shot, the missile a piece of hard cheese, wielded in vengeance by her nephew Furbaidhe for the murder of his mother Clothra.[32]

Eriu, Banbha and Fódla

This triad of goddesses, sometimes called the eponymous spirits of Ireland, were tutelary deities encountered by the Gaels or Celts, the final invaders of the land, as chronicled in the Book of Invasions. The myth is an explanation for the presence of the Celts in Ireland and includes details of how Ireland acquired its name, Erin. The three goddesses initially opposed the coming of the Gaels, but each agreed to admit them if they would promise to name the land after her. The poet Amhairghin assured Eriu that

Stone plaque depicting three mother-goddesses, one with a baby, the second with a napkin and the third with a basin and sponge. From the Romano-Gaulish settlement at Vertillum (Vertault), near Châtillon-sur-Seine, Burgundy.

it would be her name that was chosen, and so it transpired. In return, the goddess promised that Ireland would always belong to the Gaels. Nothing more is known of Fódla, the third member of the triad, but Eriu and Banbha are better-documented. Banbha was clearly an ancestor-goddess: she was the mother of Cesair, leader of the first mythical invasion of Ireland, and thus she formed a link between the Celts and their remote past. Eriu, personification of Ireland itself, was a goddess of sovereignty: she bestowed legitimacy upon mortal kings by her conferral on them of the sacred goblet of wine. Indeed, the golden cup of red wine is sometimes perceived as a solar image and, if so, it is an appropriate one since, for the Celts, the sun was closely associated with rulership, war and fertility.[33]

Anu, Boann and Etáin

Anu was an ancestral mother-goddess of Ireland who is probably, though not certainly, to be identified with Danu, the goddess after whom the mythical Tuatha Dé Danann, the 'People of the goddess Danu', were named. The Tuatha Dé Danann were a divine race of gods who occupied Ireland before the Gaels and who, dispossessed by them, created an Otherworld kingdom beneath the earth.[34] Although Anu was a pan-Irish goddess, she was particularly associated with Munster. That she was essentially a fertility-spirit of the land is indicated by the name of a mountain in Country Kerry, the Paps of Anu.[35]

The nature and symbolism of Boann has been developed further in myth than that of Anu. She appears both in the *Dinnshenchas* and in the Mythological Cycle. Boann was clearly a fertility-goddess and perhaps also a spirit of sovereignty, since she mated with several partners, including the Daghda, a tribal and fertility-deity. In this episode, the union of Boann and the Dagdha resulted in the birth of Oenghus, the god of love, an archetypal Divine Youth. In the *Dinnshenchas* the myth of Boann was constructed to explain the origin of the River Boyne. Boann was married to the god Nechtan, the guardian of a well which she was forbidden to visit. She defied him and, in punishment for her temerity, she was engulfed by the well-water which gushed out in a torrent, and she became part of the new river, the Boyne. Here we have a further instance of the association between rivers and female spirits.

Emily Lyle[36] has argued that Boann was a primal goddess, the focus of an Insular cosmogony. She bases this view upon a story in which Boann gave birth to three sons whose names were those of the three types of music traditionally played by a harper: music which induced sleep, laughter and sorrow. Lyle believes that these types of music can be linked with the three Indo-European seasons of spring, summer and winter. If this is so, then we may be witnessing an early creation – or season-myth associated with the nature of the earth and its fertility-cycle. Certainly there is reason to associate Boann with aspects of sovereignty. She took many husbands and bore several children; she was the personification of the life-force of water. Finally, her name may be significant: Boann is a 'cow' name, translated by Ross[37] as 'She who has white cows'. The goddess of sovereignty was traditionally associated with cattle.

The mythical Etáin is discussed later within the context of divine partnership (see Chapter 6). But I include a comment on her here because of her possible identity as a sovereignty-spirit. In the eighth-century *Tochmarc Etáine* (The Tale of Etáin) she is clearly presented in this role. After many misadventures, Etáin wedded the high king of Ireland, Eochaid Airem. He had previously been castigated by his people for not marrying, the implication given by the story being that an unmarried king had no authority, no right to rule. Etáin is described as the ideal of Irish femininity, white-skinned, red-cheeked, with long yellow hair. When Midhir reappeared and claimed his former love, Eochaid sacked Midhir's *sídh* (Otherworld dwelling), Brí Leith and re-claimed Etáin. This episode has been interpreted by some scholars as a seasonal, harvest-myth, similar to the Greek tale of Persephone.[38] Certainly Etáin does appear to have some elements of sovereignty: her union with Eochaid seems to have been a kind

The River Boyne, Ireland, associated in Irish myth with the goddess Boann. The river was created when the waters of a well rose up and overwhelmed Boann as a punishment for disobeying her husband.

of sacred marriage which validated his rule. If there is a seasonal origin for the myth, then Etáin was the personification of fertility and, perhaps, her yellow hair was symbolic of the ripe corn.

The Image of the Hag

The dualistic nature of the sovereignty-goddess, her concern with life, fertility and death, was symbolised by her ability to shape-shift, particularly between the image of the young, beautiful girl and the ancient, hideous hag, the *puella senilis* (the Old Girl). The crone symbolism was particularly associated with the death-aspect of the goddess. The shape-change itself was normally brought about by the sacred marriage: when the hag-goddess mated with the rightful king of Ireland, she was transformed from a wild, wandering hag into a sane and lovely girl.[39] So the partnership between goddess and king was of mutual benefit. Sometimes, there was initial conflict and hostility between hag and hero: if the man was suitable for the kingship, the hag was transformed; if he was not, then she remained a hag and brought about his downfall.

The story of Da Derga's Hostel exemplifies a luckless encounter between the goddess and the mortal king. The focus of the tale is Conaire, a king who was pre-destined to die at the hostel, which was in fact an Otherworld place. On his way there, he had met three red-garbed horsemen on red horses, harbingers of death wearing Otherworld colours. The goddess, in the form of a crone, approached the hostel and asked Conaire for admittance. She was black, naked, with a beard to her knees, and her mouth was on the side of her head. She was bleeding and had a rope around her neck. As mentioned previously, Conaire was under a *geis* or taboo whereby he could accept no single woman over the threshold after dark, and so he refused her entry. She cursed him, standing on one leg and with one hand held up in the air, perhaps a magical position for casting spells.[40] From that moment, Conaire was doomed. The image of the hag herself conveys the idea of suffering, perhaps an expression of the notion that since Conaire was unworthy of the kingship, the hag-goddess, personification of Ireland, had to remain unchanged and in abject bondage.

The story of Niall of the Nine Hostages is an origin-myth in which the dynasty of the Uí Néill, descendants of Niall, was founded. The earliest extant redactions of the tale belong to the early fifth century AD, just prior to the beginning of recorded history in Ireland. The texts were compiled in order to prove the right of Niall to rule, by linking him with the goddess of sovereignty. Niall and his four brothers were out hunting in the wilderness and were overcome by thirst. One of the brothers found a well, which was guarded by a hideous hag, who offered him water in exchange for a kiss. He was repelled by her loathsome appearance and fled in horror. All the brothers reacted in the same way except for Niall, who not only kissed the crone but had sex with her as well. As the two embraced, the hag was transformed into a beautiful woman. Niall asked her name and she replied 'I am Sovereignty'. Niall became king, his accession to the throne effected through his encounter with the goddess. In a sense, the hag represents disorder and chaos, to which harmony could be brought by the union of the goddess and the king.[41] It is surely significant that the encounter between Niall and the hag was associated with the granting of liquid by the female to the male, which may be seen as symbolic of the gift of wine from the goddess of sovereignty to the rightful king.

The hag of sovereignty appears in the form of the Cailleach Bearra in the ninth century 'Lament of the Old Woman of Beare'. The Cailleach myth is common to Irish and Scots-Gaelic folklore, but in its early form it is particularly associated with the south-west of Ireland. She was a kind of mother-goddess, linked with female guardianship of the wild, with war, death and sovereignty. The lament is in the form of a monologue spoken by the crone: in it, she speaks with nostalgia of her youth and beauty and her royal lovers, in contrast with her present lonely old age. What is especially interesting about this myth is the ambivalence between paganism and Christianity: Cailleach can mean both 'old woman' and 'nun'. It may be that the origin of the myth lies in a time when the pagan and Christian orders were coming face to face with one another.[42]

Divine Women of the Otherworld

The role of the Insular goddess as guardian of the Otherworld seems, at first glance, to be far removed from the concept of sovereignty. However, we have seen that the goddess of sovereignty possessed an infernal dimension which was symbolised by her links with war, old age and death. Conversely, the divine females encountered by heroes in the Otherworld seem to have elements of the sovereignty-character inasmuch as they appear to have needed contact with humans and were able to offer them something in return. If the nature of the Irish Otherworld is appreciated as a mirror-image of the human world, it is not surprising that parallel divine entities formed part of Otherworld myth. The sovereignty-goddesses in fact must belong to the Otherworld and, in myths of sacral kingship, they penetrated the world of humans. In the myths of the Otherworld, the reverse happened: now human heroes crossed the boundary to the realms of the infernal spirits.

There are numerous mythic episodes where human heroes were enticed to the Otherworld by supernatural women. Indeed, it was usually goddesses rather than gods who did this.[43] Sometimes their purpose in so doing is unclear, but on occasions, the presence of humans was required by the spirit-world to undertake a particular task which was impossible for its shadowy inhabitants. It may be that women were, like animals (see Chapter 8), perceived as appropriate mediators between worlds, maybe because they were deemed especially close to the natural world. Indeed, some Otherworld goddesses were closely associated with animals. Finn, the hero of the Fionn Cycle, was lured to the spirit world by a lady in the shape of a fawn, from the *sídh* of Donn mac Midir.[44] In a story of Cú Chulainn an Otherworld king, Labraidh, invited him to his realm, offering him a spirit-woman, Fand, in exchange for Cú Chulainn's agreement to kill Labraidh's rivals. This situation closely parallels an episode in the First Branch of the *Mabinogi*, where Pwyll of Dyfed, was needed by Arawn, lord of Annwn (the Welsh Otherworld) to kill another spirit-king, Hafgan[45], as if Arawn was too insubstantial a figure to fight for himself. Fand used magical birds to help gain Cú Chulainn's aid and affections, and she even took the form of a bird herself.[46]

Clíodna and Niav were two Irish Otherworld goddesses both of whom were associated with mortal heroes. Clíodna was the goddess of Carraig Clíodna in Country Cork

Clay figurine of 'Venus'; first or second century AD. From the Walbrook stream, London. Such figurines are thought to represent local Celtic divinities rather than the Classical goddess of Love.

and her domain was the Happy Otherworld. She took the form of a beautiful woman and, like Fand (and Rhiannon of Welsh myth), she possessed three brightly-hued, magical birds that could lull humans to healing sleep by their song (see Chapter 8). In her world there was feasting, sport and merrymaking; nothing evil, no death, ageing or decay. The story of the goddess' liaison with the human hero Tadg has much in common with the Voyage of Bran (see below) and, whilst Clíodna's legend survives only in a comparatively late text (fourteenth or fifteenth century), it is clear that the storyteller drew on earlier tales of the Otherworld for his inspiration. Tadg dwelt in the supernatural world of Clíodna for a while but then had to return. The goddess lent him her birds to console and comfort him and to soften his sorrow at leaving her realm.[47] As in the Voyage of Bran, the symbol of the Otherworld was the Apple Tree, upon which perched Clíodna's birds.

Niav (or Niamh) of the Golden Hair is described in the Fionn Cycle as an Otherworld enchantress, luring Oisin, son of Finn, to dwell with her in the 'Land of Forever Young', Tir na n'Og. The sting in the tail of a live mortal's sojourn in this supernatural place was that, once there, it was usually impossible to return home. Oisin conceived a yearning to revisit Ireland; Niav discouraged him and warned him that, if he were to do so, he must not physically touch the land. The hero set off on horseback but, when he reached Ireland, he realised that three hundred years of earthly time had passed, although his stay with Niav seemed quite brief. Misfortune befell Oisin: his horse-harness snapped and he was thrown from his horse. As he struck the ground, he immediately crumbled to dust, his body ageing instantly by three hundred years.[48]

The Voyage of Bran, or *Immram Brain*, is chronicled in a seventh- or eighth-century text and is a classic Insular Otherworld story, in which a human hero was enticed away by a goddess to a supernatural land. While walking near his court one day, Bran heard magical music which lulled him into a spell-bound sleep. He awoke to find placed beside him a silver apple-branch heavy with white blossom. The next night Bran saw a vision of a lovely woman who sang to him of her enchanted Otherworld, a group of islands far out in the Western Ocean which was full of happy wonders, an ageless paradise full of beauty, music and sport. The goddess gave him the apple-bough, perhaps as an entry-token to her domain and, the following day, Bran, his three foster-brothers and twenty-seven warriors set sail to find the islands of the Otherworld. The mythical status of the story is suggested by the triplism of Bran's followers: three and multiples of three were sacred and magical numbers frequently encountered in vernacular Celtic myth. Bran arrived at the Land of Women, the island of the goddess. As in the case of Oisin, Bran discovered the treacherous nature of the supernatural land: after a year had passed, his companions begged him to take them home, but the goddess warned them that disaster would befall them if they set foot in Ireland. Whilst earthly time changed, the Otherworld was timeless; a year in the Land of Women was three hundred on earth. The band of men set off in their boat and, as they approached the land, one man flung himself ashore only to succumb to the decay of extreme old age. Bran and the others continued their homeless wanderings.[49]

These Otherworld tales have a great deal in common and clearly draw upon a shared tradition. The goddess always approached the hero; she was the initiator of the contact and the instigator of the crossing of barriers. Without her invitation, mortals could not penetrate the Otherworld before they died. It is significant that in all these myths, the goddess warned her human visitors of their danger in returning home only after they were committed and were dwelling in the world of spirits. So the humans had no choice: once in the Otherworld, they generally were compelled to stay there. Tadg, in the Cliodna story, was able to go home only if accompanied by Otherworld creatures. The apparent need of humans by these goddesses may even reflect a kind of reverse sacral kingship, whereby Otherworld power was increased by the union of deities with mortals. The two worlds seem to have enjoyed a mutual dependence, a symbiotic relationship: the crossing of the boundary between them, whichever way it occurred, enhanced the potency and authority of both. Banquo in Shakespeare's *Macbeth*, expresses this ambivalence powerfully in his comment on the three witches, prophets of Macbeth's destiny of Kingship and doom:

> 'What are these,
> So witherd, and so wild in their attire,
> That look not like th'inhabitants o'th'earth,
> And yet are on't? Live you, or are you aught
> That man may question? ... You should be women,
> And yet your beards forbid me to interpret
> That you are so.'[50]

(*Right*) Gilt silver cauldron; second or first century BC. Found in a peat-bog at Gundestrup, Jutland, Denmark. The vessel was made in south-east Europe, and displays complex iconography. Its deliberate deposition in a watery context reflects the close link, in Celtic ritual, between cauldrons and water.

5 Water-Goddesses, Healers and Mothers

In times when 'going to see the doctor might be seen as a last resort rather than a first call'[1], the gods and medicine went hand in hand. Medical expertise was, at best, in a relatively rudimentary state and many afflictions must have been baffling to or misunderstood by physicians. So the Celts – as did their Classical neighbours – tended to turn to the supernatural powers for help when ill, in pain, when sight or hearing failed or when problems occurred in conception, pregnancy or childbirth.

During the last millennium BC and, indeed, even earlier, people in ancient Europe directed much ritual attention to water, casting objects – sometimes of great value – into lakes, marshes or springs.[2] There is evidence that in the Romano-Celtic period this ritual activity became sharply focused towards the propitiation of healing divinities. Watery places were especially sacred to the Celts, who perceived them as being intensely numinous. Rivers were seen as foci of the life-force, and many river-names –

Matrona (Marne) and Sabrina (Severn), for instance – reflect their personification as female spirits. Water represented liminal space, locations at the interface of the earthly and supernatural worlds. Such places were perilous and unstable but because they were 'gateways' between worlds, communication with the spirit-world was easier than elsewhere. The holy place of the goddess Arnemetia at Buxton may have been especially sacred since it was focused on two springs situated close together in the valley-floor but gushing out two kinds of water. The specific link between water and healing, and particularly between healing and thermal springs, was only fully developed during the Romano-Celtic period. The adoption of springs as religious healing centres seems to have occurred because water represented purification and a life-force and, where springs were hot, the curative power was seemingly enhanced, just as the heat of the sun was perceived as life-giving. It was recognised that some springs – at Bath, for instance – contained genuine therapeutic properties for certain afflictions. So people whose arthritis or gout was eased at the waters of Sulis might report on their cure, encouraging sufferers with other ailments to visit her sanctuary.

There was a close link between healing, regeneration and fertility, a connection which may explain why many Celtic divine healers were female and seemingly possessed generative as well as curative powers. The link between fertility and the curing of disease must also account for the association between the Celtic healing water-cults and the mother-goddesses (see below). Many of the pilgrims to the great Romano-Celtic healing sanctuaries appear to have been women: this is suggested from the nature of such offerings as spindle-whorls and hair-pins and also from the presence of anatomical votive objects such as model breasts. The nameless healer-deity at Chamalières in central France presided over a shrine to which many women came for a cure. Devotees offered more than two thousand wooden images of themselves or the parts of their bodies which required healing. One of these images, dating to the first century AD, is of a woman wearing a loose robe, a veil and a torc: she may have been a pilgrim but it is possible that she was the goddess herself.[3]

Doctors practising empirical medicine, as well as cult-officials, were present at many Romano-Celtic healing spring-shrines: the sanctuaries to Sequana at Fontes Sequanae in Burgundy and to Sulis at Bath in south-west Britain are just two examples. There is evidence that some medical practitioners were themselves women: a funerary stone set up in the first century AD at Metz in eastern Gaul depicts a female doctor.[4]

The Great Celto-Roman Healing Cults

In the Classical world the major healing centres, such as that of Asklepios at Epidaurus in the Peloponnese, were presided over by male divinities. By contrast, many of the curative spring-sanctuaries in the Celtic provinces of the Roman Empire had goddesses as their patrons. Whether this reflects differences in status between women of the Mediterranean and Celtic worlds is open to question. We have seen that the link between the female and healing water is a natural one, there being strong conceptual connections between fertility and procreation on the one hand, and healing and regeneration on the other. It is significant in this respect that many of the Celtic curative goddesses were depicted with fertility symbolism and, in addition, that the Celtic mother-goddesses were frequently venerated at spring-shrines.

Sequana of Burgundy

Sequana was a water-spirit, the personification of the River Seine at its source, Fontes Sequanae (the Springs of Sequana), where the water welled up from the ground in a valley near Dijon. From the first century BC, there is evidence that pilgrims perceived the spring-water to be beneficial in healing, even though the water possesses no therapeutic minerals but is simply pure and clear. Sequana is one of the few curative spring-deities with an iconographic presence: her bronze cult-statuette represents the goddess welcoming her suppliants with outstretched arms. She wears a diadem, indicating her high status, and the duck-prowed boat on which she stands displays her aquatic symbolism. Sequana's name is known from ten inscriptions which reveal her indigenous origin and the fact that, unlike many healer-deities, she was not equated or paired with a Roman-named divinity.[5]

In 1963, during excavation of the sanctuary-buildings of Roman date, a deposit of more than two hundred wooden votive objects was discovered in water-logged ground, apparently pre-dating the Roman levels. The inference is that these votives were grouped around the sacred spring-pool. The activity represented here seems to have centred on the spring itself, there being no evidence for any permanent Iron Age temple-structure. But shortly after the Roman conquest of Gaul, the native Celtic shrine was monumentalised and the spring-water canalised. Now an extensive religious complex – with two temples, porticoes, a dormitory and reservoirs – was constructed, though still focused upon the sacred spring-fed pool.[6] In this phase, the votive objects were made not of wood but of stone.

By analogy with what we know of Mediterranean healing sanctuaries, we may envisage cortèges of sick dedicants processing to Sequana's shrine with offerings of jewellery, money or animals, perhaps buying votive images from a special shop within the holy precinct. They would bathe in the sacred water, offer their images to Sequana in the hope that the gifts would stimulate the goddess to cure them, and perhaps sleep in the dormitory, where they might hope for a dream or vision of the healer-goddess and awake whole and well.

The votive offerings found at Sequana's shrine demonstrate the lively and important nature of the cult, even though the goddess was apparently worshipped only at this one place. Inscriptions of Roman date express gratitude for a successful cure. But it is the iconography in wood, stone and sheet-metal which allows a fascinating insight into the varied nature of the afflictions which drove pilgrims to Sequana. The idea behind healing-cults, both in the Graeco-Roman and Celtic worlds, involved reciprocity: the presiding deity would be offered an image of the ailing part of the body, in the hope and expectation that the divine power would respond by healing the dedicant. The anatomical models at Fontes Sequanae include whole images of pilgrims, internal organs, limbs and heads. Many accentuate the eyes, as if eye-disease, poor sight or blindness were major sources of suffering. Other illnesses, attested by particular carvings, include respiratory and heart disease, stomach and intestinal complaints (food-poisoning may have been common), disorders associated with breasts and genitals, and limb-afflictions, perhaps rheumatism or arthritis. Some complete images depict pilgrims carrying gifts to Sequana: young suppliants are represented with a pet dog or bird; mature dedicants are shown with purses of money.

Stone image of a blind pilgrim. From the Roman levels of the healing sanctuary to Sequana at Fontes Sequanae near Dijon, Burgundy. The goddess was especially renowned for her ability to cure eye-disease.

The animal-bones found at the site, those of both wild and domesticated species, may represent sacrifices to the goddess. Most of the devotees are portrayed wearing the typical hooded, heavy-weather coat or *sagum* of the rural peasant.

Of specifically female ailments, perhaps the most common were those associated with procreation. The presence of votive model breasts may be indicative of breast-disease (mastitis or cancer, for instance) but perhaps more prevalent were problems of lactation. The inability to breast-feed an infant would have posed a serious threat to its survival. However, Sequana was by no means a specialised healer: her devotees represent a fair cross-section of the kinds of malady suffered by ordinary people. In addition to perceptions of the goddess as a healer of physical ills, it is probable that the act of purification in the sacred water and prayer were of psychological benefit to Sequana's pilgrims. Indeed many ailments which could have been induced or aggravated by anxiety and stress may well have been ameliorated by visiting Fontes Sequanae, especially since the goddess clearly enjoyed a reputation for success.[7]

Sulis: Healer and Avenger

Beside the river Avon at Bath, hot mineral water gushes out of the ground from a set of springs at the rate of a quarter million gallons a day. Long before the Roman period, the site must have been sacred to Sulis, the personified spirit of the healing water, though we know her name only from inscriptions dating to Roman times, when she was equated with the Classical goddess Minerva. Most evidence for Sulis' cult dates from the Roman period, when the site was converted from a simple holy place to a great religious complex. However, there is possible evidence for the sanctity of the springs during the Iron Age, in the presence of Celtic coins which were cast into the water, probably as votive offerings. However, since some late Iron Age coins continued in circulation until the middle of the first century AD, the presence of those at Bath cannot be taken as concrete evidence for pre-Roman cult activity. But, in addition, a man-made causeway of gravel and stone, leading across the marshy ground from the south-west to the springs, is almost certainly a pre-Roman construction.

Soon after the Roman occupation of southern Britain, perhaps as early as the 60s or 70s AD, Roman engineers moved in to upgrade the Celtic sacred place and converted Sulis' spring to a huge temple-complex. Nothing of this remains above ground but in the eighteenth century Samuel Lysons reconstructed the elevation of its façade, with pillars and a carved pediment.[8] That Sulis was perceived as inextricably linked with the spring itself is demonstrated by an inscription on a lead curse-tablet (see below) dedicated to *Fons Sulis* (the 'Fountain of Sulis'), as if the concepts of spring and spirit were inseparable.

The adoption by the Romans of Sulis' hot springs led to the construction of an imposing Classical temple, a sumptuous set of bath-buildings, a great altar and a reservoir for the sacred spring-water. During the third century AD, the Roman writer Solinus recorded the luxurious furnishings of the springs and also commented: 'the patron godhead over these springs is Minerva, in whose temple perpetual fires never whiten into ashes . . .'[9] The temple, baths and reservoir were all constructed as part of the same building programme. The main spring, now situated beneath the King's Bath, was made into an ornamental pool enclosed by a polygonal wall and, alongside it, the bathing-complex was built so that the visitor could look across from the main hall of the baths towards the steaming spring, the living pulse of the deity. Adjacent to the baths the great temple itself, enclosed within a colonnaded precinct, was erected in honour of Sulis. The temple is buried beneath Stall Street in the centre of modern Bath, but the carved stone which survives argues for a high degree of architectural sophistication, as does the use of Graeco-Roman iconography, both in the decoration of the temple itself and in the sculpture of the great altar, which was aligned both on the entrance to the temple and the reservoir.

Whilst the original planning of Sulis' sanctuary involved the grouping of the public buildings around the visible presence of the steaming spring, major alterations in about AD 200 argue for a change in the way the cult was perceived and managed: now the temple was enlarged and, more significantly, the reservoir was enclosed in a huge vaulted hall, restricting access to the spring. This act may have been a deliberate attempt to make the focus of the cult more remote and mysterious. Whatever the reason behind the change, pilgrims were now only able to approach Sulis' spring through a dim passageway,[10] as if perhaps to simulate the transition between the earthly and spirit worlds.

Who and what was Sulis? Although she was conflated with Minerva, a female deity, doubts have been cast upon the gender of Sulis as female.[11] However, the ascription of a masculine identity is untenable, in my opinion, simply because the inscribed dedications to Sulis refer to *dea* (goddess) not *deus*. First and foremost Sulis was the native goddess of the curative hot springs. The numerous inscriptions on stone and lead or pewter attest to her equation with Minerva: the gilded bronze head which was once part of a great cult-statue depicts the image of the Roman deity, originally bearing the helmet of the warrior-goddess. Why this particular conflation was made is far from clear, but Minerva Medica was venerated at Rome and, since the Roman divinity was not only a goddess of war but also of wisdom and crafts, she may have been invoked at Bath as a spirit of the craft of medicine, just as the Irish Brigit was associated with both healing and craft-skills. (In addition, as happened with Mars in Celtic Europe, the war-element in Minerva's cult may have been transmuted to guardianship against disease.) The cult of Sulis flourished because of her reputation as a goddess of healing and because the springs produced curative hot water which could ease gout and rheumatism. Doctors were present at the sanctuary and the practice of empirical medicine went hand in hand with spiritual healing: stamps for eye-ointment found in the baths suggests that an eye-physician, Janianus, may have held a regular clinic here.[12] The many women who patronised Sulis' shrine perhaps found especial help for child-bearing disorders: the model bronze and ivory breasts offered to the goddess may have been associated with lactation, and Martin Henig has suggested[13] that the ivory ones may have been worn as an amulet by a woman until she had successfully weaned her infant when, in thanksgiving for the vital supply of milk, she gave the models to Sulis.

Healing-cults in the Mediterranean and Celtic worlds in antiquity involved specific rituals and religious perceptions. The most notable evidence for Sequana's cult in Gaul was the occurrence of anatomical models, mainly replicas of parts of the body which required the aid of the curative goddess. At Sulis' shrine, by contrast, such models are extremely rare. Apart from the miniature pairs of breasts already discussed, the life-size pewter mask of a human face is the only possible candidate. But for such a popular sanctuary, the dearth of this kind of reciprocal offering must be significant. Barry Cunliffe has suggested[14] that 'a more rational approach to healing' may be implied, because the genuine curative properties of the water, whether drunk or bathed in, were recognised. I am unsure as to how tenable this thesis is, since there are

Life-size gilded bronze head of the goddess Sulis Minerva at Bath. The great temple was built during the later first century AD on a site already sacred to the spirit of the hot springs. The head of Sulis was hacked from the body in antiquity, and the face has cut-marks, as if abused by members of a rival cult.

many important Classical healing shrines (Epidaurus in Greece and Paestum in southern Italy come to mind) where model limbs, eyes and organs were common gifts. However, for whatever reason, such gifts were not generally made to Sulis at Bath.

It is clear that the pilgrims who visited Sulis' shrine, whether for a physical cure or for refreshment of spirit, followed certain ritual procedures, immersing and purifying themselves in the sacred water and imbibing it to cleanse themselves internally and to receive the spirit of the goddess. The metal vessels found in the reservoir must have been used for this purpose and then perhaps left as gifts to the goddess. The ritual would include sleeping at the shrine in the hope of a curative vision, sacrifices, festivals and the offering of presents to Sulis in thanks or hope. The spring was the focus for personal contact with the goddess, where vows, prayers, requests and thanksgiving took place. Suppliants dedicated stone altars to Sulis and cast gifts into the spring-water, including money and more personal objects such as brooches, pins, shoes and spindle-whorls. The group of finger-rings from the oak-lined culvert may have been the offering of a *gemmarius* (gem-engraver), who perhaps cast a bag of his wares into the spring. The Roman coins show a fairly consistent level of activity at the spring from the mid first to the mid fourth century AD, when there are indications that visitor-numbers declined.[15] The 12,000 coins so far discovered seem large in number, but in fact represent only an average of between twenty-four and forty-eight coins a year in the peak period of AD 60–360. Some coin-gifts consisted of small change, but the offering of a pair of gold coins of Allectus must represent a substantial proportion of the annual salary of a wealthy person. Some of these gifts reflect the tossing in of money for good luck, to 'keep in' with the spirit-powers, but others may symbolise a deeper piety.[16]

There is some direct evidence for ritual activities associated with the veneration of Sulis: a priest of the cult, Gaius Calpurnius Receptus, served at the temple until his death at Bath aged seventy-five years: his wife, Calpurnia, who had once been his slave, set up his tombstone.[17] A *haruspex* ('gut-gazer') involved in divinatory ritual was present at the shrine, perhaps both in his official capacity and as a devotee.

Sulis may have been a solar goddess as well as a healer: indeed the two functions are by no means mutually exclusive. The name Sulis is philologically associated with a Celtic word for the sun. The finds at Sulis' sanctuary include a number of moulds for making amulets, including one which resembles a solar wheel.[18] It certainly makes sense for the goddess to be associated with the sun inasmuch as her spring-water was hot. There is also substantive evidence for a strong link between the sun and healing, as illustrated by the many curative shrines to the Celtic Apollo in Gaul.[19] Indeed, the Classical Apollo was both a sun-god and a healer. That Sulis' cult possessed a celestial dimension is implied by some of the carved decoration of her temple: a pediment depicts Luna, the Roman moon-goddess, who was associated with women and fertility. But the main temple-pediment bears a powerful image of a male Gorgon with staring eyes, whose snake- and eel-entwined hair stands out in wavy rays from his head as though to evoke both the sun and water.[20]

The evidence for the healing beneficence of Sulis at Bath is counter-balanced by a more sinister aspect of her character, namely her role as an avenger of wrongs. For more than two hundred years visitors to the sanctuary invoked the aid of the goddess against malefactors, mainly thieves, in the hope that she would punish them. These invocations take the form of 130 *defixiones* or curse-tablets, small sheets of pewter or lead inscribed with messages to the goddess, telling her the nature of the wrong done, the name (if known) of the evil-doer, and graphic details of the desired retribution. These were tightly rolled up and cast into Sulis' spring. *Defixiones* were common means, in the Mediterranean world, of bringing someone under the curser's control against their will and often without their knowledge.[21] The idea of a healing-goddess being petitioned in this negative manner seems somewhat bizarre, but the reversal of curing to cursing associated with holy water is well-documented over a long period. Francis Jones[22] notes this reversal-cult as linked to holy Welsh wells as late as the nineteenth century, where a similar process of writing a curse-message, folding it in lead and casting it into the water is recorded.

The curses invoking Sulis[23] were generally addressed 'to the goddess Sulis' or 'to Sulis Minerva', the name of the Celtic deity occurring first in all but one instance. The implication of this is that Sulis was the primal deity. The giving of the curse was an

The 'Vilbia' curse, found in a reservoir of the sacred spring at Bath. More than a hundred such curse-tablets were inscribed, rolled up and cast into the spring by victims of theft, hoping for revenge from the goddess.

important part of the ritual and, in a sense, the malefactor was being 'sacrificed' to Sulis' vengeance. An important feature of cursing was the 'fixing' of the curse, so that it was directed against the evil-doer and did not rebound on the petitioner. The Latin term *defixio* comes from the verb *defigere* (to fix). This fixing may have been achieved by means of the quasi-legal formulae in which the curses were written. The sheets were incised with crude, cursive writing, sometimes deliberately back-to-front to increase the magical effect. Lead and pewter are dark, dense and heavy metals appropriate for harming, and the poisonous properties of lead-compounds were well-understood.[24] Lead is also cheap and soft enough to inscribe and fold; its weight meant that the rolled-up curse would sink immediately to the bottom of the water. Moreover, the secrecy of the message was preserved by folding or rolling the lead: the message was for the goddess alone.

Most of the complaints recorded on the Bath curse-tablets involved theft of personal property, particularly clothes. Presumably these were items shed by bathing pilgrims and left unattended: cloaks, a cap, bathing-costumes and even a pair of gloves are recorded. Unlike the stone dedications to Sulis, not a single Roman citizen is mentioned on the curse-inscriptions. Many names, such as Lovernisca and Deomiorix, were of Celtic derivation. Did the victims know they had been cursed? If so, fear of Sulis' vengeance may have induced neuroses or psychosomatic ailments. Were the malefactors themselves pilgrims or professional thieves? If they themselves were supplicants to Sulis' sanctuary, their wrong-doing constituted a double sacrilege, and feelings of guilt may themselves have prompted the restoration of stolen property.

The *defixiones* are varied, to an extent, but certain features are common to many: in every case, the curse seems far too harsh for the crime, a fact which perhaps reflects the great sanctity of the shrine and the sacrilege implied by theft within it. The messages often ask for revenge to affect the victim's blood, eyes, fertility, sleep or bodily functions. One curse[25] requests vengeance from Sulis through the victim's blood and health and those of his family, so that they should be able neither to eat, drink, urinate nor defecate (presumably until the stolen property was returned). The language used by the cursers was often savage and emotional, and sometimes a peremptory note creeps in, as if respect for the goddess has been subsumed by the strong sense of grievance and the desire for justice.

The importance, popularity and success of Sulis' cult at Bath is attested by the architectural splendour of her religious precinct, by the abundance of dedications and offerings, by the four-century long florescence of her veneration and by her international patronage. People may have come to Bath from all over the Celtic world in search of divine aid. We know of one Peregrinus, a Treveran from Gallia Belgica, who brought with him his local cult of Loucetius Mars and Nemetona; a stone-worker from the Chartres region; Rusonia Aventina, of the Mediomatrici around Metz; and a Spanish cavalryman. People of high rank were among Sulis' devotees: one was a civic dignitary, a decurion (member of the town council) from Gloucester, who died at the ripe old age of eighty.

Sulis was arguably the most important of the British water-deities. She was a native goddess but her cult received an enormous boost from Roman patronage in the early years of Roman rule. The sight of the lavish new temple-precinct must have been awe-inspiring to local Britons used to the simple veneration of the spirit of the spring. As Potter and Johns[26] have put it:

'Bath epitomises the harmonious blend of Roman and British in a religious precinct which would have looked seemly and familiar to an urbane visitor from Italy or Greece, but which was nevertheless firmly based on the traditional beliefs and practices of the local population.'

Coventina

Perhaps the most important water-goddess from northern Britain was Coventina whose cult, like that of Sulis, was concentrated at one particular site, Carrawburgh, on Hadrian's Wall.[27] Her name is Celtic; she was the personified spirit of a spring that welled up out of the ground to feed a pool. The identity of this water-spirit is known from the inscribed dedications to her which bear her name. Coventina was not exclusive to Britain: there is evidence that devotees worshipped the goddess in North-west Spain and at Narbonne in southern Gaul.

In about AD 130 engineers contained the spring and well within a square stone-walled enclosure. Its first use was as a functional cistern but soon afterwards it 'became imbued with religious significance as the vallum-builders gave way to soldiers with Celtic superstitions and beliefs regarding springs.'[28] The coin-evidence from the well indicates that Coventina's cult reached its height of popularity only gradually, the greatest level of ritual activity taking place during the late second and early third centuries AD. By the fourth century the cult was already waning. There is evidence, however, that in the late fourth century Coventina's devotees reacted to the Theodosian Edict of AD 391, in which pagan rites were made illegal and temples closed, by trying to conceal and protect her shrine, placing building-stones on top of the well and its offerings.

What do we know of Coventina's nature, her cult, ritual and dedicants? The many votive gifts and inscribed altars bear testimony to her importance. Her high rank is indicated by such titles as 'Sancta' (Holy) and 'Augusta' (Revered), which are rare for other than Roman State goddesses. Coventina is depicted on some of her altars, and her imagery is unequivocally that of a water-spirit. Her iconography owes much to Graeco-Roman depictions of nymphs, and indeed one inscription is 'to the Nymph Coventina'. But the artistic treatment is stylised and somewhat schematic, betraying indigenous Celtic influences and tastes. On one stone, the goddess is depicted reclining on waves lapping against a bank, waving a waterlily leaf in one hand, her other arm

Stone relief of the British water-goddess Coventina, from Carrawburgh, Northumberland. The natural spring was developed as a cult-site in the second century AD. The carving depicts either the goddess and two nymphs or (more likely) a triple image of Coventina.

resting on an overturned pitcher of flowing water. On another relief a triple water-goddess is represented: this triadic form is worthy of note since near Coventina's Well was a shrine dedicated to the Nymphs, who are frequently portrayed as a triad in Classical art, and some scholars argue that the triple image found at the well in fact depicts the Nymphs rather than a triplistic Coventina. But since the stone was found in the well itself and since one dedication to Coventina equates her with a Nymph, I see no reason for doubting this image as one of the goddess, perhaps triplicated to increase the symbolism of the carving and reflective of the Celtic predilection for tripling deities of well-being (see below).

We can gain an idea as to the nature of Coventina's cult by looking at the votive offerings and other material found in or near the well itself. These divide fairly sharply into stone dedications and small items such as coins and jewellery. More than 16,000 coins were offered to the goddess and thrown into the well – a higher level of ritual activity per year than is reflected at Bath, where the cult was active over a much longer period. Many finger-rings, brooches and other trinkets were cast into the water, together with a thin bronze plaque in the form of a horse and a number of small bronze masks of human faces. There were also objects of bone, glass, lead, leather, jet and shale from the site, many of which were probably votive gifts, although some of the vessels may have been used in water-rituals associated with the cult. Some of the altars had been deposited within the well, a curious occurrence and one that apparently reflects two separate activities: some stones were carefully placed in the water, whilst others were seemingly ritually destroyed.

The fact that Coventina was a spring-goddess would appear to suggest that she was a healer-deity. However, there is very little, if any, direct evidence, from the offerings themselves, for such a function. The inscribed dedications are not specific, and only a few of the small offerings are particular to a healing cult. Pins are a feature of many curative shrines, including that of Asklepios at Epidaurus, but only two come from Coventina's Well. It is possible that the masks may represent the heads of sick pilgrims requiring a cure, but there is no firm evidence for this. The figurine of a dog allegedly found here would seem to strengthen the identification of Coventina as a healer (see Chapter 8), but there is some doubt as to the security of provenance of the Carraw-burgh dog. One of the altars from the well bears a dedication to Minerva and, mindful of Sulis Minerva at Bath, this may indicate a therapeutic connection for the North British cult. But the main reason for linking Coventina with healing is the spring itself. The connection between springs, curative cults and goddesses is sufficiently strong, especially in the Celtic world, to make a healing function for Coventina at least likely, even if this were not her sole, or even her primary, concern. Lindsay Allason-Jones suggests that she may have been an 'all-rounder' goddess, a beneficent protector against all the evils besetting humankind. That she had an infernal dimension is suggested by the offerings of leather shoes (noted also at Bath), which are often found in Romano-British graves (Curbridge in Oxfordshire is an example) and which may symbolise the journey to the Otherworld. The fragment of a human skull found in the well is unlikely to represent any sinister ritual practice but rather a reverential interment of a piece of human body, perhaps found by devotees and placed in the water to give the soul an easy passage to the afterlife.

We know a little about the suppliants who came to worship and ask favours at the shrine of Coventina. One point of interest is that the altars were dedicated by individuals and there is no evidence for corporate or official worship. The inscriptions suggest that dedicants came mainly from the Gaulish and German provinces, and most must have been associated with the army: one of the images of the goddess was the gift of the prefect of a cohort of Batavians. The impression gained from the inscribed altars is that most of the dedicants were men, but this may not reflect the true picture, since one would expect more men than women to have possessed the wealth and status to enable them to commission such relatively costly offerings. The other gifts – coins and jewellery for instance – offer no clues as to which sex was more attracted to Coventina's cult.

Virtually nothing is known for certain about the ritual activities of visitors to Coventina's Well, apart from the clear evidence for casting in offerings to the water itself. But we can perhaps envisage supplication to the goddess, prayers, vows, propitiation, to accompany the giving of gifts. Maybe sick pilgrims bathed in or drank the pure water, to gain some of the essence of the goddess. The bones of animals from the well (which were found during its original investigation but, alas, not kept) may reflect feasting, sacrifice or both.[29]

Sirona and her Peers

A group of healer-goddesses worshipped throughout Romano-Celtic Europe share a common feature, namely their possession of a male partner. The phenomenon of divine couples is discussed fully elsewhere (see Chapter 6), but it is useful here to look at some significant features of the healers and, in particular, the status of the goddess. The imagery of the female partners owes far more to native influence than that of their male companions, and the goddesses also usually bear wholly native names, whilst most of the male deities have at least some Roman element in their epigraphic identity.

Sirona was the divine healing partner of a native Celtic version of Apollo (who was sometimes called Apollo Grannus, Belenus or by some other Celtic surname). Whilst Sirona is often linked with this god, she was venerated alone at some sites, as at Baumburg in Noricum (Austria) and at Corseul in Brittany, where she was called Tsirona and where her high rank is demonstrated by her association with the *numen* (spirit) of the emperor on a dedication. If Sirona was worshipped on her own, the inference is that she was an independent divinity who existed in her own right, probably before the Roman occupation of North-west Europe.

Sirona was most popular among the Treveri of Gallia Belgica, where her main cult centre was at Hochscheid, a spring-sanctuary in the Moselle Basin. Other Treveran curative shrines dedicated to Sirona and Apollo include Bitburg, Nietaldorf and Sainte-Fontaine; and among the neighbouring Mediomatrici, the couple was venerated at Metz. But the cult was widely known throughout Celtic Europe: Sirona was worshipped in thermal sanctuaries at Wiesbaden and Mainz in the Rhineland; Luxeuil and Mâlain in eastern Gaul; Brittany in the North-west. Even further afield, Sirona's cult was followed in Noricum, as we have seen and, as far east as Brigetio in Hungary, where a temple was set up in the third century AD to Apollo Grannus and Sarana (the name perhaps resulting from local variation or a mistake on the part of the inscriber).

During the second century AD, a temple was constructed to Apollo and Sirona around a natural spring at Hochscheid. The waters of the spring supplied a small cistern, and the evidence from coins implies that the building replaced an earlier shrine, probably made of wood. The pilgrims visiting the holy spring offered presents of coins, figurines and other votive gifts to the healing water-spirits. The sanctuary was wealthy for so remote and rural a region, and its patron may have been a prosperous villa-owner who made a personal endowment to a cult to which, perhaps, he may have had cause to be grateful.

The cult-image of Apollo at Hochscheid depicts the god in Classical guise, with his gryphon and lyre, but Sirona has a snake and a bowl of eggs, showing that she was a goddess of renewal and fertility as well as healing (see Chapter 6). Clay figurines brought as gifts to the shrine by hopeful pilgrims depict Sirona seated, like a mother-goddess, with a lap-dog, a symbol of healing. At other sites, too, Sirona's imagery is that of a spirit of regenerative and fertile power: at Mâlain, she has a snake curled round her arm, as occurs at Hochscheid; at Sainte-Fontaine and Baumburg her emblems are corn and fruit (grapes at Baumburg). A final point of interest concerns Sirona's name, 'Star', which suggests a link with night and with light penetrating darkness. Stars are luminaries of the night, like the moon, and Sirona may have had similar associations with women to lunar goddesses, such as Diana, who was traditionally linked to the menstrual cycle and to childbirth.[30]

The curative spring-goddesses Ancamna and Damona are distinctive in their apparent polyandry (see Chapters 4 and 6). The imagery of both these divinities, like

Stone statue of Sirona; second century AD. From the healing spring shrine of Hochscheid, Germany. The goddess holds a bowl of three eggs, and a snake curls around her right arm.

that of Sirona, indicates that their healing function was closely linked with that of fertility. Ancamna was a Treveran deity, linked with the great healer Lenus Mars at Trier and Smertrius at Möhn, where figurines in the form of mother-goddesses were offered at her shrine.[31] Damona's name is associated with cattle, symbols of wealth in Celtic society (see Chapters 4 and 8). She was a healer-goddess who, together with her partner, Apollo Moritasgus, presided over a curative shrine and spring-pool at Alesia. Her imagery is strongly reminiscent of Sirona's: a fragmentary statue from the site shows that Damona's symbols were a snake and ears of corn. At Bourbonne-Lancy, Damona's consort was Borvo, another spring-god. An inscription from their water-shrine relates to the goddess's association with the healing sleep enjoyed by pilgrims who sought a vision or dream of the divine healers during their stay in the temple dormitory. The polyandrous character of both Ancamna and Damona show that, like Sirona, they were independent, indigenous deities whose identities were not based on their link with an intrusive Roman god. Damona was worshipped without a partner at Bourbonne-les-Bains.[32]

Numerous other local female spring-spirits were venerated in Gaul. Bormana was linked with Bormanus (also called Borvo or Bormo) at Die (Drôme) in southern Gaul, but at Saint Vulbas (Ain), a temple was set up to Bormana alone.[33] Many other spring-goddesses were, like Sequana, tied to a particular locality: Telo was the eponymous spirit of Toulon in the Dordogne, the personification of a sacred spring which became the focus of a Celtic settlement; she was sometimes linked on dedications to another local goddess Stanna.[34] Ianuaria was local Burgundian goddess who was invoked at the healing water-sanctuary of Beire-le-Châtel. We know of her from a small stone statuette depicting a young person, wearing a heavy pleated coat and holding a set of pan-pipes, which is dedicated to the goddess Ianuaria by one Sacrovirus.[35] It is unclear whether the individual represented is the deity or the dedicant, but the pipes could refer to the healing power of music, reminiscent of vernacular Celtic myths in which goddesses possessed birds with magical curative powers: the iconography at Ianuaria's shrine included stone images of birds. Icovellauna and Aveta were both venerated in eastern Gaul. 'Ico' can refer to water, and this goddess was associated with healing springs at Trier and Metz.[36] Aveta, too, was worshipped at Trier: her pilgrims, like those who visited Hochscheid, brought votive gifts to her shrine in the form of figurines of seated mother-goddesses holding fruit, infants or small dogs.[37]

Healing and Fertility

The close conceptual link between healing, regeneration and fertility has been demonstrated by the symbolism with which many curative goddesses were depicted. In addition, there is substantive evidence for the veneration of the mother-goddesses

themselves at therapeutic spring-shrines. Celtic mother-goddesses are usually portrayed seated, with symbols of abundance: babies, animals, fruit, bread, or cornucopias. A distinctive feature of these goddesses is their frequent depiction as triads.

It may have been the natural link between the mother-goddesses and childbirth
which gave them their curative function. They must have been obvious *foci* of worship
for women anxious about pregnancy, the process of birth and post-natal problems of
lactation, weaning and the thriving of infants. The mother-goddesses were perceived
as protectors and nourishers of children: the healing spring-shrine of Genainville (Val
d'Oise) produced a stone image of a mother-goddess with a cornucopia and dish to
which an infant stretches its hand, as if to take food; the two are accompanied by a
water-nymph.[38] The curative spring-sanctuary of Vertault in Burgundy produced
several images of the three mother-goddesses.[39] The goddesses venerated at Aix-lex-
Bains were called the *Matres Comedovae*, a local triad associated with the thermal
springs: their epithet, with the 'med' element, may refer specifically to health.[40] The
Matres Griselicae were the personified spirits of the local healing springs at Gréoulx in
Provence.[41] The mother-goddesses were present also in Sulis' sanctuary at Bath: a
little schist plaque depicts the three goddesses as simple, highly schematised images.
These may be the *Suleviae*, a triad of mother-goddesses to whom dedications were
made at Bath, Cirencester and Colchester, and who were also worshipped in continental Europe as far east as Hungary.[42] The oddly-named *Xulsigiae* venerated at Trier
were possibly a local variant of the *Suleviae*: they were associated with a healing spring
and had a small chapel linked with a religious precinct dedicated to the great Treveran
healer-god Lenus. It is perhaps significant that a finger-ring found at the site of
Coventina's Well at Carrawburgh was dedicated to the mother-goddesses.[43]

The association between healing and the mother-goddesses was often symbolised
by the animal-companions which accompany their images (see Chapter 8). Dogs were
common attributes of these deities in Britain, Gaul and the Rhineland: the link
between dogs and healing-cults has been referred to above and is explored in Chapter
8. Snakes, too, with their composite symbolism of healing and regeneration, frequently accompany images of the mother-goddesses: depictions at Sommerécourt and
Xertigny (both Haute-Marne) show the goddesses feeding snakes, as if they and the
reptiles are exchanging mutual regenerative energy.[44]

The Mother-Goddesses

The concept of a divine Mother was common to many ancient societies. Such cults
reflect the preoccupations of communities for whom the fertility of their crops and
livestock and, indeed, their own procreation were fundamental concerns. Margaret
Ehrenberg has suggested[45] that the universal link between fertility and a mother-
goddess may have arisen – at least partly – because in the later Mesolithic and early

Neolithic periods (*c.*5000–4000 BC in Britain) women were in charge of plant-gathering and may have discovered cultivation. It is quite likely that, when plants were first domesticated, it was the women who tended them.

For the pagan Celts of Europe during the Roman period, the mother-goddess was perhaps the most important of the supernatural powers. Images and dedications relating to their worship reflect their popularity all over the Celtic world. But it would be wrong to claim the Mothers as an exclusively Celtic phenomenon. Many Graeco-Roman goddesses possessed maternal functions.[46] The imagery of the Celtic mother-goddesses owes much to Roman art-forms and they had their counterpart in the Roman *Iunones* (the Iuno or Juno being the spirit of the female principle).

The perception of the Celtic mother-goddesses was expressed in many different ways, but common to them all is symbolism associated with plenty and fecundity. Attributes such as corn, fruit, bread, animals, cornucopias and children all show the generative power of the female and in a sense, whether the emblems of particular goddesses consist of babies or fruit, the symbolic message is basically the same. These Celtic goddesses may be depicted as single, double or triple images. This last characteristic is the most distinctive pattern of representation, but even the triadic form has its parallels in Mediterranean religious art:[47] Hecate, goddess of the dead, was perceived as a triple image, as were the Nymphs. But the widespread, recurrent depiction of the mother-goddesses in triadic form is something I would argue as being particular to the Celts. It is well-known that three had a special meaning in the Celtic world: many deities were represented in triadic form, perhaps to represent a triple function or symbolism, and the earliest written Celtic myths of Ireland and Wales contain abundant references to triplism.[48]

Although the idea of the triple mother-goddess is only represented in epigraphy and iconography during the Roman period, it is fair to assume that such divinities were venerated in some form at least during the preceding Iron Age. The three-fold goddess was perceived to be powerful in all aspects of fertility, protecting house and family from barrenness, poverty and disease in life and the spirit after death. In the Roman period evidence for the worship of the Mothers takes the form of both inscriptions and imagery. The two come together on the same monument only comparatively rarely but the dedications, like the iconography, reflect a plural goddess, the *Matres* or *Matronae*: at Lyon, for instance, a depiction of three goddesses, each with a basket of fruit and a cornucopia, is accompanied by the dedication 'to the Mothers'.[49] Some of the altars to the Rhenish mothers, such as the *Matronae Aufaniae*, also combine inscription and image.

The fundamental importance of the mother-goddess cult is expressed both in its wide, pan-Celtic distribution and by its popularity among all echelons of society. The geographical spread of the cult may be aptly expressed by reference to a dedication from Winchester to the 'Italian, German, Gaulish and British Mothers'.[50] The link between the goddesses and the land is sometimes very clear from the topographical nature of their names. The Rhineland Mothers, who may have strange, Germanic-sounding titles, like the *Vacallinehae, Aufaniae, Boudunniehae*, are generally interpreted as goddesses who presided over specific localities. This occurs further south and west in Gaul: the *Nemausicae* of Nemausus (Nîmes), the *Glanicae* of Glanum (near Saint-Rémy-de-Provence) and the *Griselicae* of Gréoulx were all spirits of healing springs in southern Gaul. This close tie with the landscape is significant in that it appears to reflect similar concepts to those present in early Irish myth, whereby the goddess of sovereignty personified the land itself, its fertility and prosperity (see Chapter 4).

The Multiple Mother-Goddesses

Study of four regions within the Celtic world – the Rhineland, Aquitaine, Burgundy and the British West Country – serves to demonstrate the similarities and differences in perception of the roles, functions and concerns of the Mothers as plural divinities.

Among the Santones of Aquitaine in western Gaul, the mother-goddess was distinctive in being expressed in double form, rather than as a single or triple image. Saintes and Poitiers have produced sculptures of two mothers, seated side by side, bearing symbols such as fruit and cornucopias. A particular feature is a marked age-differential between the two goddesses, as if various stages of womanhood are expressed. This is something which occurs also in Burgundy.

Stone sculpture of three mother-goddesses. From the Romano-Gaulish town of Alesia, Burgundy. Each goddess is accompanied by a naked male infant and, on the right of the stone, a fourth naked child sits in a boat, accompanied by a swan.

The Burgundian mother-goddesses appear to have had complex, multi-faceted roles; indeed, the imagery of triadic groups in this region appears to demonstrate a belief-system that perhaps consisted of several levels of profundity. The mothers were here expressly concerned with the nourishment and protection of children. A relief at Alesia in Burgundy depicts the goddesses with a group of naked infants playing at their feet. There is a marked age-difference between the three, the central one being the youngest and one of her companions being much older than the other two. While the two younger deities have bared right breasts, as if to suckle babies, this older one is fully-clothed and she wears a mural crown, perhaps in reflection of her status as the personification of Alesia itself. Like other Burgundian images, these three goddesses may represent the three ages of womanhood: old age, maturity and nubile youth and so, by extension, the three main periods of earthly life of all humankind. They may have been perceived as guardians of children until death and beyond: here, an infernal role for the mother-goddess is perhaps reflected in the occurrence of her images in graves, underground rooms and caves (see below).[51]

A sculpture from Vertillum (modern Vertault) depicts three seated goddesses each with the right breast and shoulder bared for suckling: one woman holds a swaddled baby on her lap; the central one unrolls a swathing-band or napkin; the third has a basin and sponge. This homely imagery of baby-care is repeated on other Burgundian iconography, but with subtle changes which call into question the apparently simple message of domestic concerns. The central goddess on an image at Saint-Boil bears a napkin and a balance-beam; two sculptures at Nuits-Saint-Georges show yet more complexity: on both, the central goddess has an attribute which resembles a scroll rather than a napkin. On the first, the central goddess is depicted as much older than her companions, with lined cheeks, withered neck and sunken eyes, whilst her sisters have youthful, rounded faces. On the second, the central female has a cornucopia as well as her scroll and on the ground by her feet are a steering-oar, the prow of a boat and a globe. Her companion has a second cornucopia and an offering-dish.[52] The presence of such symbols as the balance-beam and scroll redirects our focus away from the straightforward domestic imagery expressed by the Vertault sculpture. Such symbols, which are visually almost identical to each other, may imply a conceptual shift and point to a more profound expression of belief. Thus the humble wash-basin may become an offering-dish and the napkin turns into a scroll. The prow, rudder and globe are symbols proper to the Roman goddess Fortuna. The parchment and balance-beam seem to reflect the idea of a spirit of destiny, like the Roman *Parçae* (the Fates), unrolling the scroll of life and weighing human souls. Some Treveran mother-goddesses hold spinning equipment, which may equally be interpreted both as sym-bols of domestic life and of the thread of life spun by the Fates until they decided to cut it.[53] At Nuits-Saint-Georges it is the eldest, most senior, goddess who holds the Book of Life, perhaps the most important attribute of the goddesses. This symbolism, viewed as a whole, seems to suggest that the Burgundian Mothers not only presided over human fertility, and the protection and nurture of children, but also over the passage between life and death. Perhaps these goddesses had a complex role, guarding the new-born infant, with the cornucopia symbolising earthly prosperity; and they had charge of the Book or Scroll of Life, with its inexorable one-way journey towards death. The boat may be present to carry the soul to the Otherworld, but Fate and Fortune decided on the destiny of humans during life and after death and Fortuna's rudder symbolises the arbitrary direction of human existence. The double symbolism of napkin/scroll is deliberately ambiguous and it is unnecessarily simplistic to interpret the motif as being one or the other: the two ideas are not mutually exclusive. The napkin signifies the beginning of life, whilst the scroll took the child right through to the end of earthly being.

The imagery of the Rhenish Mothers displays a marked contrast to that of Burgundy. Firstly, the carved and inscribed stones are generally of extremely high quality, arguing for a wealthy, sophisticated clientèle. Whilst we know little of the Burgundian dedicants, the Rhineland goddesses had devotees of high rank in the Roman army or civil administration: an altar was set up to the *Aufaniae* in Bonn by an urban treasury official of Cologne in AD 164.[54] The Rhenish mother-goddesses form a distinct and homogeneous group whose imagery makes no direct reference to human reproduction. The maternal title *Matronae* is linked with numerous topographical epithets, such as the *Aufaniae* around Bonn and the *Vacallinehae* of the great hill-top sanctuary of Pesch in the Eifel.[55] The iconography of these goddesses follows a consistent pattern: their symbols consist of bread, fruit, corn or money and their altars are often festooned with carved floral and faunal motifs. The deities themselves are depicted in a distinctive manner: a young central goddess with long, free-flowing hair, smaller than her companions, is flanked by two older divinities who wear curious beehive-shaped headdresses. This age-differential, already noted in Aquitaine and Burgundy, may reflect a similar expression of progressive stages of womanhood but, although three goddesses are present on the Rhenish images, two ages only – youth and maturity – are represented. It may be that the third goddess is present for artistic symmetry or, more likely, because triadic symbolism was a fundamental and potent part of the mother-goddess cult.

The epigraphy and iconography of the Rhineland goddesses tell us something about the cult and its adherents. One altar to the *Aufaniae* from Nettersheim depicts each of the Mothers carrying a work-box, and the central one also bears a distaff. As commented upon above, this may reflect simple domestic pastimes of spinning and clothes-making but, on another level, the distaff may allude also to human destiny. The great sanctuary at Pesch contained many temples and ancillary buildings grouped round a sacred tree, which seems to have been the cult-focus. This link between the Germanic Mothers and trees is repeated on an altar at Bonn, the rear of which is decorated with a tree entwined by a snake.[56] The pilgrims who worshipped at Pesch were mainly soldiers in the Roman army: they dedicated over 160 altars to the *Vacallinehae* and the images of these goddesses show their main emblem to be bread (the staple diet of the legionary).

Apart from monumental dedications to the Rhenish goddesses, there is evidence of a cheaper, more individual aspect of the cult, in the form of small clay figurines representing either the triad of the monuments or a single goddess, but still with the distinctive beehive headdress.[57] A difference in the small images is that some of the single ones nurse babies and, on many statuettes, the goddesses wear lunar amulets round their necks.[58] One of these single goddesses of Rhenish type, with the beehive headdress and lunar crescent, has recently been discovered in a child's grave at Arrington, Cambridgeshire.[59] The lunar motif is generally interpreted as a symbol of fertility; the Roman moon-goddess Diana protected women in childbirth.

Where there is evidence, most of the inscribed dedications to the Rhineland Mothers were made by men: this accords with the high status of the cult, as displayed by the superb quality of many monuments. But an altar to the Mothers of the Gesationes (a Rhenish tribe) from Rödingen was dedicated jointly by a man and a woman,[60] and images of supplicating devotees show participation by both sexes.[61] In general, the German mother-goddesses attracted high-ranking, perhaps intellectually sophisticated devotees, and there must have been more to their cult than a simple message of domestic well-being and fecundity. The cult may have offered deep comfort and satisfaction both in the world of the living and in the unknown journey to the Otherworld.

Some fifty dedicatory inscriptions and images relating to the mother-goddess cult are recorded from Britain. As with the Rhenish Mothers, the British goddesses attracted relatively high-ranking worshippers: an *arcarius* (municipal treasury official) at Chichester and a ship's pilot of the Legion vi at York are two examples.[62] An inscription from London refers to the restoration of a shrine to the mother-goddesses by a district, which is testimony to corporate worship. The Backworth (Northumberland) treasure dedicated to the Mothers must have been the gift of a wealthy patron: a silver skillet was filled with coins, spoons and jewellery and covered with an old silver mirror as a lid. One of the finger-rings in the hoard was inscribed 'to the *Matres Coccae*' (the 'Red Mothers'). Coin-evidence suggests that the cache was deposited in about AD 139.[63]

Of the many objects associated with the mother-goddess cult in Britain, the most interesting form a discrete group in the Cotswold region, centred on the tribal capital of Cirencester (Gloucestershire). One carving from the town depicts a lively scene of three ladies chatting on a bench, each accompanied by a small boy, one of whom reaches up to his mother's breast. The central goddess holds a lap-dog, so perhaps the image combines concepts of fertility and healing. A second Cirencester stone depicts the three goddesses, the middle one with a baby in her arms, the other two with trays of fruit. Here the imagery embraces the fecundity both of humankind and of the earth itself. The three wear different hairstyles, supporting the view that the goddesses were perceived as three separate entities. The central figure is the largest and her two sisters incline towards her as if in deference. This and her possession of an infant may indicate her seniority within the triad. A third sculpture portrays three ladies sitting stiffly side by side, each with a tray of bread or fruit which is slightly different from that of her companions. Again, the varying hairstyles suggest individuality rather than the mere triplication of a single image.[64]

A distinctive aspect of the Gloucestershire mother-goddess cult is the association of these deities with another god-type, the *genius cucullatus* or 'Hooded God', who occurs in both British and continental contexts, but only in Britain in triadic form. In the Cotswolds, mother-goddesses and *genii cucullati* are frequently represented together but, when thus associated, the goddess loses her triple form and the triadic concept is instead displayed by means of her three hooded companions. One stone from the vicinity of Cirencester depicts a mother-goddess seated in a high-backed chair, with a loaf or egg in her lap; she receives a gift from one of the three *cucullati* who stand before her. The goddess's name, inscribed on the base, is 'Cuda', a reference to prosperity and good fortune. Another sculpture presents the divine mother sitting next to three standing hooded gods, two of whom carry swords.[65] Both images appear to show the goddess in a dominant relationship to the hooded deities with her. On the first, she accepts a gift from them, as if they are suppliants; on the second, her companions are armed, perhaps to defend and guard the goddess and her devotees from barrenness or disease.

The Mother-Goddess as a Single Image

Not all depictions of the divine mother present her as a triad; she was often venerated as a single entity. She appears thus on a small stone statuette found near the base of a deep pit in the vicinity of a Romano-Celtic temple at Caerwent (Gwent).[66] The context may imply an infernal function for the goddess, but her symbols are a small round fruit held in one hand and an ear of corn or palm-leaf in the other. Corn and fruit reflect abundance but, if the second object is a palm, then this motif may be a symbol of victory (as it is in Classical iconography). Another mother-goddess image found underground is the large stone statue from a house-cellar, which has been interpreted as domestic shrine, at Alesia: the goddess wears a mantle, torc and diadem and she sits in a basket-chair with an enormous heap of different fruits, the epitome of the earth's bounty.[67]

Two goddesses, from Naix (Meuse) and Chatonrupt (Haute-Marne), show certain similarities to each other.[68] Both carry fruit-baskets and both are flanked by young girls or children. The companions of the first goddess are two girls with jugs of wine and keys, the latter perhaps symbolising the opening of the temple-doors and, maybe, at the same time the gate to the Otherworld, just as Epona's key may open the door to the stable and to heaven (See Chapter 8). The Chatonrupt Mother appears with a little girl who playfully inserts her arm under the goddess's wrist to snatch a piece of fruit from her lap. This charming tableau reflects the benevolent complicity of the mother-goddess, who looks on unperturbed at the child's greedy antics. This sculpture dates to about AD 50.

Small figurines of goddesses may represent offerings in temples or private shrines. A rare wooden image of what may be a mother-goddess comes from Ballachulish (Argyll). The oak figurine, which may date as early as the seventh century BC, is of a naked female; it was found in a peat-deposit in which there is evidence of a wattled structure, perhaps a small shrine. Her interpretation as a fertility-goddess is suggested by the emphasis of the pudenda.[69]

Clay figurines of seated goddesses, found on domestic sites, in graves and temples, are sometimes known as *deae nutrices* ('nursing goddesses') because they are depicted suckling one or two infants. The imagery may derive from that of Italian nursing goddesses, or indeed from representations of the deified Roman empress, who was sometimes portrayed as a fertility-goddess nourishing her empire. The Romano-Celtic *deae nutrices* were mass-produced in Rhenish and Gaulish factories particularly during the second century AD, and were traded widely in western Europe.

That the *dea nutrix* was perceived as a divine protector of the home is indicated by the domestic context of many finds. But she was also venerated in sanctuaries at such places as Alesia and at Dhronecken near Trier, where a shrine was apparently dedicated to the nursing goddess. Here numerous images both of her and the children she protected were offered in hope or gratitude, perhaps for the gift of children, health or prosperity. The sepulchral context of some figurines suggests that the goddess also acted as a guardian of dead souls: she may have been buried in such graves as those at

(*Left*) Clay figurines of a mother-goddess, known as the *Dea Nutrix*; first or second century AD. From London. Such statuettes were imported from workshops in Central Gaul and the Rhineland, and were buried with the dead or placed in private shrines.

(*Right*) Clay figurine of a Rhenish mother-goddess, buried with a baby boy at Arrington, Cambridgeshire; second century AD. The nine-month-old infant, who died of hydrocephaly, was interred in a lead coffin with aromatic resins. With him was a wooden box containing several statuettes, including those of animals.

Hassocks (Sussex) and Ballerstein (Alsace) as a comfort to the dead and the bereaved, and to symbolise the hope of rebirth beyond the tomb.[70] The clay mother-goddess of Rhenish type at Arrington, already mentioned above, accompanied the body of a child who had died of hydrocephaly: he perhaps needed especial help in his journey to an afterlife where he might be reborn whole. These hints at a funerary function accord well with some of the symbolism already noted in respect of the triple mothers. The context of a small bronze figure of a nursing mother from the Culver Hole Cave in Gower (West Wales) may also be relevant to an underworld function: her deposition in a cave is reminiscent of that of the stone goddess at Alesia in a cellar.

Nerthus and Carriage-Borne Mother-Goddesses

Tacitus[71] alludes to a Germanic mother-goddess, Nerthus, whose sanctuary was an island-grove in which stood a sacred wagon 'draped with a cloth which none but the priest may touch'. This cart was then drawn round her territory to a place of celebration: merrymaking went on for several days, during which no-one went to war and all iron objects were locked away. At the end of the festival the goddess was returned to her shrine by her priest 'when she has had her fill of the society of men', and the cart, cloth and 'believe it if you will, the goddess herself' were purified in a sacred lake. After this lustration-rite, the slaves attending the goddess were sacrificed by drowning in the lake, because the sight of the holy could only be admitted to dying eyes.

Although there was apparently no image of the goddess herself in anthropomorphic form, it is tempting nonetheless to link Nerthus with the iconography of one plate on the Gundestrup Cauldron, which depicts the bust of a woman flanked by two wheels.[72] The Danish cult-wagons found with a female burial at Dejbjerg (See Chapter 7) may also have been associated with such a goddess. The sixth-century AD Bishop Gregory of Tours[73] alludes to a third-century rite, involving celebratory singing and dancing, which took place in the Burgundian town of Autun: a goddess named Berecynthia was carried round the countryside in a wagon 'for the preservation of their fields and vineyards'. Of possible significance in this context is a fragmentary stone image of three mother-goddesses riding in a horse-drawn cart at Essey in Burgundy.[74]

The Symbolism of Mother and Sun

In discussing Sulis, it was noted earlier that healing-cults and the sun were sometimes associated. There is some evidence that some domestic goddesses could also have a solar dimension. This is represented above all by a group of clay figurines made in the same workshops as the *deae nutrices*. The statuettes have the outward form of the

Roman Venus but, because of their context and associations, some scholars believe these images to represent a humbler native Celtic goddess of fertility and domestic well-being.[75] Such figurines occur in houses, shrines (especially healing spring-sanctuaries, such as Vichy, Nuits-Saint-Georges and Springhead) and in graves. Pierre Lambrechts makes the point[76] that the substantial number of figurines found all over Gaul, the Rhineland and Britain, does not accord with the very few monumental sculptures of Venus in Romano-Celtic contexts. In any case, the presence of small clay statuettes of the goddess as votive offerings in shrines and as grave-goods argues for a more universal and domestic appeal than is appropriate for the Roman goddess of love. The Venus-form may have been chosen to represent a Celtic personification of fertility. Venus would adapt readily to such a role, since she was originally an Italian spirit of the fertile soil.[77]

One group of 'Venus' figurines is distinctive in that they bear solar symbols – wheels, circles and radiate motifs – in relief. The main centres of manufacture for these images were around Rennes in Brittany and in the Allier region of Central Gaul. One figurine, from a Breton grave at Caudebec-lès-Elbeuf, bears intense sun-symbolism which is concentrated on the breasts, belly and thighs, as if to emphasise a link between the sun and fertility.[78] This image is representative of many in the sun-decorated group, in the sheer density of the solar motifs that often appear both on the front and rear of the figure. The fertility association is evident not only from the positioning of the symbols near the genitals, on the breasts and abdomen, but the breasts themselves may be decorated so that they themselves become quasi-sun motifs.

The presence of these solar-decorated images of domestic goddesses in graves perhaps represents the comfort of light in the dark tomb, which was perhaps perceived as the 'womb' of the earth. But in addition, the veneration of a 'solar' goddess may be an acknowledgement of the marriage between a celestial god and the mother-goddess, the sky and the earth. This is a feature of many mythologies and religious systems, notably those of Egypt and the Classical world.

The Significance of the Mother-Goddess Cult

The importance of the divine mother in Celtic belief is demonstrated by the widespread distribution and the large number of cult-objects relating to her worship. Her devotees came from all ranks of society: there was some rich patronage, but she was also invoked by humble rural communities. The monumental dedications may have often been those of men, but this probably reflects the generally higher and wealthier position of men rather than that men were particularly attracted by the cult. Women may more often have made smaller, more personal offerings to her. Sometimes dedications were made jointly by men and women: the Rödingen inscription to the *Matronae* of the Gesationes has already been noted; and a dedication to the *Matres*

Ollototae (the Mothers of Other Peoples) was set up by one Julius Secundus and Aelia Augusta.[79]

That the cult of the Mothers was by no means an exclusively female concern raises questions as to the perceived role of these goddesses. The intimacy with which they were regarded by some dedicants is indicated by an epithet which occurs on inscriptions especially in southern Gaul: the *Proxumae* (the 'Very Near Goddesses').[80] The context, dedications and the iconography of the Mothers present us with evidence for a complex, hierarchical cult. Some of the goddesses appear to have been concerned with straightforward fertility of people, livestock or crops, but the imagery of others hints at a deeper symbolism in which life and death, the destiny of humans and the inexorable progression from birth to death were clear concerns of devotees. The context of some cult-objects shows the Mothers to have been involved in healing and as companions to the dead. Guardianship and well-being in all its manifestations seem to have been their predominant role and, as such, the cult would have been of equal appeal to women and men.

We need to examine the significance of the triplism that is such a prominent iconographical feature. Study of the images reveals that, in many cases, it is not simply a matter of intensifying the symbolism to the power of three which is intended. The goddesses show differences from each other not only in their fertility-emblems but also in their personal features and their ages. It is clear that both plurality and threeness are significant: there is a great deal of evidence for the sanctity of the number three in the pagan Celtic tradition.[81] Triplistic imagery may embrace many different concepts, involving deliberate fluidity, ambiguity and personal choice on the part of worshippers. There may have been perceptions of three goddesses or of one deity with three aspects, or three intensifying images, offering triple honour to the Mother. Triple concepts which may have underlain this multiple imagery include the spatial: sky/earth/underworld, or before/here/behind; the elemental: earth/air (or fire)/water; or the temporal: past/present/future. All or some of these ideas may have been present. The age-differences discernible on some images may be associated with the three ages of womanhood. We should remember also the Irish goddesses – the Morrigán, for instance – who were multi-functional spirits of war, fertility and territory. The mother-goddesses of Romano-Celtic Europe may, indeed, have possessed some elements similar to that of the Insular sovereignty goddess (see Chapter 4), in that they were equally concerned both with fertility in all its forms and were closely linked with the land. The Celtic mother-goddesses may also have influenced early Christian cults, such as those of the Virgin Mary and certain female saints (see Chapter 9).

6 Love, Marriage and Partnership among the Goddesses

In early Irish and Welsh law, women enjoyed a certain independence: they could own property and could not be married without their consent. If a woman possessed equivalent wealth and social status to that of her partner, she was perceived as equal to him.[1] Accordingly in early medieval Wales and Ireland, marriage did not mean complete subservience of the woman to the man. The evidence from early myths and from pagan Celtic iconography presents us with pairs of supernatural beings whose basic equality may often be discerned. The Irish mythic tradition contains numerous examples of divine love and, even in cases where the man was a god and the woman apparently mortal, she herself possessed some elements of the supernatural and frequently set the pace for the relationship, thereby demonstrating her sexual power over her partner. The same is true of some divine lovers in Welsh myth, like Pwyll and Rhiannon (see Chapter 3). A recurring pattern in the Insular myths is one of jealousy incurred by the rivalry between an ageing suitor and a young lover over a girl. It was the girl who had the real power; she was able to manipulate the men, whilst seemingly a passive onlooker; she was the temptress whose beauty could cause chaos and catastrophe. She rejected her elderly admirer in favour of the man whom *she* chose.

No close links can be made between the lovers of Irish myth and the divine partners evidenced by Romano-Celtic iconography. Nevertheless, the images of these paired deities have certain characteristics in common which, once again, are indicative of their basic equality. Thus, most importantly, the male and female are often represented as being of the same size. This lack of distinction in male and female body-sizes (which goes against realism) may therefore have been symbolically important. Indeed, the emblems or attributes belonging to the goddess tend to fall within a more restricted range than those of her husband which may be very varied; the implication of this may be that we are dealing with goddess-forms which have essentially similar functions, whilst the gods are more diverse. In addition, a pattern may frequently be distinguished in the iconography (and sometimes also in epigraphy) whereby the goddess appears to belong to a more native, local Celtic tradition, while her partner is demonstrably of Roman origin. It is almost as if the imagery expresses allegorically the idea of 'marriage' between Celt and Roman, the conquered and the conqueror.

Temptresses and Treachery in Irish Myth

The story of Deirdre and Naoise is chronicled in a ninth-century text which was later integrated within the Ulster Cycle as a foretale of the *Táin Bó Cuailnge*. The tale of Gráinne and Diarmaid first appears in the tenth-century Book of Leinster and later became part of the Fionn Cycle. Both mythic stories are concerned with love, jealousy, honour, sexual power and the challenge presented by youth to old age. In both tales it was the females, Deirdre and Gráinne, who initiated the love-affair and who rejected ageing suitors because they had been imposed upon them. There is a possible parallel here with Blodeuwedd in Welsh myth, who spurned Lleu in favour of Gronw. In both the Irish episodes, the love-triangle ended in disaster for the young hero for whom the jealousy of his elderly rival proved his downfall. Both young lovers, Naoise and Diarmaid, were initially reluctant to have anything to do with the girls who were to cause them so much trouble, because each was inhibited by his honour-code which made him hesitate before challenging the older suitor, who was of superior political and social status to himself. It was Deirdre and Gráinne who persuaded them to elope, against their better judgement, imposing upon them a more compelling issue of honour than that which held them back.

Deirdre and Naoise

Fedlimid, chief bard or storyteller at the court of King Conchobar of Ulster, was the father of a baby girl, Deirdre. Before she was born, Conchobar's druid Cathbadh prophesied that, though the child would be extremely beautiful, she would cause nothing but sorrow and disaster to Ulster. On hearing the druid's pronouncement, the king's noblemen demanded that she be killed as soon as she was born, but Conchobar demurred: he decided to rear her secretly as her foster-father until she was of marriageable age and then take her for his wife.

The child was brought up in isolation from society, with the companionship only of a few women, of whom Leabharcham the poetess was her chief confidante. One day, the two of them were together, being visited by Conchobar, who had slaughtered a calf and was busy skinning it outside in the snow. A raven perched nearby, drinking the calf's blood, and the watching Deirdre exclaimed at the juxtaposition of the three colours: white snow, red blood and black raven. She foretold that the man she married would have this colouring, and Leabharcham informed her that such a man existed, with black hair, red cheeks and white skin. He was Naoise, one of the three sons of Uisnech, and Deirdre was determined to marry him.

Deirdre broke out of her sequestered life and contrived to meet Naoise, but he knew she was promised to the Ulster king and his honour demanded that he reject her advances. Deirdre was persistent and challenged his honour as a man, proving her own power to be greater than that of his bond to Conchobar. Naoise yielded and the two eloped, escaping from the Ulster court in company with Naoise's two brothers Ainle and Ardan. The lovers fled first to Ireland and then to Scotland, where the men sought military service under the Scottish king. All was well for a while, until the king began to lust after Deirdre but, as she and Naoise prepared to flee once again, news reached them of a pardon from Conchobar, who recalled them to Emhain Macha, sending to Scotland the great heroes Ferghus and Conall Cernach as his ambassadors, pledges of good faith to the fugitives. Only Deirdre divined that the pardon was false and that Conchobar was seeking to lure them back by treachery, in order to destroy them. Naoise and his brothers believed in Conchobar's pledge and returned home. Ferghus accompanied them to ensure their safe conduct, but before the party arrived at the royal court the Ulster champion was lured away by an invitation to a feast: Ferghus was under two sacred bonds or *geissi*, one to protect Naoise and Deirdre, the other never to refuse a feast, the latter being of more longstanding and therefore the more powerful. No longer under Ferghus' protection, the three brothers were trapped and killed by one Eoghan: Deirdre was imprisoned by Conchobar for a year, after which he asked her to name the individual she loathed most, and she immediately spoke of Eoghan, the killer of her lover. In an exquisite act of vengeance, Conchobar announced his intention of giving Deirdre to Eoghan as his wife but, rather than wed her lover's destroyer, Deirdre killed herself, leaping from the chariot in which she was travelling with Conchobar and Eoghan, and dashing out her brains against a rock.[2] The prophecy of disaster was ultimately to prove correct because it was Conchobar's treachery that caused the defection of three great Ulster champions (Ferghus, Conall Cernach and Conchobar's own son Cormac) to the rival court of Connacht, thereby leaving Ulster vulnerable to attack from Queen Medb, and leading to the devastation of Ireland.[3] Conchobar was both Deirdre's salvation and the cause of her destruction. His lust kept her alive as a child but also brought about her death. Deirdre herself was no mere passive facilitator of events, like Branwen or Olwen of Welsh tradition. She took control and proved stronger than Naoise, pitting her honour-code against his and winning. Deirdre was the initiator; she chose her lover, thus triggering the jealousy of the rejected king which brought doom to them all. Deirdre not only had a strong personality but she also possessed powers of perception denied to Naoise: only she could see through Conchobar's false message, though she could not halt its consequences. By contrast, Naoise was a colourless figure, brave but less clever than his mistress. Deirdre's character is rounded, vivid, three-dimensional, whilst that of Naoise seems simply to be an archetype of the young lover, necessary to complete the mythic triangle of girl, youth and older male rival.

As to the status of Deirdre herself, it is difficult to ascertain whether she was goddess or human, but there are undoubted elements of the supernatural about her and her story. Her birth and life were pre-ordained by a holy man; she was associated with heroes and beings who were themselves of superhuman rank. Conchobar was a prophet; Ferghus and Conall were huge and far more powerful than normal mortals. Archetype or individual, Deirdre's place in Insular myth is assured. She stands out among other Irish mythic females in having the power to challenge the strict honour-codes of males. She was also associated with the sacred number 'three': she was involved with the three sons of Uisnech, though only the character of Naoise was developed; and she caused the defection from Ulster of three great heroes. In the end, however, Deirdre's power could not prevail and she succumbed to male dominance.

Gráinne and Diarmaid

The mythic triangle of older suitor, young challenger and initiating young girl recurs in the Fionn Cycle story of Gráinne, Diarmaid and Finn, leader of the heroic war-band the Fianna. Finn's role is similar to that of Conchobar: he was a powerful, though ageing leader; his jealous anger at losing Gráinne at the moment of their wedding caused him to act with dishonour in his treatment of Diarmaid, an action which led ultimately to the young man's death.

The story begins with the pre-wedding feast of Finn and Gráinne, his betrothed, at which his young bride-to-be caught sight of Diarmaid, a handsome young lieutenant of the Fianna, and with whom she immediately fell passionately in love. Like Deirdre, Gráinne took the initiative and approached Diarmaid, who recoiled from her advances because of the oath of loyalty he had sworn to his war-leader Finn. Once again, the boy's honour-code was successfully challenged by the girl, who mocked his manhood. Gráinne overpowered his bond to Finn, binding him to her with a stronger *geis* of her own, a magical tie which forced Diarmaid to take her away from the royal court of Tara. The strength of the sexual bond imposed by Gráinne on Diarmaid is demon-strated by the reaction of Diarmaid's warrior-companions, who urged him to break his pledge to Finn in favour of his new bond to the girl.

Like Deirdre and Naoise, Gráinne and Diarmaid fled from the wrath of the jilted elderly suitor, and they were pursued by Finn for many years. The pair were helped by Oenghus, Diarmaid's foster-father, the god of love, who hid Gráinne when she was in danger of capture, lured Finn's men away from Diarmaid by taking his form, and advised the pair how to survive in the wilderness. One warning imparted by Oenghus was never to rest for more than one night in any one spot. The two wandered into an enchanted wood, the Forest of Duvnos, which was presided over by a supernatural monster, a one-eyed giant named Sharvan the Surly. In the forest there grew a tree of immortality, the centre of the wood's enchantment, the consumption of whose berries granted eternal life, and Sharvan was especially anxious to guard the tree against would-be immortals. But Gráinne urged Diarmaid to get her some of the fruit: the young man did her bidding, slaying the near-immortal Sharvan in the process, and both lovers ate some of the magical berries. Oenghus now had to aid the couple once more, since Finn discovered their hiding-place in the forest; he again spirited Gráinne away to safety. Finn was exhausted by the seven years of pursuit: he declared himself reconciled to the loss of his bride, and she and Diarmaid married and produced five children. But Finn's defeat festered in his mind and he resolved to destroy Diarmaid by treachery, inviting him to participate in a boar-hunt in which he knew, by prophecy, that the young man would perish. (Although Sharvan's berries had endowed Diarmaid with immortality, he could, like Lleu of Welsh myth, be killed by magical means.) The hunted animal was the Boar of Boann Ghulban, an enchanted creature, Diarmaid's transformed foster-brother. Two versions exist of this fatal confrontation between Diarmaid and the boar: in one, the animal killed the hero; in the second, Diarmaid slew the boar but then pricked himself on one of its poisonous bristles. Finn's betrayal was now compounded: he could have saved his dying rival by fetching him water cupped in his hands; twice he brought the water but, in his hatred, he let it fall through his fingers before Diarmaid could drink; the third time he decided to save the youth but it was too late, and Diarmaid died.[4]

As in the case of Deirdre, Gráinne was not necessarily herself divine but she was hedged about by elements of the supernatural. She had a stronger personality than her lover and she initiated their affair, happily betraying Finn to elope with Diarmaid. Finn was undoubtedly a supernatural hero (this is indicated by many episodes in the Fionn Cycle) but his character was flawed by jealousy, dishonour and treachery which, in the end, caused his own downfall. Gráinne herself wielded a strong bond or *geis*, stronger than that of Finn. She had a close link with the god Oenghus, and both she and Diarmaid gained immortality in the Forest of Duvnos. Indeed, the only way that Diarmaid could be destroyed was by enchantment.

Finn was himself killed by the breaking of one of his *geissi*, a taboo on drinking from a horn. Trying to prove himself vigorous enough to continue his leadership of the disaffected Fianna, he tried to leap the Boyne and perished in the water. We hear little more of Gráinne herself, though she had achieved immortality by eating the berries, and she certainly survived both her lovers. Gráinne's character alone demonstrates her supernatural status: she was able to cause two powerful heroes to break their honour-codes and thus proved herself to possess greater potency than both of them.

Mixed Marriages: Gods and Mortals

Oenghus and Caer

Oenghus of the Birds was an Irish god of love, a member of the Tuatha Dé Danann, the race of gods whose activities are chronicled in the Book of Invasions. Oenghus mac Oc (the 'Young Son') was so-called because of the circumstances of his conception and birth, being born as a result of an illicit union between two deities, the Dagdha and

121

Fragmentary ceramic dish, ornamented with red-painted swans; made in about 400 BC. From Radovesiče, (formerly) Czechoslovakia.

Boann. Wishing to conceal Boann's pregnancy, the two deities put an enchantment on the sun so that it stood still in the sky for nine months, and Oenghus was therefore conceived and born on the same day.

Oenghus was a help to young lovers, to Gráinne and Diarmaid, as we have seen, and to Etáin and Midhir, as is discussed further below. But he himself could also fall prey to passionate love. The 'Dream of Oenghus' chronicles his desire for a mortal woman, Caer, who was under a shape-shifting spell causing her to be transformed, every other year on the Feast of Samhain, from human to swan form.[5] The story does not tell us why Caer was under this spell, but she was possibly enchanted by her father Ethal Anbual so that she could not marry. Certainly he refused Oenghus' request for her hand even though Ailill, a divine arbiter, interceded on his behalf. This paternal opposition to a daughter's marriage recurs in the Welsh myth of Culhwch and Olwen (see Chapter 3). But Ethal had his own *sídh* or Otherworld dwelling-place, which must imply his divinity and therefore his immortality. Caer's status may be that of half-human, half-deity, and it may be partly this instability that caused her to shape-shift at Samhain. Details of Caer's zoomorphic enchantment are explored in Chapter 8. What is interesting here is that it was possible for gods and mortals to marry. Caer was not fully divine, though she had strong connections with the spirit-world; she was a victim of another's malice and appeared to have no power over her own destiny. The spell cast upon her was so strong that Oenghus had to join her in her swan-guise in order to

122

possess her. Unlike that of the Irish war-goddesses, Caer's shape-shifting was involuntary, and this marks her as of less than divine rank. Oenghus was able to break the enchantment, but only by the substitution of Ethal Anbual's power over Caer with his own. Without Oenghus, Caer was condemned for life to her split identity.

Etáin and Midhir

Like Caer, Etáin was a victim, not a goddess but closely associated with the supernatural world. She was linked with two gods of the Tuatha Dé Danann: Oenghus, the god of love, who helped her and Midhir, who was in love with her. Etáin was mortal and her problems would seem to stem from her relationship with the god Midhir. The love he had for her excited the jealousy of his wife Fuamnach, who cast a spell upon the girl, changing her first into a pool of water (just as the Morrígán punished Odras for daring to mate her bull with the goddess's cow) and then into a purple fly. That the transformed girl herself possessed some supernatural power is implied by her ability to lull Midhir to sleep by her humming, and to warn him if an enemy approached. Fuamnach's revenge on Etáin was not complete: she conjured up a magical wind to blow the fly away, but she found a refuge with Oenghus, who was able partially to lift Fuamnach's spell and restore Etáin to human form between nightfall and dawn. Oenghus sheltered her for some time but Fuamnach still pursued her and she was blown far away. Etáin's first existence drew to a close when, still in the form of a fly, she fell into a goblet of wine and was swallowed by the wife of Edar, a war-champion of Ulster. The woman conceived and bore a child, who was a new Etáin, reborn more than a thousand years after her original life.

Midhir was, of course, an immortal, to whom time was irrelevant, and he had been searching for Etáin over all the long period of her enchantment, death and rebirth. It was his wife's spell over Etáin which, paradoxically, caused her to break the normal boundaries of mortality: her transformation may have frozen time for her. Midhir finally rediscovered his love as the wife of Eochaidh, king of Ireland, but her past had been wiped from her memory and she remembered neither Midhir nor any of her trials. Midhir contrived to win Etáin from Eochaidh by trickery: he challenged the king to a board-game which he won: the stake was a kiss from Etáin, which was reluctantly honoured by her husband. When the former lovers exchanged a kiss, Etáin remembered their passion and her love for Midhir was rekindled. The pair fled from Eochaidh's court with the king in hot pursuit. Midhir had transformed them both into swans (like Oenghus and Caer) and thus they made their escape from Tara. When the king got too close, Midhir magically conjured fifty girls, all identical to Etáin. Eochaidh made his choice, but he made a horrific error and slept instead with his own daughter, thus committing the appalling act of incest.[6]

Etáin was supposedly human and mortal, yet her supernatural symbolism was intense. Loved by one god, helped by another, she was the victim of jealous revenge that led to an involuntary transformation. However, she was the subject of a long-standing destiny, and she was reborn, still with her old identity, though with no memory of her past. There is also an element of the sovereignty-goddess (see Chapter 4) about Etáin: she was married to the king of Ireland and his union with her was perhaps necessary for the legitimacy of his rule. Midhir was divine but he sought a partner of apparently mortal status. Etáin's identity is unclear: although she is presented in the myth as human, the implication is that she was somewhat above human status. There was even a triadic dimension to her identity, which links her with the triplistic nature of some of the unequivocal Irish goddesses, like Macha and the Morrígán. In a sense, there was one Etáin but, in another, it is possible to distinguish three: the original subject of Midhir's love; the wife of Eochaidh; and the daughter whom the king mistook for his wife.

Divine Partners in Romano-Celtic Europe

The epigraphy and iconography of pagan Celtic Europe present us with a bewilderingly wide range of coupled deities, some of whom were venerated over very broad regions involving several tribes and others, by contrast, very localised indeed, occurring perhaps at just one or a few sites. Those couples who are represented iconographically reflect their functions and concerns by means of the symbolism with which they are depicted. They therefore give far more information about their cults and the perceptions of their worshippers than those whose existence is known only by names on inscriptions. We can deduce very little, for instance, about Veraudinus and Inciona who appear only at Widdenburg in Luxembourg[7] or Luxovius and Bricta at Luxeuil,[8] though the latter pair were venerated at a healing sanctuary. Sometimes, indeed, context gives us our only clue to function: Ucuetis and Bergusia, worshipped at Alesia, may have been craft-deities: a large bronze vessel bearing a dedication to the couple was found in the cellar of a large building, along with countless bits of bronze and iron scrap, perhaps the work-debris of metalsmiths. The cellar may not itself have been a workroom but was possibly an underground sanctuary to a divine couple who watched over the craftsmen and their work.[9]

The relationship of goddess to god may be suggested by epigraphic evidence. Generally speaking, the name of the male deity is mentioned first, and this may or may not be significant for their relative status. The order may simply be convention and, in any case, if reference is made to two deities, someone's name has to come first. On the other hand, there may be an implication of the superiority of god over goddess, although this is not indicated by iconography. But what is fascinating is that where an overt epigraphic conflation between Roman and local names exists, the male deity frequently has either a Roman name or he may have a bipartite title which is half-Roman, half-Celtic, while the goddess's name is entirely Celtic. Thus we have Mercury and Rosmerta or Apollo Grannus and Sirona. Sometimes, as in the case of Ucuetis and Bergusia or Sucellus and Nantosuelta, both names are of indigenous origin.

The iconography of divine couples shows them to have possessed a wide range of functions. Their attributes display varied symbolism which may be associated with war, plenty, wine, business or healing. But even within this diversity, the female shows greater consistency, often possessing symbols which are indicative of a role as a goddess of domestic prosperity, fertility and abundance, akin to the mother-goddesses. The male partner, on the other hand, has a wider variety of imagery: he may carry a spear, a sword, a hammer or a wine-goblet. But, like the epigraphy, the iconography shows that the goddess has a more native identity than her consort: images of Mercury and Rosmerta or Apollo and Sirona indicate that the iconography of the god is entirely classical: there is nothing to localise him apart from his partnership of the goddess. The divine female's prosperity-function may be symbolised by attributes which perhaps have their origin in the Classical world – the cornucopia (horn of plenty) for instance – but her imagery is not lifted wholesale from Graeco-Roman artistic tradition as is sometimes true of her mate.

Rosmerta and Mercury

In this book we are primarily concerned with the identity and role of the goddesses, so my inverting of the usual name-order is deliberate. This couple is one of the few whose iconography is, on occasion, accompanied by an epigraphic dedication, thereby enabling a positive and unequivocal link to be made between imagery and name: carvings of the couple accompanied by dedicatory inscriptions occur, for instance, at Eisenberg and at Metz.[10] The images are sufficiently idiosyncratic for their appearance alone to identify them as Rosmerta and Mercury. Typically, the god appears in his classical guise with his *petasos* (winged cap), *chlamys* (short cloak), money-bag and *caduceus* (herald's staff). He may be accompanied by some of his sacred animals, the goat or ram, tortoise and cockerel. Mercury's Celtic role is particularly associated with fertility and with commercial success; the ram and the goat were fertility-symbols in classical iconography, and Mercury's purse is entirely appropriate. A local Gaulish attribute of the god is a money-chest. Rosmerta's symbolism, like that of many Celtic deities, is expressed not only by her imagery but also in her name which means the 'Great Provider'. This is an all-embracing title which can mean beneficence in almost any form. She is, above all, a goddess of prosperity, who is depicted with a *patera* (offering-plate) and a cornucopia, promising the good things of life to her suppliants. Her consort's role complements hers and his close relationship with a native goddess is shown by his frequent adoption of native attributes or symbols, such as the Celtic torc at Trier[11] and the ram-horned snake, symbol of regeneration, at Néris-les-Bains (Allier).[12] A stone relief from Mannheim depicts Rosmerta herself feeding a snake from a purse, as if she is the source of life, nourishment and regenerative power.

Rosmerta's relationship with Mercury is complex. She sometimes shares his attributes of the purse and the *caduceus*. But the imagery of a stone at Wiesbaden appears to express Rosmerta's pre-eminence: the god offers the contents of his purse to Rosmerta, who sits enthroned before him.[13] The Wiesbaden iconography accords well with some other evidence that, far from being a mere female extension of Mercury's cult, Rosmerta enjoyed an essential independence. British representations, at Bath and Gloucester, depict Rosmerta with a curious bucket-like vessel, which does not appear in Gaul or the Rhineland. I suggest in Chapter 8 that this vessel may be associated with the craft of butter- or cheese-making, although Hilda Davidson and Graham Webster[14] have had this idea before me. The Gloucester monument is especially distinctive

Stone plaque of Mercury and Rosmerta; first or second century AD. From Glanum, near Saint-Rémy-de-Provence, France. Rosmerta holds a cornucopia, symbol of abundance, and Fortuna's emblems of rudder and globe; Mercury has a caduceus, goat, purse and tortoise.

126

because here the goddess not only has a bucket and ladle but, in her other hand, she holds a peculiar sceptre-like object, a long staff surmounted by a pelta-shaped head,[15] perhaps a kind of wand of authority. Rosmerta's independence of Mercury is shown by an image of the couple at Glanum in Provence, in which the god appears in his normal guise but Rosmerta has borrowed the attributes of Fortuna, a rudder on a globe, as well as a huge cornucopia.[16] This link with Fortuna recurs on a second image at Gloucester, where the couple are joined by a third divinity, a goddess who bears the imagery of Fortuna. The two females carry torches, Fortuna's upraised, Rosmerta's inverted, as if they represent light and darkness, life and death. Imagery like this indicates that Rosmerta has a more profound cult-role than that of a mere carbon copy of Mercury or of a simple fertility or prosperity goddess. Like some of the mother-goddesses (see Chapter 5) and perhaps also like Nehalennia (see Chapter 8), Rosmerta's role may be to protect humans in the chancy circumstances of earthly life. That she may also be associated with rebirth is suggested perhaps by her British bucket-symbol which may, at one level, be a butter- or cheese-making vessel but, at another, a cauldron of regeneration.

Mercury has no consort in Graeco-Roman tradition, so Rosmerta's very presence is indicative of Celtic influence, as is her symbolically explicit name and her idiosyncratic imagery. But the goddess's independent status is suggested above all by her veneration alone, without Mercury. The Burgundian tribe of the Aedui worshipped the unac-companied Rosmerta at Escolives (Yonne) and Gissey (Côte d'Or). At both locations, the image of the goddess was dedicated to Rosmerta and the emperor. At Escolives, she is depicted standing in a niche with a dish and a cornucopia: none of Mercury's attributes is present. But at Gissey, Rosmerta was the spirit of a sacred spring.[17] The high status of the goddess among the Aedui is indicated by her link with the Imperial Cult, and for this tribe Rosmerta was clearly a divinity of considerable rank and importance, whose potency did not depend upon her partnership with Mercury.

The function of Rosmerta, with or without a consort, is not only suggested by the symbolism of her name and the attributes with which she is portrayed. Sometimes context implies a role which is concerned not only with fertility but with healing. We have seen this at Gissey; Rosmerta appears also at major curative spring-sanctuaries, such as Bath.[18]

The popularity of the cult may reflect the multifarious issues with which this divine couple concerned themselves. Images and dedications reveal that people venerated Rosmerta and Mercury over a very wide area of Celtic Europe, with concentrations of monuments in central and eastern Gaul, both banks of the Rhine, and with an outlying cluster among the Dobunni of the British West Country, centred on Glou-cester. The reason for this widespread worship may have been partly because, in the Celtic world, Mercury was particularly associated with commerce. But Rosmerta's symbolism suggests a more profound concern with fertility, prosperity and well-being in both earthly life and the Otherworld. Rosmerta appears with the cornucopia, the cauldron of rebirth or the bucket of milk, the snake, the torch and the symbols of Fortune. So her attributes conveyed an immediate message of her deep concern for the human condition and its needs.

Nantosuelta and Sucellus

On a stone monument at Sarrebourg, near Metz, the tribal capital of the Mediomatrici, a divine couple is depicted standing side by side in a niche. The goddess wears a long robe and has flowing hair surmounted by a diadem. In her right hand she holds a dish over an altar and with her upraised left hand she steadies a long pole on top of which is an object like a miniature house, with two window-like openings and a gabled roof; at her feet are three honeycombs. Her partner is a mature man, older than his compan-ion, with curling hair and beard. He wears a cloak, a belted tunic and boots. Cradled in the crook of his right arm is a large pot and in his left he holds a long-shafted hammer or mallet, working-edge uppermost. The stance of the pair is very similar and the hammer and house-model are both on the ends of poles which are identical in height, as are the divinities themselves. Beneath the couple is a raven; above is an inscription which dedicates the stone to Sucellus and Nantosuelta.[19] The names of these deities are entirely Celtic: the god is called the 'Good Striker', an appropriate epithet for a hammer-god; the goddess's name means 'Meandering Stream'. Like Rosmerta, Nanto-suelta was venerated alone in eastern Gaul: on a carving at Speyer, she appears with her house-sceptre and raven and, on another depiction from Teting near Trier, she is portrayed with a pot and her house-symbol.[20] These representations of the goddess show a certain homogeneity: the house-motif, honeycombs and pot suggest a basi-cally domestic, homely symbolism, indicative of a concern for providing the necessities of life, shelter, food and drink. The raven may be a chthonic, infernal image (see Chapter 8) which is perhaps suggestive of an Otherworld dimension to the goddess's function.

It is debatable whether or not it is correct to identify the many nameless represen-tations of the hammer-god and the domestic goddess with Sucellus and Nantosuelta, but the distinctive long-shafted hammer of the god is so idiosyncratic and so relevant to his name that the identification is probably valid. What is noteworthy about the couple is the regional diversity of their imagery which is combined with the consis-tency of the hammer-motif.

In continental Europe the hammer-couple was popular in distinct areas, notably Burgundy, the Lower Rhône Valley and the Rhineland. Only one British carving is recorded, at Thorpe in Nottinghamshire, although Sucellus alone appears more than once. The Aedui and Lingones of Burgundy were the couple's most ardent wor-shippers, and here the partners were venerated above all for their association with

Stone relief of Nantosuelta and the hammer-god Sucellus; Romano-Celtic period. From Sarrebourg, near Metz, France. There are many representations of a hammer-couple with similar attributes; this one bears an inscription naming the two deities.

wine-growing. The imagery of the goddess is very consistent: she is a nourishing divinity of plenty, with a cornucopia and offering-dish and sometimes fruit.[21] Her male companion's symbolism has greater diversity: his hammer identifies him, but he often has a pot, an amphora-like jar, a wine-barrel or a sack of grapes. One of the many images of the pair from Alesia depicts a wine-barrel between the two deities, and at Dijon and Bolards, a great wine-jar occupies the same position.[22] One image at Alesia displays Nantosuelta playing a leading role in the wine-symbolism: she pours liquid from a *patera*; and she wears the mural crown of a tutelary (protective) divinity, the guardian-spirit of the city itself.[23] On another relief from the town, Nantosuelta is depicted with the rudder of Fortuna as if, like Rosmerta and other goddesses, she has a dimension as a divinity of Chance, steering human lives through the capricious waters of earthly existence. In Burgundy the couple's main overt concern was viticulture and the florescence of the wine-harvest. But the symbolism of wine and wine-vessels may have had a more profound meaning, that of resurrection or rebirth after death, which was perhaps reflected by the blood-like colour of red Burgundian wine.

The imagery of Nantosuelta and Sucellus is distinctive both in southern Gaul and in the Rhineland because of the presence of a dog as a companion. The Lower Rhône group is exemplified by an image at Marguerittes (Gard), where the couple stand side by side, a small dog gazing up at them.[24] The Rhenish iconography is essentially similar, but on a stone at Mainz the hammer-god's partner appears in the guise of a huntress, with a bow and quiver.[25] There may be combined infernal and regenerative symbolism in both groups of images: the dog may evoke messages of death, hunting, healing and guardianship. Hunting may be indicative of a dualistic relationship between life and death, with its overtone of nourishment through sacrifice.

It is difficult to determine the general relationship between Nantosuelta and Sucellus from their images alone. The individuality of the god, and the fact that he appears many times on his own[26] suggests that he is the dominant partner. Certainly it is his hammer-symbol which identifies the couple. He is always represented as older than his partner which, again, might accord him seniority. But she often wears a diadem, which reflects high status, as does the torc around the neck of the British depiction of the goddess. Both divinities bear symbols of prosperity: the hammer is an enigmatic attribute but the name 'Good Striker' implies protective beneficence, and the wine-symbolism of Burgundy points unequivocally towards plenty and well-being. Nantosuelta's emblems place her firmly within the great group of fertility-goddesses: sometimes her cornucopia is enormous, as if to emphasise her potency as a provider. The water-symbolism implied by her name is not clear from her imagery but if we remember the liquid-pouring motif at Alesia, and the general association with liquor on the Burgundian carvings, it may be that water or liquid represents the life-force, the source of Nantosuelta's power. That the goddess may have had an infernal dimension to her persona is suggested by the companionship of the dog and the raven; water itself can be a dualistic motif of life and of death; and Nantosuelta's link with the symbolism of Fortuna is suggestive of just such an element in her identity.

The dominant function of the couple was as purveyors of prosperity, whether it took the form of food, wine or life itself. Most of their images were set up by ordinary people, as individual acts of worship rather than as part of a corporate act of devotion. They were personal deities venerated in the home, not generally in public temples. This pattern of worship accords well with Nantosuelta's house-symbolism which seems to display her representation as the essence of domestic life.

Wine, Fertility, Health and Protection

The Aedui of Burgundy and some other Gaulish tribes during the first few centuries AD venerated a divine couple who were represented iconographically but for whom we have no names. Their imagery indicates that their major concerns, like those of the hammer-god and his partner, were fecundity and abundance. It may even be that, though the distinctive hammer-symbol is absent, we are dealing with the same divine pair. Certainly among the Burgundian Gauls, a concern for viticulture, as well as general well-being, is strongly evidenced by the symbolism of these partnered deities. Preoccupation with the prosperity of vineyards is here reflected by the motifs of wine-jars, goblets, grapes and even wine-tending implements: on a relief at Vertault, the couple is represented with a dish of grapes and a hoe.[27] The wine-imagery may be very intense: on a monument at Volnay, the male deity exhibits distinct signs of drunkenness as he staggers, clasping a wine-cup in both hands, while his female companion supports him.[28] On an image at Alesia, wine-motifs are again dominant with the divine couple accompanied by three wine-barrels.[29] Sometimes bread and wine symbolism expresses the basic needs of Aeduan peasants: the relief at Vitteaux near Alesia depicts the goddess with a large loaf of bread and the god with a wine-goblet;[30] and this combination of motifs recurs at Alesia.

On occasions, the fertility-symbolism of the Burgundian couples is emphasised: at Autun, a very large cornucopia is depicted, and the virility of the god is made evident by his lifted tunic and bared genitals,[31] while a goddess at Alesia exposes her right breast in readiness to suckle an infant.[32] This kind of depiction perhaps reflects the perception that it is the partnership of the divine couple that promotes the fecundity of the earth: their own union brings the land to life. Certainly the couple's close relationship is sometimes stressed, as at Saint-Boil, where the two divinities turn their heads to each other in companionship, and at Alesia, where the two hold hands and share a cornucopia.[33]

Among the Leuci of eastern Gaul and the Santones of the west, the divine couple's symbolism is reflected by zoomorphic imagery. At Saintes in Aquitaine, an antlered god is accompanied by a female partner with one or more cornucopiae, signifying her association with plenty.[34] The Aedui venerated a divine couple with a snake-companion, represented by carvings at Alesia and Autun.[35] The Aeduan sculpture at Santosse in Burgundy expresses the perception of the divine partners as master and mistress of animals: they sit surrounded by stags and horses (representatives of wild and domesticated nature). The deities offer goblets of wine to the horses as they caress them, and their feet rest on the backs of the stags.[36] So the relationship between goddess, god and animals is extremely close. The wine which is so important to Aeduan symbolism is offered to the beasts as a sign of nourishment, while the stags receive blessing from the touch of the two deities. The duality of the couple is reflected also in the depiction of the creatures in pairs.

The idea of a divine couple as guardians and protectors of humankind is evidenced in iconographical and epigraphic representations where the goddess is accompanied by a god who possesses the attributes of a warrior. He is not a war-god in the accepted sense but a fighter against such evils as barrenness and disease. Once again, this partnership was most popular among the Burgundian tribes, perhaps with a cult-centre at Alesia: on one image from the town, the couple closely resemble the hammer-god and his partner; they sit side by side, the goddess holding a cornucopia, a dish and a basket of bread or fruit, while the god bears a spear, point uppermost, like a sceptre.[37] A second depiction at Alesia shows that this warrior-image could indeed be equated with the hammer-god: he has both a hammer and a sheathed sword, signifying that he is not an offensive fighter but a peaceful protector; she wears a mural crown and is clearly the tutelary goddess of the city.[38] A third carving shows the same couple: he has a spear and she carries a cornucopia so heavy that she needs both hands to support its weight.[39] The warrior-partners were venerated also at Autun, where the shield and spear of the male are balanced by the goddess's fertility-emblems of the dish and the horn of plenty.[40] On this relief the god is naked, as if at one and the same time he reflects both virility and the ritual of nude combat which was recorded as a Celtic custom by some Classical sources.[41] One significant difference between the Aeduan 'warrior' deity and the hammer-god is in age: the hammer-bearer is almost invariably mature, in the prime of life, but the weapon-bearer is young, as befits a soldier. It may be that what we are witnessing is imagery of one and the same divine entity represented at different ages. His role as a young warrior is that of guardianship, of the fecundity of the land, the well-being of his people and, perhaps, even of the goddess herself who is the personification of fertile beneficence.

War-couples outside Aeduan territory may reflect similar perceptions of protection: a British goddess is accompanied by a mounted war-god at Calcot in Gloucestershire.[42] The war-imagery may be associated with a dedication to Mars: this occurs among the tribe of the Triboci in the vicinity of Strasbourg, where the war-god's traditional role is again belied by his goddess-companion who has a pot (perhaps of wine).[43] The Mars link is present, too, at the Burgundian therapeutic spring-sanctuary of Mavilly, where a god wearing chain-mail and equipped with a shield and spear is accompanied by a goddess whose closeness to her mate is exhibited by her resting one hand on his shoulder and the other on his shield.[44] This god is accompanied by a ram-horned serpent, present here, perhaps, for its regenerative, healing symbolism. The deities at Mavilly were invoked especially for their power to cure eye-afflictions.

In early Roman religious tradition, Mars' war-function was a secondary role, which he acquired through his identification with the Greek Ares. Originally, Mars was an agricultural spirit, protector of fields and boundaries, and his popularity in Romano-Celtic contexts often reflects perceptions which are close to Mars' initial Roman concerns. For the Celtic Mars, protection against ill-health was an especially import-

Stone altar dedicated to Loucetius Mars and Nemetona, by Peregrinus, a citizen of the Treveri (of the Moselle Valley); Romano-Celtic period. From Bath.

ant role and one in which he was frequently venerated with a goddess-companion. Among the Treveri, the popular healer-god Lenus Mars was worshipped with his female partner Ancamna (see Chapter 5) at his great sanctuary in Trier. But Ancamna was invoked with another healer-companion, Mars Smertrius, at Möhn nearby.[45] The title 'Smertrius' derives from the same Celtic root as Rosmerta, and again reflects a role as a provider, this time presumably of health as well as plenty. Ancamna's apparent marriage with two gods has implications of polyandry among the goddesses, a tradition followed also by another deity, Damona. At the Möhn shrine, Ancamna was offered small clay images of a mother-goddess, as if healing and abundance were closely linked in the religious perceptions of her followers.

The healing function of some divine couples is evident (see Chapter 5). The most important partnership is expressed in the veneration of the Classical god Apollo who, judging by his several indigenous Celtic titles or epithets, was clearly fully absorbed into the Gaulish pantheon. The Graeco-Roman Apollo was a multi-functional divinity whose concerns included healing, hunting and prophecy; he was also associated with light and the sun. Celtic worshippers invoked Apollo mainly as a curative spirit, but his solar and oracular functions also manifested themselves at some therapeutic cult-centres. The Celtic Apollo was associated with a number of female partners. He himself

Bronze group of the divine healers Apollo and Sirona; Romano-Celtic period. From Mâlain, Burgundy. The base is inscribed with a dedication to the couple.

adopted several indigenous titles, such as Grannus, Belenus or Vindonnus, but his companion's name is wholly native. Thus Apollo Grannus and Sirona were venerated at many European sanctuaries: their main cult-centres, as we saw in Chapter 5, were among the Treveri of the Moselle Basin.[46] At these sites, the god is represented as an entirely Classical figure, but images of Sirona (whose name is philologically linked to 'star') show greater independence of Mediterranean tradition, although there are some resemblances between Sirona and Hygeia. The Celtic healer-goddess is depicted with a snake curled round her arm, and that she was associated with fertility as well as regeneration and healing is implied by her attributes of eggs and corn[47] (see Chapters 5 and 8). Sirona's name, which reflects light in darkness, is significant, since one of Apollo's epithets was Belenus, another title meaning 'brilliant light'. Apollo Vindonnus at Essarois in Burgundy was also connected with clear light and this may reflect his role as a healer of eyes and poor sight. It is possible that Sirona's name implies comparable symbolism.

Damona was another Gaulish goddess who was linked with a version of Apollo, Moritasgus, at Alesia in Burgundy,[48] where the couple had an important healing sanctuary. Like Ancamna, Damona possessed more than one husband, being associated with another healer-god, Borvo[49] at Bourbonne-les-Bains and elsewhere. Borvo himself, sometimes also called Bormo or Bormanus, could also swap partners and was linked with another goddess, Bormana. Damona was in fact coupled with a third male partner, the native god Abilus, at the Burgundian shrine of Arnay-le-Duc.[50]

The Divine Marriage: Partnership and Polyandry

Certain general issues concerning the pairing of female and male divinities remain to be addressed. A distinctive feature of the vernacular mythic tradition is, as we have seen, the triangle of girl, youth and older, jilted suitor (or father). The dominant themes are love, jealousy and resulting disorder, sometimes with catastrophic consequences for all concerned. The norm is for the woman to be claimed by two men, one young, one old. It is perhaps possible to see here an allegory of seasonality, the death of the old year and the beginning of the new, reflected in the ascendancy of youth over age. There may also be a connection between these love-myths and that of sacral kingship (see Chapter 4), the marriage of the goddess of sovereignty and the rightful king. If this is the case – and it would certainly appear to be so with the story of Etáin – then the great conflict between the young man and the established suitor comes sharply into focus as a challenge for the kingship. The sovereignty-myth involves the universal female spirit of territory and fertility who unites with successive mortal rulers, this union resulting in prosperity for the land.

It is worthwhile to speculate as to whether we may legitimately make links between the myths of Ireland and the divine couples of the European Celts in the early first

135

millennium AD. What can be said with confidence is that all the iconography emphasises benevolence, well-being, prosperity and plenty, and this symbolism is reflected,
above all, in the imagery of the goddess. It is clear that the potency of these paired
divinities lay in their union: their partnership or marriage was the main factor in their
successful provision of health, fertility or protection. It is usually impossible to distinguish one partner as dominant: they are the same size and the symbolism of each is
equally intense. On occasions, their affection for each other and their mutual dependence is quite plain. Since the god's imagery argues for a wider variety of functions and
that of the goddess is more consistently associated with plenty, it is possible that we are
witnessing a religious tradition which has much in common with the Insular sovereignty-goddess who has many different partners. The Burgundian images of divine
couples may be especially relevant in this respect, since the male is often depicted with
a cup of wine, which is reminiscent of the goblet of liquor given by the Insular goddess
of sovereignty to her mortal mate, a human being elevated to supernatural rank by his
union with a divinity. The goddess of the divine partners represented in the European
iconography may be a similar universal deity of territory, who marries a number of
local gods for the well-being of the land and its people.

In the context of sovereignty, polyandry may have a special place. We find this
tradition in Irish sovereignty-myths, and it occurs also in the pagan European
material. Thus Damona and Ancamna are shared by several deities. What we do not
know is whether different names always represented different gods or whether a
certain divine entity could possess more than one name, depending on locality or
function. Indeed, it is not always clear from the iconography whether the gods or
goddesses with different sets of attributes represent one pair of deities or several.
Polygamy may occur with both male and female divinities, but the apparent polyandry sometimes displayed among divine couples may reflect a tradition which had
elements in common with later Insular myth. There may, indeed, be further connections between Irish tradition and the European iconography: sometimes, as we have
seen, the goddess's male companion is of mature years, sometimes young and beard-
less, as if perhaps she, like the young girls of the Insular stories, is coupled with both
youth and age, spring and winter. The divine couples of pagan Celtic iconography are
separated by a wide spatial and chronological gap from those of Irish mythic tradition,
and so any apparent links between them must be treated with caution. But to me it
seems at least possible that we are dealing with a common tradition and that some of
the concepts behind the early continental pairs of divinities may have contributed to
perceptions which appear in later vernacular myth.

Stone sculpture depicting a mother-goddess accompanied by a hooded male figure (a *genius cucullatus*) carrying an egg; Romano-British period. From Cirencester, Gloucestershire. The egg is a symbol of fertility and regeneration.

7 Priestess, Prophetess and Witch

This chapter explores the involvement of human females in religion and ritual, whether as official religious functionaries (priestesses) or in other roles, including those of witches or sorceresses and enchantresses. In this sphere, the distinction between the human and the supernatural is not always clearly defined: an enchantress may belong to this world or the Otherworld. The female prophet or divinator is important in this respect: she often combined the role of priestess with that of seer, and it is clear that she, like her male counterpart, acted as a mediator between the spirit-world and that of earthly beings. In a sense, she was both human and divine, yet set apart from both. The realm of sorceresses or witches was that of magic and superstition, areas not necessarily closely linked with actual divinities or with religion in the strict sense. Sorceresses were involved with a murky sub-system of belief based largely upon fear and maleficence, the dark side of the spirit world, where the practitioner herself was as dreadful as the powers she controlled. The main argument for the existence of such women in Celtic Europe is speculative, based upon extremely rare inscriptions, upon the treatment of some female bodies after death and upon some tentative evidence for female human sacrifice, especially in northern Europe.

The evidence for Celtic priestesses derives mainly from ancient literature, especially that of the Classical world. Early Celtic vernacular literature speaks of prophetesses and other females involved in ritual practices. But archaeological findings bear sparse witness to the existence of female priests. The problem is that, whilst there is evidence in the form of liturgical regalia and in the suggested provision of priests' houses attached to religious sites, yet no sexual distinctions are possible: a headdress or sceptre may equally be the property of priest or priestess.

Priestesses

Female Druids

Caesar's long description of druids in Gaul[1] and the other main Classical references to druidism speak of the priesthood as if it were exclusively male. However, there is some early literary reference to females who were closely associated with druidism and, in the Roman texts and Irish sources, there are definite references to druidesses. Tacitus[2] describes in graphic detail the reception committee which met the soldiers of the Roman governor Suetonius Paulinus when he attacked the druidic stronghold of the

Island of Mona (Anglesey). His testimony is relevant to us because of his allusion to women who, if not themselves druids, certainly had a close relationship with them.[3]

On the shore stood the opposing [British] army with its dense array of armed warriors, while between the ranks dashed women in black attire like the Furies, with hair dishevelled, waving brands. All round the druids ... scared our soldiers ...

These ladies howled curses, brandished torches and caused psychological havoc by their wild appearance. They were also associated with human sacrifices, the remains of which Tacitus records as decorating the Britons' altars in a grisly display of blood and entrails. Who were these women? Were they druids, prophetesses or simply ordinary people caught up in the frenzied excitement of the day? Their description reminds us of the Irish war-furies haunting the battlefields in the *Táin* (see Chapter 2).

Lindsay Allason-Jones[4] has made a suggestion concerning the possible association between women and druidism in early Roman Britain. Aulus Plautius, the first governor in the Claudian conquest-campaign, brought his wife Pomponia Graecina with him to Britain. She was later apparently accused of practising a 'foreign' religion. 'The distinguished Pomponia Graecina, wife of Aulus Plautius ... was charged with foreign superstition ...'[5] It is just possible that the cult concerned was druidism, to which Graecina might have been exposed during her sojourn in Britain with Plautius.

The *Scriptores Historiae Augustae* (the Augustan Histories) are late Roman documents written by a number of authors in the fourth century AD. They are not generally considered particularly reliable as historical sources,[6] but they contain illuminating comments concerning druidesses. The Histories consist of lives of various Roman emperors and in three – those of Severus Alexander, Aurelian and Numerian – there are references to encounters between emperors and female druids who, in each case, were also seers, predicting the future of each ruler.

One author, Flavius Vopiscus of Syracuse, makes two references to the prophetic powers of Celtic druidesses. In one,[7] he chronicles an episode concerning the late third-century emperor Diocletian, which was apparently related to Vopiscus by his grandfather. When Diocletian was serving in the Roman army as an ordinary soldier among the Tungrians (of Belgium), he happened to encounter a druidess when settling his bill at a tavern. She castigated him for his greed and parsimony and he retorted flippantly that he would be more generous when he was emperor. The druidess chided him for his levity and informed him that once he had slain 'the Boar', he would gain the purple. The reference to the boar was a play on words: *aper* means boar but was also the name of the prefect of the Praetorian Guard.

Vopiscus' second reference to druidesses occurs in his Life of Aurelian.[8]

On a certain occasion, Aurelian consulted the druid priestesses in Gaul and inquired of them whether the imperial power would remain with his descendants, but they replied ... that none would have a name more illustrious in the Commonwealth than the descendants of Claudius ...

139

The emperor Severus Alexander had a less favourable encounter with a druidess, who prophesied his betrayal and downfall when he was in Gaul:

Furthermore, as he went to war, a Druid prophetess cried out in the Gallic tongue 'Go, but do not hope for victory, and put no trust in your soldiers.'

This prophecy was apparently one of many portents and omens foretelling the death of Severus Alexander, and it was correct, for he was murdered by some of his own troops. The episode was recorded by another contributor to the Histories, one Aelius Lampridius.[9]

All these references make strong links between druidesses and prophecy: these women were both priestesses and seers. The alleged encounters between native Gaulish religious functionaries and Roman emperors may be entirely fictional, the idea perhaps being to use a kind of stock character, representative of an alien and outlandish cult, to enhance the image of the emperor as one whose power was gained not only from Roman divine will but also from a wider spiritual theatre. However the details of these episodes may be interpreted, what comes across clearly is the existence of female Celtic religious functionaries with proven oracular powers, who were sufficiently important to offer advice to the ruler of the Roman world. Whether or not the encounters recorded actually took place, the two fourth-century chroniclers regarded the presence of druidesses as not beyond the bounds of reality.

References to female druids are not confined to late Roman texts: they occur also in the early Irish mythic literature and, here again, are particularly concerned with prophecy. The Fionn Cycle contains reference to the rearing of the quasi-divine hero Finn by a druidess and a 'wise woman' (presumably a seer). Finn's mother Muirna was the wife of Cumhaill (otherwise known as Cool), the leader of the Fianna, a renowned war-band who guarded the king and his lands. Cumhaill was betrayed by Goll mac Morna, who wrested the leadership of the Fianna from him by trickery. Muirna was afraid for the infant Finn's safety, so she entrusted him to her two bondswomen so that he might be reared by them in secrecy. The two foster-mothers, the druidess and the seer, trained Finn in hunting, fishing and war-craft and, even when he was a youth of fourteen, continued to protect him, warning him of his danger when threatened by his father's usurper Goll.[10] The story of Finn is significant: here the functions of druidess and seer were split between the two women, although they were closely linked and both of them trained, guarded and warned him. Moreover, we have an association here between prophetesses and warrior-training, a connection also discernible in the Ulster Cycle, where the female teacher and prophet Scáthach trained Cú Chulainn in war-craft (see Chapter 2). Finally, Finn's foster-mothers have an ambiguous status in that, although they possessed supernatural power, they were in a subservient position in Muirna's household, little better than slaves. Were they deliberately hiding their true identity perhaps even from Muirna herself or was the family of Finn of such high and, by implication, divine status that the subordinate rank of the women was appropriate?

Other Priestesses

There is evidence for female priests in both ancient literature and archaeology. Classical commentators refer to Celtic religious functionaries, a tradition which was also present in the Classical world: in Greek culture, religion was virtually the only public role open to women.

Both Pomponius Mela and Strabo allude to the presence of Gaulish priestesses living on islands: this may or may not be significant, but in early vernacular mythic

Bronze figurine of a young woman playing a *tibia* (flute); Romano-British period. From Silchester, Hampshire. The statuette may represent a participant in a religious ceremony, associated with music and dancing.

tradition, islands were perceived as liminal places, belonging both to the human and the supernatural worlds, and islands were sometimes sites for the Happy Otherworld. In the seventh-century AD Voyage of Bran, humans were enticed to a group of islands, the 'Land of Women', the Otherworld.[11]

Pomponius Mela[12] describes a group of islands called the Cassiterides, which were situated in the 'British Sea' facing Finistère: he was probably referring to the Isles of Scilly. Mela comments that one of the islands, Sena, possessed a Gallic oracle attended by nine priestesses whose sacred nature was symbolised by their eternal virginity. They were powerful women who could control the elements, cure all diseases, shape-shift and predict the future. The reference to virginity has its parallel in the Vestal Virgins of Rome, who tended the goddess Vesta's holy, ever-glowing fire. In the early Welsh mythological story called *Preiddeu Annwn* ('The Spoils of Annwn'), which survives in a thirteenth-century manuscript, the British hero Arthur sought to steal a magical cauldron of regeneration belonging to the king of the Otherworld. The cauldron was capricious and powerful: it would not cook food for a coward, and it would only boil if heated by the breath of nine virgins.[13] The repetition of the number nine in both the Welsh myth and in Mela's account may be significant, in that three and multiples of three are known to have been sacred and magical in Celtic tradition.[14] The association of priestesses and virginity may lie partly in the importance of purity for the service of the spirit world, but also perhaps because virginity symbolised the undissipated sexual energy of the female, which was thus very potent. (We have encountered this idea already in Chapter 3, the story of Math).

The Greek geographer Strabo, who lived between about 40 BC and AD 25, has left us a fascinating account of the priestesses living on an island off the west coast of France, which is worth quoting in full:

He [Posidonius] also says that there is a small island in the ocean, not far from the land, lying off the mouth of the Loire; and the women of the Samnitae inhabit it; they are possessed by Dionysus and propitiate the god with initiations and other sacred rites; and no man may land on the island, but the women themselves sail out from it and have intercourse with men and then return. It is their custom once a year to remove the roof from their temple and to roof it again the same day before sunset, each woman carrying part of the burden; but the woman whose load falls from her is torn to pieces by the others, and they carry the pieces around the temple crying out 'euoi', and do not cease until their madness passes away; and it always happens that someone pushes against the woman who is destined to suffer this fate.[15]

There are several points of interest in this passage, which may be an account based upon the observation of a genuine rite or some mythic story. These women were not virgin, but they belonged to an all-female community who shunned the company of men except for occasional sexual unions, for which the women sought out the men rather than the reverse. The cult involved was not, of course, that of the Greek Dionysus but of a Gaulish equivalent whom Posidonius identified with a god familiar to him. The Maenad-like rites of the women, who were clearly possessed by the god and were in an ecstatic trance when they performed their symbolic roof-renewal and sacrifice, are described by someone who was perhaps familiar with *The Bacchae*, a play written by the fifth-century BC Greek dramatist Euripides. In this play a group of women, enthralled by Dionysus, took to the mountains, where they ran amok, tearing wild beasts apart with their bare hands and, as the culmination of the tragedy, dismembered their king Pentheus, whose mother led the maddened women. The play emphasises the contrast and conflict between *nomos* (man-made law and order) and *physis* (wild, untamed nature, epitomised by the female). The third point of interest in Strabo's account concerns the annual temple-ceremony: there are few unequivocal literary references to roofed pre-Roman Celtic sanctuaries, but the Loire shrine is a definite example. The annual unroofing and re-roofing rite is a curious custom, which may have some kind of seasonal symbolism. It was apparently of ritual importance that the activity was completed within a single day, as if the temple must not be left open to the sky during the hours of darkness. Fourthly, Strabo's account is significant in its description of human sacrifice, unique in that it involved one of the functionaries themselves. The sacrifice must therefore have been considered an especially valuable gift to the god. The Graeco-Roman distaste for human sacrifice may be showing itself in the linking of this savage rite with an abnormal group of religious women. Strabo makes reference elsewhere[16] to human sacrifice carried out by priestesses who were also prophetesses (see below). These were women of the Teutonic Cimbri, who officiated in the sacrifice of prisoners of war. The Cimbri were not themselves Celtic but appear to have had some customs in common with the Celts (including ritual head-hunting, divinatory human sacrifice and the use of sacred cauldrons). These Cimbri are known to have invaded southern Gaul in the late second-century BC, and thus perhaps adopted some of the cult-practices they encountered there.

There are few unequivocal references to priestesses attached to specific temples in the early Celtic literature. Loch Erne in Ireland was named after Erne, chief priestess of Queen Medb at her royal court of Cruachain: Erne and her assistants were drowned in the lake after being frightened by a monster, Olcai.[17] A legend of Saint Brigit of Kildare contains a reference to the foundation by her of a Christian monastery jointly for men and women, on the site of a pagan temple. The pre-Christian sanctuary was apparently tended by women who kept vigil over a sacred fire which, like that of the goddess Sulis, mentioned by Solinus (see Chapter 5), was never allowed to go out.[18] The rite described bears a marked resemblance to that of the Roman Vestals, whose task it was to tend the sacred hearth.

The archaeological evidence for priestesses consists primarily of iconography and epigraphy and is occasionally represented by some female burials. Iconography occasionally displays images of women who were probably either priestesses or at least involved in formal ritual activity. These carvings all date from the Romano-Celtic period so, unless a Celtic cult is clearly indicated, it is impossible to tell whether such women belonged to the Roman or Celtic religious tradition. The bronze figurine of a priestess at South Shields (Tyne and Wear) looks very Classical in style: she is robed, with her mantle draped over her head ready for sacrifice, and holds a *patera* in one hand and a round object, perhaps a cake or an apple, in the other.[19] By contrast, the naked bronze female dancer from the mid first-century BC religious hoard at Neuvy-en-Sullias (Loiret) may represent a local cult-celebrant, perhaps an official of the shrine at Fleury nearby.[20] The fine wooden first-century AD image of a lady, with draped head and a great buffer-torc round her neck, from Chamalières (Puy-de-Dôme), could be a representation of a visitor to the great healing spring-sanctuary but she could equally have been a cult-official, her torc signifying her high rank.[21]

Bronze statuette of a priestess, holding a *patera* (offering-plate). From South Shields, Tyne & Wear. The veil over her head signifies the woman's participation in a sacrificial ceremony.

Some Gaulish iconography depicts women – probably official priestesses – at altars which may have been associated with native cults. A lady holding a *patera* on a stone carving at Metz stands by an altar; and another, from Bourges, throws incense onto a flaming altar.[22] These two are significant because the women are depicted alone, unaccompanied by male participants; most sacrificial scenes portraying women show them as the companions of men, who take the primary role.[23] The Celto-Germanic mother-goddess cult of the Rhineland, naturally enough, had some female cult-officiants, and images of these women exist. Organised worship is implied on a relief at Bonn, where a procession of women is depicted;[24] on a second Bonn sculpture the local Mothers, the *Aufaniae*, are shown seated, flanked by two groups of female officials or devotees who, like the Mothers themselves, carry baskets of fruit to offer to the goddesses.[25] A third altar from Bonn, dedicated to the *Matronae Aufaniae* by the Quaestor (Finance Officer) of Cologne, shows the three mother-goddesses seated in a row and, behind them, the busts of three women, apparently sitting in an upper gallery, as if perhaps they are novitiates of the cult.[26] A female devotee or priestess of the mother-goddess cult is depicted on a stone at Cologne carrying a napkin, as though she were a participant in some kind of ritual, perhaps a sacrifice.[27] In all of these instances, it is impossible to be sure whether the women in attendance at the cult-ceremonies were actually priestesses or simply devotees. But where they appear to be involved in such formalised ritual as sacrifice, then it is likely that they were genuine professional 'clergy' attached to particular temples.

There is epigraphic evidence for Gaulish and British priestesses, but they were not all associated with Celtic religion. The British priestess Diodora was an officiant of the Oriental cult of Herakles of Tyre.[28] Forty-three Gaulish female priests of the Roman Imperial Cult are recorded. That these were priests in their own right, not the wives of male officiants, is clear from their tombstones: one municipal *flamen* from Nîmes was Licinia Flavilla, to whom a tombstone was erected in the late first century AD. Her husband's name is also recorded on the stone, but her name comes first.[29] These *flamines* were ethnic Gauls but they served a Roman cult the nature of which was quasi-religious and quasi-political. Other examples of Roman deities served by Gaulish women include Mercury at Berthouville in Normandy, where three women are recorded as having offered gifts to the god: Julia Sibylla dedicated a *patera* to him, Germanissa two *paterae* and Camulognata a vase.[30] The latter two ladies have Celtic names and their gifts were presumably in fulfilment of a vow. A native Celtic goddess called Solimava was given a temple by Firmana, daughter of Obricius, a Gaulish woman from Bourges.[31] She was presumably a wealthy patroness who had reason to be grateful to her special goddess. An inscription found near Vindolanda in North Britain reads 'to the goddess Sattada the assembly of the Textoverdi willingly and deservedly fulfilled the vow'.[32] We can only speculate as to whether this local goddess was perhaps attended by female priests.

The interpretation of burials as being those of priests or priestesses is necessarily extremely tentative. Human remains of females in pagan Celtic Europe are occasionally interpreted as having some kind of sacral association, either because of the location of the grave or because of features associated with the nature of the deposition itself. The presence of a single human burial at a religious site could argue for its possible identification as that of a cult-official associated with that site. The ritual enclosure at Libeniče in Bohemia dates to the fourth century BC: it consists of a long, sub-rectangular enclosure bounded by a ditch, some 90 m × 22.5 m in dimension. At its south-east end was some kind of subterranean shrine, perhaps roofed; this focus of cult-activity contained a stone block (perhaps a sacrificial table or altar) and two post-holes close together, near which were the remains of two burnt timber uprights and two bronze torcs. The implication is that the two posts may have been roughly carved into human form, adorned by the necklets. Deposits of human and animal bones suggest that sacrifices took place on the site. The floor of the sunken inner sanctum had successive pits dug into it over a period of about twenty-four years, probably representing repeated, perhaps seasonal, religious ceremonies. Within the enclosure a woman was interred; she may have been a sacrificial victim or a priestess who had presided over the sacred place.[33]

Lowbury Hill, Oxfordshire, has long been recognised as a Romano-Celtic temple-site: rubble from the shrine structure indicates that it had walls of flint and mortar, a tile floor and a slate and tile roof. Votive objects include a clay figurine of a cockerel, brooches, eight functional spears, deliberately blunted spear-heads, a model sickle and coins ranging from the first to the fifth century AD. Recent excavations on the site have revealed a large outer stone-bound *temenos* (sacred enclosure) and an inner one defined by a palisade. Deliberately deposited in the precinct was the body of a woman aged between thirty and forty years. Before her burial, she had been subjected to a mutilation-ritual involving the removal of her facial bones.[34] This defacement bears resemblances to certain rites associated with the interment of elderly women in late Roman Britain, and also with the disfigurement of some of the female Iron Age bog-bodies of northern Europe (see below).

It is possible that the two late Iron Age ritual carts buried in a Danish peat-bog at Dejbjerg were associated with the funeral-rites of a priestess. The two vehicles, which were constructed as ceremonial, non-functional wagons in the first century BC, are thought by some scholars to be of Central European origin[35] and by others to have been made locally in Denmark but decorated using Celtic art-styles.[36] Each cart had a throne-like structure in the centre and both were dismantled and placed in a single mound with a cremation-burial, thought to be that of a female.[37] The ritual surrounding her interment suggests that she may have possessed some kind of cult-status.

The burial of high-ranking women with rich grave-goods in the late Hallstatt Iron Age (sixth century BC) is usually interpreted as representing the interment of the female members of an aristocratic élite.[38] But the wealth represented by these tombs could be a mark not just of secular rank but also perhaps religious status. The two are not mutually incompatible; cult-functionaries were traditionally held in high esteem in the highly stratified society of Caesar's Gaul.[39] André Pelletier[40] is of the view that the tomb of the 'princess' at Vix in Burgundy, who died at the end of the sixth century BC, could have belonged to a high priestess who perhaps combined that role with that of a high-ranking woman in a dynastic chieftain's family. The lady interred beneath the great cairn at Vix must have lived in the aristocratic stronghold on Mont Lassois nearby. She was in her mid thirties when she died and she went to her grave amid great ceremony, borne on a four-wheeled hearse to a wooden mortuary chamber later to be surmounted by a mound 42 m in diameter and 6 m high. When the cart bearing her body reached the tomb, it was dismantled, the wheels leant against the chamber-wall and the woman placed on the body of the cart. She was accompanied by sumptuous grave-goods, including exotic imports from the Mediterranean world. She wore brooches and a solid gold torc weighing 480 g, which was decorated with winged horses and was probably made by a Greek or Etruscan goldsmith. Placed with her were an Attic black-figure ware dish and Etruscan bronze vessels. The most spectacular tomb-furnishing was a massive bronze *krater* (wine-mixing vessel) 1.64 m high, surmounted by a strainer decorated with a statuette of a woman. It was imported from the Greek world, maybe from Corinth, probably not as a complete vessel but in its component-parts, assembled after its journey to Burgundy. Hilda Davidson has suggested[41] that the Vix *krater* could have been for sacrificial blood, and cites Strabo's allusion[42] to great bronze containers used by Cimbrian priestesses to catch victims' blood. Apart, perhaps, from the fabulously rich sixth-century BC chief's burial at Eberdingen-Hochdorf in southern Germany, the Vix tomb is arguably the most wealthy grave of this period yet discovered in Central Europe. Whilst there can be no positive argument in favour of its owner's religious status, it is not beyond all reason to infer that the lady of Vix may have been special, even in aristocratic circles, and may have enjoyed more than simply secular rank. Similarly, the lady buried with the comparatively rich grave-furniture at Wetwang Slack in Yorkshire in the third century BC could perhaps have been a priestess. It has been suggested[43] that the curious sealed bronze box which accompanied her body could have contained a special substance such as holy water or oil.

Prophetesses

The link between priestesses and prophecy has already been referred to. Both druids and druidesses were closely involved with divination, and their power, at least partly, depended upon their ability to predict the future successfully. It is clear from the comments both of Classical authors and from the early mythic tradition of Ireland that prophecy was an important function of religious officials in the pagan Celtic world. Many of these prophets were women. The nine virgin priestesses of Pomponius Mela's island of Sena[44] were able to foretell the future; the three druidesses alluded to by Vopiscus and Lampridius in the Augustan Histories were notable for their predictions to the emperors Diocletian, Severus Alexander and Aurelian. Ammianus Marcellinus[45] describes an episode concerning the apostate emperor Julian: when he entered the town of Vienne in AD 355, an old blind woman, in the crowd pressing against the city-gates to welcome him, prophesied in a loud voice that Julian would restore the temples of the gods.[46]

Tacitus, Caesar and Strabo all speak of prophetesses among the Germans, some of whose religious customs were closely akin to those of the Celts. Tacitus[47] recounts the Germans' belief that women had a particular sanctity which endowed them with the gift of prophecy. He mentions some of these ladies by name: one was called Valeda, a formidable woman whose power was such that she represented her tribe in political negotiations and was accorded almost as much honour as a goddess.[48] Caesar[49] speaks of a Germanic tradition whereby the senior women of the family used divinatory means to decide upon the efficacy of waging war. This association between prophetesses and warfare recurs in an account given by Strabo[50] already mentioned briefly above. He says this of Cimbrian holy women:

They were grey with age, and wore white tunics and over these, cloaks of the finest linen and bronze girdles. They were bare-foot. These women would enter the camp, sword in hand, and go up to the prisoners, crown them, and lead them up to a bronze vessel which might hold some twenty measures. One of them would mount a step and, leaning over the cauldron, cut the throat of a prisoner, who was held up over the vessel's rim. Others cut open the body and, after inspecting the entrails, would foretell victory for their countrymen.

This passage is worthy of comment since, once again, we have a link between priestesses and human sacrifice, a phenomenon we met earlier when discussing Strabo's Maenad-ridden island off the mouth of the Loire. The Cimbrian women, like the Gaulish druids referred to by Caesar[51] and others, are particularly concerned with prophecy, and here it is the outcome of battle which is the main issue. Strabo's account makes it clear that the sacrifice of war-prisoners will ensure victory, the consultation of the victims' intestines being a mere formality!

The role of the prophetesses in early Irish myth shows a striking resemblance to that of the Gaulish and German holy women of Caesar, Strabo and the other Graeco-Roman chroniclers in that they, too, are closely associated with warfare. One of the most important females in the Ulster Cycle is Scáthach, the daughter of Ardgamm, who appears in the *Táin*. She was first and foremost a trainer of young heroes in war-craft, running an academy of battle-skills in Ulster. Her most famous pupil was Cú Chulainn, to whom she gave his most fearsome weapon, the Gae Bulga, a barbed spear that always killed. Scáthach's name, 'Shadowy One', implies her supernatural status, and she taught Cú Chulainn in Alba, the part of north-west Britain facing Ireland, but probably in this context perceived as the Otherworld. Scáthach was a prophet: she was able to foretell Cú Chulainn's fate in his conflict with Queen Medb of Connacht.[52] The link between female prophecy and war recurs in the Fionn Cycle (see p. 140), where the young hero Finn was fostered by holy women, who taught him war-craft and warned him of future dangers.[53]

One of the most influential seers associated with the Irish royal court in early myth was Fedelma, a poetess and prophet belonging to the entourage of Queen Medb. At the time that Medb planned her campaign against Ulster, in the *Táin*, Fedelma warned the queen of Cú Chulainn's prowess as a warrior and she predicted that he would devastate Ireland, killing most of Medb's forces in the process.[54] This is a description of the first meeting between Medb and Fedelma:

They [Medb and her charioteer] saw a young grown girl in front of them. She had yellow hair. She wore a speckled cloak fastened with a gold pin, a red-embroidered hooded tunic and sandals with gold clasps ... Her teeth were like an array of jewels between the lips. She had hair in three tresses ... She held a light gold weaving-rod in her hand, with gold inlay. Her eyes had triple irises. Two black horses drew her chariot, and she was armed.[55]

Once again we see a direct link between prophecy and battle. Fedelma is described as a beautiful young girl but she bore weapons, like a warrior. She also clearly belonged to the supernatural world: the triplistic imagery of the hair and eyes is a strong indication of her divine status, and her speckled cloak, too, implies her Otherworld origins. Supernatural animals in both Welsh and Irish myth were speckled, and the Cwn Annwn, the hell-hounds of the Welsh Otherworld, were speckled greyish-red. More-over, Fedelma announced that she had been learning poetry and prophecy in Alba, Scáthach's Otherworld realm. This is the conversation which took place between Medb and the prophetess at their initial encounter; the queen asked her first who she was:

'I am Fedelm, and I am a woman poet of Connacht'
'Where have you come from?' Medb said.
'From learning verse and vision in Alba,' the girl said.
'Have you the *imbas forosnai*, the Light of Foresight?' Medb said.
'Yes I have.' the girl said.

Medb then asked her to foretell how her army would fare:

'Fedelma, prophetess; how seest thou the host?'
'I see it crimson, I see it red.'

149

Fedelma repeated this refrain several times, in spite of Medb's refusal to accept the prophecy. She then chanted a long prophetic poem which began thus:

'I see a battle: a blond man
with much blood about his belt
and a hero-halo round his head
His brow is full of victories...'[56]

Medb was clearly haunted by Fedelma's warnings, which she recalled over and over again when things were going badly. When Medb's druids counselled her against joining battle with the Ulster forces because the omens were not favourable, she was troubled and was reminded of Fedelma's prophecy. Again, when Fergus, the defecting Ulster champion, warned Medb of Cú Chulainn's power, she thought of Fedelma:

As Fergus spoke, Maeve [Medb] bethought herself of the prophecy of Fedelma, the woman from the Fairy, about the youthful Cuchullin'.[57]

Enchantresses and Witches

Witchcraft, or sorcery, is concerned with the dark side of religion and ritual practice. We are here dealing with magic, superstition, the occult, which are not necessarily associated with the world of goddesses and gods.[58] Cursing, spell-casting and entice-ment all relate to the control and snaring of humans, often by other humans who may claim – or possess – Otherworld powers but who are certainly not themselves of divine origin. These wielders of magic are very often women. Another category of females met in myth is the enchantress, the spirit-woman who lures humans, mainly men, across the boundary of the earthly world to her Otherworld place. Like witchcraft, the action of the enchantress usually brings misfortune to humans. Sometimes the identity of the sorceress or enchantress is ambiguous, and we are not quite sure to which world she belongs.

Several enchantresses are recorded in the mythic tradition of early Ireland. Pre-served in manuscripts of the thirteenth and fourteenth centuries but referred to in texts dating back to the tenth century is a legend, possibly even earlier in origin, about Muirchertach, a king of Ireland.[59] The story is that, while out hunting, Muirchertach had an encounter with an enchantress in the guise of a lovely young girl called Sin (a highly appropriate name, as we shall see). She agreed to accompany him to his court at Cletech, but only if he would promise to do anything she asked and would never let a Christian priest enter his house. Sin arrived at the king's palace and immediately banished Muirchertach's wife and the royal children from the court. The ousted queen appealed for help to Bishop Cairnech, who threatened the king with dire punishment, but in vain. The bishop cursed him but – revealingly – he used not a Christian formula but one belonging to a pagan druidic ritual. Now Sin revealed her true character: she

150

was a sorceress, and she cast a spell upon the king so that (like Macha's curse on the Ulstermen) he suffered great weakness and troubling visions. One night, he woke from one of these dreams to find the house on fire. Still under Sin's curse, he tried to quench the blaze with a vat of wine but fell into it and drowned. Sin's action revealed itself as motivated by revenge: it seems that her father had met his death at the hands of Muirchertach. But the character of Sin is ambiguous: she loved both her father and her lover, and she died of grief at the latter's death, torn between the bonds of love and vengeance. Both she and Muirchertach were victims of destiny, and it may be that the bishop's curse was in the end stronger than Sin's spells. In a sense, Sin is an archetype identifiable in other myths: she, like Macha and the Delilah of the Old Testament, could use her femininity to deprive a man of his virile strength. Jean Markale[60] suggests that Sin is perhaps a mythic character similar to the Welsh Blodeuwedd, rebelling against male domination. But I see a closer resemblance between Sin and Olwen who, again, was caught in a triangular and conflicting relationship between her father and her suitor Culhwch. Perhaps of greater interest than Sin herself is the juxtaposition of paganism and Christianity in the Irish story. Sin was a pagan sorceress, who pitted her magic against a Christian cleric. The priest, however, did not use God to help him but the old religion of his pagan antecedents, the druids, as if good 'magic' was the best weapon against bad.

The bewitching of mortal men and their enticement by Otherworld women may be amply demonstrated in many other Insular myths. The Ulster hero Cú Chulainn was lured to the spirit-world by Fand, a woman from a *sidh* (Otherworld dwelling-place). Finn's son Oisin was likewise enticed by Niav (Niamh), daughter of an Otherworld king. In the seventh-century tale the Voyage of Bran, a lady of the Otherworld appeared to Bran in a dream, luring him and his followers with music to her realm in the Island of Women (see Chapter 4). The enticement was perilous to mortals in that, once in the Otherworld, they were trapped there because, if they tried to return home, they would find that hundreds of years had passed on earth, and they would succumb to old age.

Irish and Welsh myths occasionally refer specifically to witches. Queen Medb turned the six posthumous children of Cailitín into witches and warlocks, destroying one arm, one leg and one eye of each. She arranged their training in magic, and then sent them all over the world to learn further sorcery. They acquired spears from Vulcan, each destined to slay a king, and they were the instrument of Cú Chulainn's death.[61]

The early Welsh myth of Peredur contains allusions to witches, who were predominantly evil but who were both teachers of war-craft and prophets, like Scáthach and other Celtic seers. Peredur was a young hero who, in the course of his travels, was warned by a lady to be on his guard against the Nine Witches of Caer Loyw (Gloucester), who had laid waste all the land around except the lady's castle. At dawn on the day after the warning, Peredur encountered one of the witches attacking the watchkeeper, and he struck her hard on the head. The witch knew him and hailed him by name, proclaiming that it was her destiny to be injured by Peredur, and announcing that he should learn war-craft from her. He forced her to swear not to harm the lady's lands further, and he dwelt for three weeks with the witches, learning battle-skills. Later, Peredur met the nine women again and learned that they had harmed his family, killing his cousin and maiming his uncle. Peredur, Arthur, Gwalchmai and a war-band of heroes fought the witches, who predicted correctly that they would perish at Peredur's hands.[62]

There are many resemblances between this episode and those of Insular myth which concern female prophets. Their destiny was linked with heroes, whom they instructed but to whom they were subservient. The number nine recurs: we have already noted the nine priestesses of Mela's Cassiterides and the nine virgin cauldron-keepers of *Preiddeu Annwn*. But the Welsh witches were different from the Insular ones in that they were inherently harmful. They combined the functions of the Irish female seers and the enchantresses, with an additional streak of malice. This may be the result of medieval Welsh Christian influence, which may have altered the myths and may

Lead curse tablet from London. The victim was a woman: 'I curse Tretia Maria and her life and mind and memory and liver and lungs mixed up together, and her words, thoughts and memory, thus may she be unable to speak what things are concealed'.

152

have portrayed some of the supernatural females in the stories in a deliberately negative manner.

Is there any evidence for the existence of witches or sorceresses in the archaeological record of pagan Celtic Europe? An early Gaulish inscription from Larzac in southern France provides fascinating information concerning the existence of female magicians. Inscribed on a lead sheet, it describes two rival groups of *mnas brictas* ('women endowed with magic'). One group had apparently practised harmful magic on another, and the latter used wise women to counter the adverse effect of this charm.[63] The other suggestion of such a presence lies in the mute testimony of some female human remains, which had either been subjected to abnormal treatment after death or which show some signs that they may have been sacrificial victims. If a woman was suspected of being a sorceress, it is quite likely that efforts would have been made to prevent her spirit from lingering in or near the body after her death. There may have been a fear that she might continue to influence the affairs of living humans, and still be able to curse or cast spells. Certainly the Romans were fearful of ghosts and had ceremonies and rituals designed to neutralise their earthly power: the specific function of the festival of the *Lemuria* was to drive away spirits.[64]

Decapitation

In late Roman Britain, certain people were subjected to decapitation which probably – in most instances – took place after death rather than causing it, although punitive execution cannot be entirely ruled out. Whilst both sexes (including infants) were thus treated on occasions,[65] there is a definite bias towards the occurrence of decapitation among middle-aged or elderly women. There is too much evidence to examine every instance here but a few are of special interest. The late Romano-British cemetery at Lankhills, Winchester, produced seven burials of elderly women who were beheaded and the heads placed by their legs. All were associated with either elaborate or abnormal graves of other individuals, and one woman was buried with two dogs, one of which had been dismembered and the ends of the bent-over backbone tied together. The decapitation-process was performed according to a precise ritual, always from the front, using a knife to sever the vertebrae in exactly the same place.[66] In order for such precision to be possible, the victim must either have been already dead, drugged or restrained: the bodies show no evidence of having been bound. Burials of females at Curbridge and Stanton Harcourt (Oxfordshire), Kenchester (Hereford and Worcester) and Orton Longueville (Cambridgeshire) followed very similar ritual patterns: the heads of all the women were placed either between the legs or at the feet.[67]

A rite specific to Dorset involved the burial of old ladies accompanied by spindle-whorls. They were decapitated, their lower jaws removed and the skulls placed by the feet. It is not clear whether the ligaments of the mandible were cut immediately after death or whether the head was exposed until disarticulation occurred naturally. At Kimmeridge two females were interred together in the late third century AD: one was placed in a stone cist, her head placed near to her foot, the lower mandible removed, and a spindle-whorl placed with her; on top of the cist was the body of a second woman, the jaw from the first burial placed by her knees and with another spindle-whorl.[68] The decapitation of these women may have served two functions: the head may have been removed and placed by her feet in order to point the woman's way to the Underworld, so easing the passage from one world to the next. The removal of the lower jaw would seem to point to a desire to stop the woman from speaking, even when dead. At both Kimmeridge and at the site of a similar burial, at Guilden Morden (Cambridgeshire), skeletal evidence shows that the beheaded women had suffered badly from arthritis, a condition which may have made them ill-tempered and snappish: Lethbridge[69] and Merrifield suggest that this may have caused people to perceive them as witches. Even if these crones were merely nags or scolds, this may have been sufficient to taint them with the stigma of abnormality or even possession; if their medical condition deformed them in any way, this could likewise have been interpreted as the mark of evil.

Sometimes only the skull of a woman was interred, but in curious circumstances. Two such heads are recorded as coming from wells. One came from Headington (Oxfordshire), deposited with half a sheep and associated with a late third-century AD potter's workshop.[70] The second, from Odell (Buckinghamshire) had been deliberately placed behind the wicker lining of a well, and must therefore have been put there at the time it was constructed.[71] Such behaviour may have resulted from a belief not that the women were witches but that the power of their skulls would be positively beneficial to the well-water, perhaps even endowing it with healing properties. The link between heads and wells is documented in both the pagan and early Christian Celtic worlds[72] (see Chapter 9).

When examining the phenomenon of female decapitation, it is necessary to place it within the context of the ritual as a whole. Not only middle-aged or elderly women were so treated: the beheading of infants cannot be explained in terms of either witchcraft or a punitive killing and, in any case, the decapitated burials are too numerous at some cemeteries for them to have all been witches or criminals; at Dunstable, one in ten bodies were so treated.[73] Philpott[74] believes that the beheading of bodies prior to burial must bear a ritual significance, and he suggests links between this phenomenon and the display of severed human heads during the Iron Age. His view is that severing the heads of the dead may reflect a rite of passage, a liminal ceremony which may have been a substitute for human sacrifice and he argues that such a rite may have taken place in cases where it was felt that the individual required assistance moving between worlds. He makes the further suggestion that decapitation concentrated all the individual's power in the head, making it a potent force for

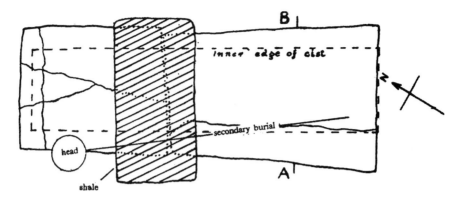

Fig. 1 Plan of cover stones with secondary burial above.

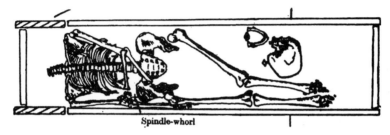

Fig. 2 The primary burial.

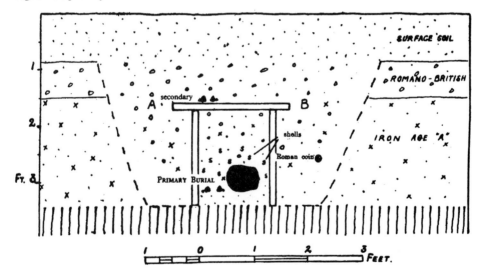

Fig. 3 Section through cist and grave pit.

The body of an elderly decapitated female was buried with a spindle-whorl in a stone cist at Kimmeridge, Dorset, at the end of the third century AD. The head, minus the lower jaw, was placed by her feet. Above the cist was a second female.

155

healing. There is a considerable body of evidence for the Celts' belief in the power of the human head.[75] This could account both for the association of severed heads with water and for the fact that some decapitated burials accompanied other bodies which show evidence of injury or violent death. Female deities played a prominent part in the cults of healing and the predominance of female severed heads in graves may reflect a similar belief in the curative power of the female.

Whatever the precise beliefs behind decapitation-ritual, the application of the rite especially to the bodies of, usually older, women must be significant. As we have seen, the removal of the lower jaw may be linked with the notion that speechlessness symbolised death and transition between worlds. Thus the Welsh mythic Tale of Branwen alludes to dead warriors resurrected in the Cauldron of Rebirth whose Otherworld status is retained and reflected in their inability to speak, although they could fight. Decapitation may have taken place for a number of reasons but, where elderly women were the subjects of such ritual, especially where the jaw has been removed, it is reasonable to suspect that spell-casting or cursing may have prompted a symbolic attempt to prevent speech after death. The decapitation of sorceresses is known in some modern traditional societies, such as the Plains Indians of North America.[76] The face-mutilation of the Lowbury Hill priestess has already been noted. The same thing occurred with the face of a beheaded woman at the Dunstable cemetery. This mutilation is perhaps explicable inasmuch as a witch may have had the evil eye and therefore the potency of her facial expression had to be neutralised. Where the face had not been interfered with, the rite could even have been positive in intent, the mark of a wise woman or a healer whose spells were efficacious and whose head was severed to retain its power. Both groups – witches and wise women – may have required a specific ritual to help them enter the Otherworld.

Female Human Sacrifice

Discussion of female decapitation-rituals leads directly to the question of whether we can identify evidence of human sacrifice among Celtic women and, if so, what the reasons might be. If women were sacrificed, then this may be associated with punishment, the execution of a sorceress or an adulteress. A fertile woman could have been sacrificed to persuade the spirits to make the earth plentiful, or a barren woman because she brought ill-luck to a community. Women could have been chosen as sacrificial victims for any number of reasons: in Greek myth Iphigeneia was sacrificed to Artemis by her father, King Agamemnon, in order to induce a fair wind for the sea-voyage to Troy.[77] Celtic women may specifically have been sacrificed to female divinities. We know from ancient literature that goddesses sometimes demanded human victims: Tacitus refers to the British Andraste[78] and to Nerthus of the Germans.[79] Strabo discusses the human sacrifice of women in his account of the all-female religious island-community off the mouth of the Loire.[80] Caesar comments on an obsolete ritual in Gaul involving 'suttee', whereby the dependants of a dead Gaulish man were buried with him at the end of his funeral.[81] Such a practice may explain the apparent interment of an entire Iron Age family at Hoppstädten in Germany.[82]

There is little unequivocal archaeological evidence for human sacrifice in pre-Roman Europe but, occasionally, women seem to have been the victims of ritual murder. A ceremony took place in the sixth century BC at Bycískála in Bohemia which involved the burial of forty people, mainly women, usually with the heads, hands and feet missing. Two horses were sacrificed, and other offerings included grain, wagons and vessels, including a cauldron containing two skulls, one of which had been made into a drinking-cup.[83] This is an irresistible reminder of the comment made by Livy about the hapless Roman general Postumius, whose head was cut off and made into a drinking-vessel by the Celtic Boii of North Italy in 216 BC.[84] The people at Bycískála may have died as a result of war, epidemic or – perhaps – human sacrifice to the infernal powers perceived to dwell in the dark cave. What may have been a punitive but also ritual killing took place in Iron Age Britain, at Garton Slack in Yorkshire, where the bodies of a youth and a thirty-year-old woman were buried pinned together by a wooden stake driven between them and impaling their arms. The woman had been pregnant: beneath her pelvis was a foetus, expelled from her womb perhaps when she was unconscious. The couple were probably buried alive,[85] perhaps as a punishment for adultery, maybe even incest.

Lindow Man has been well-publicised as a British Iron Age bog-body: found in a Cheshire marsh, the young man had been garotted, struck hard on the head and his throat cut before being pushed, naked, into a bog-pool. The similarity of religious custom between Celts and the Germanic tribes has been mentioned already. Some of the Danish bog-victims were women and the unique preservation of their bodies reveals important evidence of the ritual accompanying their deaths. The lady at Juthe Fen in Jutland was about fifty when she died: like a number of other bog-women, she was buried wearing a woollen skirt, a lambskin cape and a bonnet (clothing very similar to that of the goddess Nehalennia in the Netherlands, and possibly typical local North European female dress). Juthe Fen Woman was plump and grey-haired, and she may have died violently, in that her arms, legs and stomach were pinned tightly to the underlying peat with heavy wooden branches, one of which caused the left knee-joint to swell where it was fixed. Her facial expression was described by her discoverers as one of despair.[86] Like Lindow Man, she was no working peasant: her small, delicate hands and feet suggest high birth. One point of considerable interest is that she was deposited immediately above a powerful natural spring, as though she were a gift to the spirit of the water-source, the living heart of the marsh. An article which appeared soon after her discovery, 'Light Reading for the Danish Public', suggested that Juthe

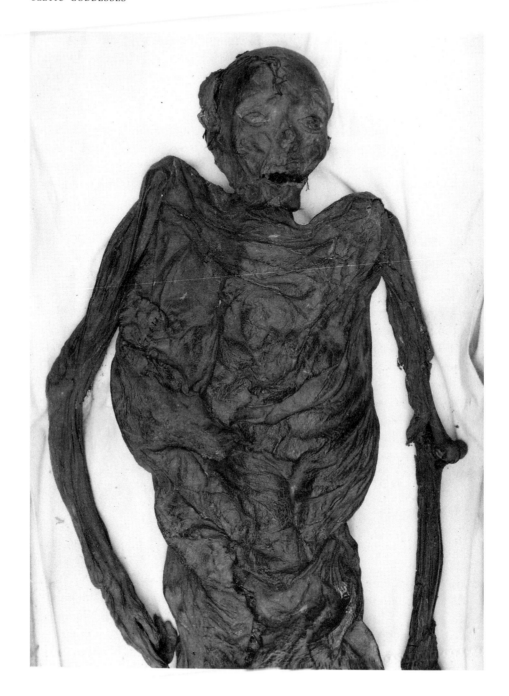

The Iron Age female bog-body at Juthe Fen, Jutland, Denmark. The high-born, middle-aged woman was clothed in skirt, cape and bonnet. She was the victim of a ritual murder, being pinned down in the marsh while still alive.

158

Fen Woman was a witch, weighted down so that she stayed put in her marsh and did not wander among humans. The ritual of pinning women down in a bog recurred at Auning Fen, where the victim again wore a cape and skirt. At Borre Fen, a man and woman had both been strangled and placed naked in the marsh; the female had an infant with her, and part of an Iron Age pot: she was symbolically pinned with three sticks. Another woman, found at Huldre Fen, was pinned by a willow stake, her Iron Age date confirmed by the comb which accompanied her. The bodies at Auning and Huldre showed evidence of maltreatment before death, perhaps the result of torture: limbs had been broken and heads battered. A young girl at Windeby in Schleswig Holstein was consigned to the bog in the first century AD: she was stripped naked, the left side of her head shaved, and blindfolded before being led out, with a collar round her neck, and drowned. The nakedness and, particularly, the shaven head of the Windeby girl call to mind a comment of Tacitus on a Germanic custom: 'Adultery . . . is rare . . . punishment is summary and left to the husband. He shaves off his wife's hair, strips her in the presence of kinsmen, thrusts her from his house and flogs her through the whole village.'[87] Tacitus also remarks that severe punishment, including execution, was not merely punitive but in obedience to the gods.[88] Most striking of all is Tacitus' comment which relates directly to bog-murder: 'The punishment varies to suit the crime. The traitor and deserter are hanged on trees, the coward, the shirker and the unnaturally vicious are drowned in miry swamps under a cover of wattled hurdles.'[89] Could it be that 'unnaturally vicious' could cover the ritually-murdered bog-women, who may have been judged guilty of adultery, incest or sorcery?

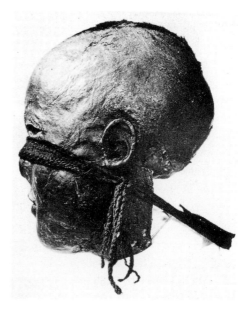

The head of a young girl, drowned in a bog at Windeby, Schleswig Holstein during the Iron Age. She was blindfolded with a brightly-coloured headband, and led out to her death naked, but for an ox-hide collar.

8 Mistress of the Beasts

The religious system of the ancient Celts, like that of many pre-industrial societies, was underpinned by a fundamental belief in the sanctity of nature and the natural world. This led inevitably to a respect and reverence for the creatures inhabiting what must have been perceived as a sacred landscape.[1] The veneration of both domestic and wild animals led to the worship of divinities whose role it was to protect these beasts and to promote their fertility and well-being. But the function of these deities was complex and could involve the destruction of their sacred creatures in the hunt as well as their protection.

The Celtic love of animals had its roots in the close secular relationship between humans and the creatures they hunted or those raised by farmers as providers of food, wool, hides, milk and cheese, draught and transport. This was a rural society, where the well-being of crops and livestock was crucial to a community's very existence. So it is understandable that goddesses and gods who were closely linked with animal-symbolism formed an important group within the Celtic pantheon.

There was an especially close affinity between animals and the goddesses, an affinity that manifested itself in a rich and complex gynaecomorphic iconography, where the images of female and beast were intimately associated. In the Romano-Celtic period, and occasionally even in the pre-Roman Iron Age, the animal symbolism which accompanies the images of goddesses suggests that their identity was, to some extent, dependent upon this zoomorphic association.

Cattle, horses, pigs and dogs all had their divine protectresses, as did the wild creatures: deer, bears, snakes and birds. The iconography of the Roman period, which displays visual images of these zoocentric female deities, appears to belong to the same mythic tradition as the later Celtic stories of Ireland and Wales, which abound in episodes demonstrating a strong link between animals and divine females. To this vernacular group of myths belong the skin-turners, shape-shifters who related to the supernatural world and who could transform themselves from human to animal form. Many of these divine shape-changers were female, and where the change was voluntary the most common creatures involved were birds. We cannot know whether or not the females and their animals represented in the earlier European iconography were shape-changers or not. For instance, was Epona an anthropomorphic goddess of horses or was she essentially a horse which sometimes appeared in human form? Are we seeing Classical traditions, based upon the belief in the supremacy of the human form, being imposed upon a Celtic system where, conversely, no rigid boundary between humans and animals was perceived? For a Greek or Roman no divinity could be envisaged as fully zoomorphic: that would offend the fundamental Classical tenet that man was the measure of all things. Even the goat-legged god Pan was regarded as a dangerous personification of the wild, a demon rather than a high-ranking member of the Greek pantheon. But the Celts had no such inhibitions. For them, an animal-image could have as much sanctity as that of a goddess or god in human form.

For Greek dramatists such as Euripides, man represented order, *nomos*, while women and animals stood for *physis*, wild, untamed nature and, by implication, lawlessness. This is amply illustrated in *The Bacchae*, in which the god Dionysus is attended by Maenads, ladies of the Theban court of Pentheus, who are possessed by the god and become wild, like the beasts of the mountains on which they range in ecstasy, driven by the intoxication of Dionysus. This link between women and wildness, and a perceived (by men) inability to think or behave rationally, may partly account for the circumscribed status of Greek women who, perhaps, were considered to need protection by men against their untamed natures. The Classical attitude to both women and animals appears to have been different from that of the Celts. To them, the natural world was numinous: *physis* was more important than *nomos*. Both goddesses and animals were perhaps perceived as being especially close to the sacred landscape.

Goddess and Animal in Iron Age Art

Strettweg

In the seventh century BC, a Hallstatt knight died and was cremated at Strettweg in Austria, his remains and some of his possessions interred beneath a mound. Among the accompanying grave-goods were an axe, a spear and three horse-bits, indicative of the man's high status as a member of the aristocratic warrior-élite of early Celtic society. Also buried with him was a unique and beautiful cult-object, a bronze model wagon consisting of four wheels supporting a platform on which the enactment of a ceremonial scene is depicted. The theme of this ritual imagery appears to be a stag-hunt presided over by a goddess. She stands in the centre of the platform, holding a great bowl high above her head. Behind and before her are two groups each comprising two women who grasp the huge antlers of a stag which stands between them. Behind these animal-attendants are a woman wearing large earrings and a man with erect phallus, wielding an axe. Surrounding these groups are pairs of mounted warriors with spears, shields and conical helmets.[2]

It is clearly extremely difficult to offer any close interpretation of the scene on the Strettweg wagon, but the imagery does suggest certain themes and beliefs. The stags may be the victims of a hunt or a sacrifice (or both): the presence of armed men implies

161

the former, the presiding goddess the latter. What is most interesting in the present context is the feminine focus of whatever ceremony is depicted: the central figure, larger than anyone else, is female, and she holds the great dish towards the sky, as if she is perhaps receiving her supplicants' offering of blood or wine. The attendants holding the stags are also female. Hunting, sacrifice, war and fertility are all seemingly present. The stag was venerated by the Celts as the essence of wild nature and the forest, its huge spreading antlers evocative of the great broad-leaved trees of the woodland and its aggressive spring-time virility perhaps symbolic of the re-awakening of the fertile earth after winter. The imagery of fertility is enhanced by the phallic symbolism of the male attendant or suppliant, who may even have represented the dead man himself: he was accompanied on his journey to the next world with an axe and horse-trappings.

If a stag-hunt is represented at Strettweg, the presence of a goddess may be significant: in many religious systems, including that of the Celts and some North

American Indians, the divine hunt was associated not simply with killing but also with nourishment and regeneration. The act of hunting destroys but also provides food so that others may live. The spilling of blood could also initiate new life and, if the correct rituals were observed, the slain animal would be resurrected to repopulate the land for the hunter. For this to happen, it was necessary for hunter and hunted to enter into a special relationship with each other, an association based upon mutual respect. It may be that the Strettweg goddess had a role as an arbitrator, ensuring that the hunt abided by the cult-rules and only accepting the blood-offering if the hunt was fairly conducted. It is interesting that the second century AD Greek writer Arrian, commenting upon the hunting-practices of the Celts,[3] mentions a hunter-goddess to whom sacrifice had to be made on her birthday. The gift to the goddess neutralised the theft from the natural world engendered by the act of hunting.[4]

Reinheim

In 1954, as a result of digging operations in a sandpit, a rich female La Tène burial of fourth-century BC date was discovered in a tomb overlooking the river Blies at Reinheim in Germany. The grave was in an oak-lined chamber, under a mound which had originally been one of a group of tombs. The woman appears to have been of high rank, perhaps even a dynastic princess, for she was interred with signs of great wealth,

(*Left*) Bronze model cult-wagon from a chieftain's grave; seventh century BC. From Strettweg, Austria. A central goddess holds up a large vessel; with her are warriors or hunters, some mounted, and women holding two stags with huge antlers.

(*Right*) Detail of a gold armlet, depicting a woman with a large bird perched above her head; fifth to fourth century BC. From a rich female grave at Reinheim, Germany.

including gold armrings and a torc and, indeed, what may have been the entire contents of her jewel-box, about two hundred pieces made of gold, bronze, amber, coral and glass.[5] Both the torc and one of the bracelets are decorated with iconography which is suggestive of imagery associated with a goddess of birds: the upper half of a woman's body is depicted, on whose head perches a great bird, the piercing eyes, hooked beak and wings clearly visible. A great deal of Celtic decorative metalwork is largely abstract in its artistry, though based ultimately on floral and faunal forms, and this very definite image on the Reinheim jewellery stands out as exceptional. The identity of the Reinheim goddess, if goddess she is, can never be known, but she is clearly closely linked with predatory or carrion-birds. It is difficult not to be reminded of the Irish battle-goddesses who shape-shifted at will between raven and female form (see Chapter 2).

Outer plate from the silver Gundestrup Cauldron, Denmark; second or first century BC. A goddess is depicted with a bird perched on her thumb, two eagles and a small terrier-like dog which rolls at her feet.

Animal-goddesses depicted on jewellery appear elsewhere in early Celtic art. The recent great find of torcs from Snettisham in Norfolk[6] includes one decorated with a goddess of beasts. Scenes like these must represent myths which are entirely lost to us but which were meaningful symbols within the context of religion in Iron Age Europe.

Gundestrup

Despite the recent claims of an Indian origin for the Gundestrup Cauldron,[7] it is clear that much of the religious imagery on this great silver vessel is Celtic, although oriental influences are undoubtedly also present. The find-spot of the cauldron is a Danish peat-bog and the date is now regarded as probably second or first century BC.[8] Amongst the incredibly rich iconography decorating the inner and outer surfaces of this vessel are scenes of a goddess accompanied by animals. One of the outer plates depicts a goddess accompanied by a much smaller male figure (his size perhaps suggestive of his inferior, human status), who wrestles with a large cat-like creature, perhaps a leopard or cheetah. Another outer plate depicts a goddess with a small bird perched upon her thumb; above are two eagles, and beneath her breast is a small dog lying on its back, as if rolling for joy at the proximity of his divine mistress. The third goddess-plate portrays the bust of a female with braided hair, flanked by wheels, as if to symbolise a cart: Tacitus[9] alludes to a Teutonic goddess, Nerthus, whose image was borne in a wagon during ceremonies in her honour. The divine women on the Gundestrup Cauldron, like some of the male deities, wear heavy torcs, which appear to indicate high rank.[10]

Boars and Bears: Arduinna and Artio

Both Artio and Arduinna were Gaulish goddesses of wild animals who are known, albeit rarely, from both iconographic and epigraphic evidence: hence our knowledge of their names. Both divinities appear to have been patronesses of their particular animals but also, perhaps, acted as benefactors and guardians of the humans who hunted them. Arduinna, as is indicated by her name, was a topographical goddess, the personified spirit of the Ardennes Forest in northern Gaul. On a bronze figurine, she appears as a boar-goddess and a huntress, dressed in a short tunic and boots, like the Roman huntress Diana, riding bare-back on a great galloping boar with curving tusks and raised dorsal crest. Arduinna bears a quiver at her back and a small spear or hunting-knife in her hand.[11] The statuette displays the ambivalence of some Celtic divine hunters towards their prey: Arduinna carries hunting-weapons, but her attitude to the boar is itself unaggressive. She rides him like a horse and is clearly at one with her mount. She is both huntress and goddess of the forest, protectress of its denizens, a spirit who must be appeased and propitiated by human hunters if their expeditions were to be successful and without mishap. The hunting of boars was dangerous and the correct rituals would have to be observed.

From a study of the faunal evidence from a number of Iron Age sites in Britain and Gaul, it seems as if wild boar was not part of the normal diet of early Celtic communities.[12] But boars were hunted, probably as a sport of the élite and also as practice for war. Arrian alludes to hunting as an aristocratic pastime but speaks of the Celts' use of the hunt as an exercise of bravery and skill in many ranks of society.[13] It may even be that boar-hunting, as a particularly dangerous pastime, was used as an initiation-test for manhood. If this were so, then the presence of a boar-goddess may symbolise a sexual element in the hunt, whereby the young men of the community equated the killing of the boar with sexual maturity and the 'conquest' of the female.

Bears are rare in the archaeological record of Iron Age Europe, though they must have been common. Bear-teeth were occasionally buried in graves, as at the cemetery of Mont Troté in the Ardennes, where the teeth formed the 'beads' of a necklace.[14] A late Iron Age aristocrat, whose remains were interred at Welwyn in Hertfordshire, was accompanied in his grave by a bearskin.[15]

In the Roman period, evidence for bears in ritual is equally sparse: small jet bears occasionally accompanied burials in North Britain. But Gaulish Celts venerated a bear-goddess: she was Artio, her very name, 'Bear', indicative of her ursine identity. As is the case with Epona, whose name is likewise based on the Gaulish word for horse, Artio was clearly a divine protectress of bears, but so closely identifiable with her animal that her *persona* cannot be separated from that of the creature itself. Artio was

Inscribed bronze group of the goddess Artio, accompanied by a bear; Romano-Celtic period. From Muri near Berne, Switzerland.

166

invoked among the Treveri of the Moselle Valley, where her name was scrawled on a rockface; and at Muri, near Berne in Switzerland, a figurine of the goddess is inscribed with a dedication to her. The statuette depicts Artio sitting opposite a large bear which stretches its head towards her, as if seeking food from her basket of fruit. The beast stands beneath a tree which is perhaps symbolic of the animal's forest-habitat.[16] The relationship between the goddess and the bear is one of intimacy, mutual respect and equality: the animal does not appear to be subservient to Artio, nor does it threaten her. The goddess appears as a benevolent patron rather than a huntress of the bear; the fruit she carries nourishes it. But, by implication, Artio is a goddess of universal plenty and well-being who promotes wild nature and provides sustenance for the forest and its inhabitants. Arduinna is an ambiguous divinity, who hunts as well as protects her wild creatures; this is not evident in the case of Artio from the evidence of the imagery at Muri.

The Deer-Women

The early Iron Age cult-wagon at Strettweg is one of the few pieces of Celtic iconography which demonstrates a clear relationship between a goddess and deer. In addition, there are rare instances of images which depict goddesses wearing antlers, although this is usually the prerogative of male divinities.[17] But there are two supernatural females in the early Irish myths who did have a close affinity with deer. Flidhais was a goddess of wild nature who is represented as a deerherd, treating the animals as if they were domestic cattle. Flidhais appears in the Ulster myths as sexually vigorous, the only woman apart from the promiscuous Queen Medb who could satisfy the voracious appetite of the great hero Ferghus. In the absence of either of these two ladies, Ferghus had to resort to the attentions of seven normal women.[18] Flidhais appears to have been both herder and hunter of deer and other wild creatures, the personification of raw nature, and she possessed imagery of both sexuality/fertility and destruction, like the Insular battle-goddesses.

The second deer-woman of Irish myth is Sava, who appears in the Fionn Cycle. Sava was a shape-shifter, but an involuntary one. She was a young woman who had been changed into a fawn as an act of vengeance by the Black Druid, because she repelled his advances. Finn, the hero of the Cycle, encountered her and, because he himself had supernatural powers, he was able (temporarily at least) to cancel the enchantment, and he married her. But the deer-symbolism was retained: Sava produced a son and it is unclear whether or not Finn was his father: The child was named Oisin, which means 'Little Deer', and he had a close affinity with stags; he was even perhaps a skin-turner himself. Finn found Oisin abandoned in the wilderness; his mother Sava had been reclaimed and seized by the druid. The boy grew up, as Finn's son, among the famous war-band the Fianna. Interestingly, Finn himself is presented as having close links with the natural world and with stags in particular; he hunted them and they sometimes tried to lure him to the Otherworld.[19] So the meeting between Finn and Sava may not have been entirely fortuitous, although clearly the hero had no part in her enchantment.

Sava was probably not herself a goddess, but she was touched by the spirit-world in that she attracted the unwelcome attentions of one who had supernatural power. Her transformation to deer-form seems to have been a meaningless act of revenge, the behaviour of a thwarted lover, who tried to ensure that if Sava would not accept him, she should never have a husband. There is a parallel in Classical myth: Aeschylus' drama *Prometheus Bound* tells the story of the hapless mortal girl Io who was pursued by the lecherous Zeus. Her refusal of him caused her transformation to the form of a cow, condemned to roam the world tormented by a stinging gadfly. Sava and Oisin, with their continuing deer-associations, bear certain resemblances to other mothers

Bronze statuette of an antlered goddess, holding a cornucopia; Roman period. Unprovenanced, but probably Gaulish. She is a rare example of a female version of the stag-god Cernunnos.

and sons in Celtic mythology: in the Welsh story of Rhiannon, both she and her son Pryderi had a recurring link with horses (see Chapter 3). But Sava was a deer and, as such, it was appropriate that she was 'hunted' by Finn, a hero who had close associations with the world of wild nature.

The Snake-Goddesses

The iconography of Romano-Celtic Europe presents a number of images of female deities whose main attribute is a serpent, which may curl round a tree, encircle the goddess' arm or be fed from a bowl of food which she offers it. In order to understand the role of the snake in association with the goddess, we should examine the symbolism of the creature itself in both a Celtic and Roman context. This is complex and contains messages which are both positive and negative, based partly on observation of the behaviour of the snake in the wild.

Snakes are carnivorous; they are hunters, and they kill violently, by a poisonous bite or by constriction. Their predatory nature perhaps gave rise to negative, fearful perceptions of the snake, particularly if the danger to humans were fully recognised. The snake is essentially an earthbound creature, gliding close to the ground with a rippling, water-like motion, able to insinuate itself in and out of minute cracks or holes in rocks. Maybe this behaviour created a link in people's minds between the snake and infernal symbolism. Fertility-imagery was also associated with the serpent: the female gives birth to a large number of young at once; the male has a multiple penis; and of course the shape of the reptile may have endowed it with phallic symbolism. Finally, the practice of skin-shedding was seen as an allegory of regeneration and rebirth. So death, the underworld, fertility, healing and renewal could all be symbolised by the image of this one beast.

The association between serpents and the goddesses seems to have been principally concerned with the symbolism of fecundity, healing and regeneration. Several of the curative goddesses venerated at healing spring-sanctuaries have snake-imagery. Sometimes the snake depicted is naturalistic, but on occasions it is the idiosyncratic, hybrid image of the ram-headed serpent that is present. In Classical symbolism, the ram represented fertility. The ram-headed snake belongs essentially to the Celtic imagination, and its iconography occurs mainly in north-east Gaul, where it is especially associated with the divine lord of animals, nature and plenty, the antlered god Cernunnos.[20] Of the healer-goddesses who are accompanied on iconography by snakes, Sirona is perhaps the best-known (see Chapters 5 and 6). Her stone cult-image at the spring-shrine of Hochscheid near Trier depicts her with a snake coiled round her right arm (highly reminiscent of portrayals of the Greek healer-goddess Hygeia), stretching its head towards the bowl of eggs she holds in her left hand. This imagery is repeated on a bronze group at Mâlain in Burgundy.[21] Another Gaulish healer-deity,

Damona, was depicted as a serpent-goddess: the fragmentary image from a shrine of Apollo Moritasgus and Damona at Alesia consists of a stone head of the goddess, crowned with ears of corn, and a hand entwined with a snake.[22] Both Sirona and Damona are thus demonstrably associated with both healing and fertility: they were both venerated at curative sacred springs; each bears a snake-attribute; and the eggs and corn evoke the idea of the earth's bounty. The snakes would seem to be symbols of regeneration and the renewal of body or spirit under the power of the divine healer. Indeed, Sirona's eggs are themselves not only symbolic of fertility but also of rebirth, since eggs have to be broken to liberate new life or to provide nourishment.

Other Gaulish healer-goddesses possessed snake emblems: the therapeutic spring shrine of Mavilly in Burgundy was the home of a goddess perceived as an image with snakes and a torch.[23] In a shrine whose main power seems to have been to heal eye-afflictions, the torch may reflect light after the darkness of disease and clear vision in place of defective sight. Mavilly also produced a carving of a god and goddess accompanied by a ram-headed serpent, as did the curative water-sanctuary of Néris-les-Bains in central Gaul, where the serpent's symbolism of well-being is enhanced by its depiction gazing towards a large bag of money held by the god.[24]

We have seen that the serpents associated with the healer-goddesses sometimes appear to seek nourishment from their divine companions. This occurs at Hochscheid and at Néris. Similar imagery occurs with other Gaulish goddesses: the female divinity depicted on a carving at Sommerécourt (Haute Marne) sits cross-legged, with a large cauldron of mash and fruit in her lap. Her symbolism as a spirit of plenty is emphasised by her cornucopia, and her pomegranate may suggest rebirth, as it does in the Classical world. The goddess is encircled by a large ram-headed snake which eats from the great bowl on her knees. The carving was found with a companion-piece which depicts an antlered god feeding two similar snakes from a large dish of mash.[25] A stone figure of a goddess at Xertigny nearby bears similar imagery: here she sits with a small ram-horned serpent curled up in her lap, like a pet dog.[26]

One British snake-goddess is of particular interest: she may be Verbeia, the personificatory spirit of the River Wharfe at Ilkley in Yorkshire. Her stone image is of a standing woman, with a snake grasped in each hand. The snakes are depicted unrealistically, as stiff, zig-zag shapes falling from her hands[27] and the images may represent both snakes and the water of the river itself: an altar dedicated to Verbeia was found nearby. The water-associations of the snake perhaps reflect similar ideas to those of the spring-sanctuaries of Gaul, where the serpent, with its regenerative symbolism and its rippling shape, represented the spirit of life-giving, purifying water which could cleanse and heal. Water itself was perceived to possess dual symbolism: it could both give life and destroy it; it could fertilise crops but also inundate them; it quenched thirst but also drowned the unwary. Like water, the snake's symbolism may also have been multi-faceted, with life and death closely linked.

The light and dark aspects of the snake's symbolism are perhaps manifest also in its appearance with the Romano-Celtic mother-goddesses, especially in the Rhineland. These Celto-Germanic maternal triads are sometimes associated with the image of a snake curled round a tree, symbolism which resembles that of the serpent and Tree of Knowledge encountered by Adam and Eve in the Garden of Eden of the Old Testament. On the reverse of one Rhenish altar to the local mother-goddesses, the *Aufaniae*, a great tree, perhaps an oak or willow, stretches its branches to the sky, its trunk encircled by a snake.[28] The image may be that of the Tree of Life, guarded by the serpent and reflective, perhaps, of the link between the upper and lower worlds: the tree depends both on its branches and its roots; the serpent is earthbound, crawling along the ground, but it can also climb; the tree 'dies' in winter and is reborn in spring; the snake also 'dies' each time it sloughs its skin. The mother-goddesses themselves (See Chapter 5) presided over both life and death and the well-being of humankind on earth and in the Otherworld.

The concept of the snake as a beneficent symbol of renewal is by no means confined to the religious systems of the pagan Celts. The great Graeco-Roman healer-god Asklepios/Aesculapius is depicted with a serpent-entwined staff: he was both a curative and a chthonic deity, and his serpent reflected both these roles.[29] Likewise, his daughter Hygeia is often depicted with a serpent coiled around her arm. The Classical Mercury combined the functions of divine herald and promoter of prosperity, but he was also a god who led the souls of humans to the next world and his most important emblem was the *caduceus*, a rod entwined with two interwoven serpents which, again, reflect the essential dualism of Mercury's role.[30] The goddesses of healing and fertility had the snake as their attribute because it symbolised the close ties between life, fertility, healing, death and regeneration, just as the roles of the goddesses themselves embraced these interdependent concepts.

Birds and Shape-Shifters

Both iconography and the early written myths – especially those of Ireland – provide rich evidence for bird-goddesses. The vernacular tales contain a recurrent theme which concerns the transformation of women, generally supernatural women, into birds, a process which could either be voluntary or a punishment. The birds involved were generally either ravens/crows or aquatic/wading-birds, such as swans or cranes.

Bird-Goddesses in Celtic Europe

Because of their ability to fly, birds have been perceived in many cultures as symbols of the freedom to leave the bounds of earth: thus birds could be allegories of the human spirit released from the body at death. In the Celtic system, however, particular birds

171

were considered sacred because they somehow epitomised the personae of the divinities with whom they were associated. Frequently such birds were the companions of the goddesses. Sequana of the Seine is a good example of this link: she was a healer-spirit of the spring, the personification of the river at its source (see Chapter 5), and she appears at Fontes Sequanae sailing in a duck-prowed boat, in recognition of her aquatic symbolism.[31]

The imagery of the Gaulish bird-goddesses indicates that the raven or crow was their most common companion. The iconography of the raven-goddesses expresses nothing of the destructive battle-symbolism with which ravens and female deities are associated in the early Insular myths (see Chapter 2). Instead, the message conveyed is of the raven as a beneficent creature, companion of divinities whose main concerns were healing and prosperity. Most of the European goddesses are not identifiable by name because of a lack of epigraphic evidence that can be matched with the imagery. An exception is Nantosuelta, the female partner of Sucellus, the Gaulish hammer-god. She appears with a raven at Sarrebourg near Metz and at Speyer in Germany.[32] The general symbolism and context of Sucellus and Nantosuelta suggests that they were deities of well-being and plenty, especially associated with wine-production. Other domestic goddesses sometimes had raven-emblems: a group of images from Luxembourg depicts a mother-goddess seated within a house-shaped model shrine accompanied by a raven,[33] the link with house-symbols recalling Nantosuelta's emblem of the house borne on a pole. It is difficult to interpret the nature of the link between ravens and these peaceful goddesses of well-being. They may have been oracular birds: ravens had this association both in Classical religion and in the Celtic myths. But their black plumage and carrion-feeding habits may have endowed these creatures with infernal symbolism, and it is well-known that the mother-goddesses possessed a chthonic aspect to their cult: images of these deities are sometimes found in graves or at the bottom of wells. Depictions of the horse-goddess Epona are occasionally accompanied by ravens: she appears thus at Altrier in Luxembourg[34] and she certainly possessed a chthonic function (see below).

Geese and doves were both sometimes linked to goddess-cults: the goose is an aggressive, watchful creature, as effective as a guard-dog, and this may be why the bronze war-goddess at Dinéault in Brittany wears a goose-crested helmet. Doves appear to have been particularly associated with peace and with healing. Their 'voices' have led to their being linked, like ravens, with prophecy, and they were connected with the cult of Venus in Classical symbolism, probably because of the loving behaviour of paired doves. Their association with healing-cults in Gaul was perhaps because they represented peace and the harmony of the spirit, which may have been perceived as beneficial to physical and mental health. Certainly many of the great curative cult-establishments of Gaul contained images of doves, sometimes carved in groups of up to six birds. The spring-sanctuary of the goddess Ianuaria at

Beire-le-Châtel in Burgundy yielded examples of this kind of offering, presumably brought to the temple by hopeful or grateful pilgrims in expectation of or gratitude for a cure.[35] Visitors to Sequana's shrine, too, brought doves as offerings to the divine healer: some images of the pilgrims show them bringing doves as gifts to the goddess.[36]

Birds and Goddesses in Celtic Myth

The great group of Irish warrior-goddesses with the ability to shape-shift from human to raven form are fully discussed in Chapter 2. It is useful here to remind ourselves that the raven's scavenging habit of feeding off dead things, its black colour and its reputed cruelty towards other birds made this bird a fully appropriate associate of these Insular goddesses of death and destruction. Battle-furies such as the Morrigán and Macha were also prophets, and ravens, too, were linked with oracular powers.

Cranes were similarly often associated with unpleasant females in the Insular myths.[37] Some of these women were transformed into cranes as a punishment for antisocial behaviour, especially for nagging or scolding, which may have been compared to the crane's screech. The Irish sea-god Manannán possessed a bag full of treasure made from the skin of a crane which had once been a woman who had been metamorphosed because of her jealousy. Three cranes guarded the *sídh* (Otherworld dwelling) of the god Midhir, and they not only protected him against intruders but they could also unman warriors, depriving them of their courage to join battle. This 'bad-luck' symbolism may have given rise to the taboo on the consumption of the flesh of cranes noted by Giraldus Cambrensis.[38] The Irish hero Finn had a close relationship

Celtic bronze coin; first century BC or AD. From Maidstone, Kent. The obverse shows two cranes facing each other (the reverse has an image of a stag and boar). In Celtic myth, unpleasant females were sometimes metamorphosed to crane-form.

173

with cranes, which were associated both with death and with salvation. In a story called the 'Hag of the Temple', Finn encountered cranes of death: the hag had four sons who were under the curse of crane-shape, a spell from which they could only be released if an enchanted bull were sacrificed and the blood sprinkled over them.[39] But in another story Finn, as a small boy, was saved from death by his grandmother, who shape-shifted to crane-form and caught him as he fell off the edge of a cliff.[40]

Cranes were associated, for the most part, with harshness, meanness, jealousy, old age and death. They were not transmogrified divinities but they were closely linked with the supernatural, and they had an influence on the spirit-world. The punitive element in bird shape-shifting occurs with other birds: in the *Mabinogion*, Blodeuwedd, the Flower-Woman, could not be punished by death for betraying and killing her husband Lleu since she was a magical being, but she could be transformed to an owl, condemned to hunt alone at night.[41]

Swans and swan-women had a very different image in the Irish mythic tradition. Whilst it is true that the transmogrification form girl-to swan-form may sometimes be punitive, the image is overwhelmingly one of love and innocence. The birth of these swan-myths may well have been due both to the purity of these creatures, symbolised by their white colour, and to their habit of mating for life: most of the swan-stories are associated with sexual love, often between god and swan-maiden. The 'Dream of Oenghus' demonstrates this theme particularly well. Oenghus mac Oc ('Oenghus, the Young Son') was a member of the Tuatha Dé Danann and, specifically, was a god of love, helper of such 'star-crossed lovers' as Midhir and Etáin and Diarmaid and Gráinne (see Chapter 6). In the 'Dream', Oenghus himself was smitten with love for Caer, a swan-girl whose enchantment caused her to shape-shift to bird-form every alternate year at the great autumn festival of Samhain held on 31 October and 1 November. When Oenghus first saw Caer, she was with her 150 female swan-companions at a lake. Each pair was linked by a silver chain but the tallest swan-girl, Caer, was decorated with a chain of gold, indicative of her special status. The fact that the transformation took place at Samhain is significant, since it was a time of danger and instability, when the normal boundaries between the real and spirit worlds were temporarily dissolved, where time and space were suspended and both humans and

Bronze flesh-fork decorated with swans and cygnets; seventh century BC. From Dunaverney, Co. Antrim, N. Ireland. In Celtic mythic tradition, swans symbolised divine love.

spirits could move freely between worlds. Samhain represented a breakdown of normality and order, which were replaced by chaotic imbalance. Why Caer and her companions were under this shape-changing enchantment is not clear from the story, but it may have something to do with Caer's father, Ethal Anbual, who forbade Oenghus to marry his daughter. Oenghus was divine and so able to enter Caer's shape-shifting world: by approaching her at Samhain and taking swan-form himself, he could bring her away from her lake and wed her, presumably breaking the spell as he did so. The tale ends with the two swan-lovers flying around the lake three times, singing everyone to sleep for three days and nights, while they escaped to Oenghus' *sídh* at Brugh na Bóinne.[42]

Caer was quite clearly a woman of supernatural status, although she does not appear to have been a goddess. She was the victim of an enchantment that could only be undone by the love of a god and, to achieve this, Oenghus had to join her in her transformation. By doing this, Oenghus was, in a sense, accepting her status; it was a symbolic act of equality without which Caer's spell could, perhaps, never have been broken. The story of two other lovers, Midhir and Etáin, has a similar theme of immortal and mortal, though superhuman, woman. After many vicissitudes (see Chapter 6), involving punitive shape-shifting and rebirth, Midhir and Etáin escaped from the court of Etáin's husband, the king of Ireland, by taking the form of swans and flying from the royal court of Tara.[43]

The theme of swans linked together by chains is a recurrent one. It appears in a myth of the Ulster hero Cú Chulainn, with whom a girl called Derbforgaill fell in love. Cú Chulainn had the reputation for being a somewhat reluctant lover, being too preoccupied with warfare for dalliance. Derbforgaill and her maidservant pursued the champion, having transformed themselves into a pair of swans, joined by a chain of gold. Cú Chulainn shot one of the birds with a sling-stone; as she fell to the ground, badly injured, she regained the human form of Derbforgaill, apparently because of the shock of the blow or the fall. Cú Chulainn tended her wound, sucking out the stone but, as he had tasted her blood, he could not mate with her, being bound by some kind of blood-taboo. There is an early Breton story which closely resembles this one: a shepherd saw three swans which, as they touched earth, were changed into young girls.[44] The chains with which the birds were joined, in many swan-myths, must have a particular symbolism: they may denote the swans as being the victims of enchantment, a kind of talisman that ensured their continued link to the real world of humans; without these chains, it may not have been possible for them to regain their woman-form. It is worth noting that very similar swan-girl stories exist in Germanic myth and folklore: Swan Lake is perhaps the best-known example.

The final link between mythic birds and goddesses concerns magical singing birds which could bring healing sleep by their music. This theme is recurrent in the Celtic traditions of Ireland, Wales and Brittany. The birds were not of any known species and, indeed, they were clearly supernatural creatures with few earthly characteristics at all. The Breton legend of the Princess Marcassa is of unknown date but is possibly quite early: it refers to a magical bird called the 'Dredaine-Bird' whom an elderly, ailing king had to touch before he could be healed.[45] Two brief references to the singing birds of Rhiannon are present in the Welsh myths: reference is made to them in the Tale of Branwen, where they were heard by the companions of Brân in their sojourn in Harlech, after the great battle between Wales and Ireland (see Chapter 3). The birds were far away across the sea and yet the men could hear them clearly, and their song soothed their physical ills and spiritual anguish.[46] The birds of Rhiannon reappear in the Tale of Culhwch and Olwen: in order to win Olwen, one of Culhwch's tasks was to acquire these birds for Olwen's father.[47] In this myth, the birds were clearly regarded as being unattainable, because they belonged to the supernatural world.

The Irish Otherworld goddess Clíodna (See Chapter 4) possessed three magical singing birds which could cure sick or wounded humans by lulling them to sleep with their healing music. They lived on two islands in the sea, and they are described in the story of Tadg, a mortal who dwelt for a time in this Happy Otherworld, the realm of the goddess. Tadg encountered a group of beautiful women led by Clíodna, and saw the three birds perched on an apple-tree (a peaceful symbol of the supernatural world). The birds were similar to blackbirds, though larger, but they had glorious, multi-coloured plumage: one was blue with a purple head, the second purple with a green head, the third speckled and with a head of golden feathers. When Tadg and his men went back to their own world, Clíodna sent the birds with them, their song softening the sadness of leaving the enchanted spirit-world. These magical birds laid wonderful eggs of blue and crimson: if eaten by humans while in the Otherworld, the men grew feathers themselves, but the effect was temporary and the feathers dropped off when they washed their bodies.[48] The relationship between Clíodna and her birds was close, but they were her attendants rather than her *alter ego*. It must be assumed that their healing properties reflected the persona of the goddess herself and, whilst she herself did not leave her realm, her birds could do so and return safely; perhaps it was easier for birds to traverse both worlds because they had the power of flight.

The Hound of Nehalennia

The multifarious nature of dog-symbolism, in both Graeco-Roman and pagan Celtic religion, results from the nature and behaviour of these domestic animals which have such a close relationship with humankind. Dogs scavenge; they are the companions of hunters; they act as guard-dogs and sheep-dogs; they are killers but are faithful to their owners, sharing hearth and home and protecting the family. They have long held the reputation of being able to heal themselves with their own saliva. So we find dogs as symbols of several cults concerned with hunting, death, healing and guardianship.

176

Stone altar to Nehalennia, a goddess of the North Sea. From Colijnsplaat, Netherlands. She is depicted with a fruit-basket, her foot on the prow of a boat, accompanied by her dog, a symbol of fidelity and protection.

We saw in Chapter 5 that many of the healer-goddesses were associated with dogs. Sirona at Hochscheid and Aveta at Trier are two examples of curative goddesses to whom small clay figures of seated women nursing lap-dogs were offered at their shrines.[49] Stone carvings of the British triple mother-goddesses at Cirencester and London depict dogs as their companions.[50] Figurines of seated female deities carrying lap-dogs occur over wide regions of Celtic Europe, from Canterbury to Cologne. The association of small dogs with goddesses of health must result, at least partly, from the symbolic link between healing and dogs. The Classical healer Asklepios had live sacred dogs at his great sanctuary of Epidaurus in central Greece, and shrines to the god both here and in Rome attest the miraculous curative powers of his animals.[51] The lap-dogs nestling on the knees of the European goddesses may also symbolise the comfort of warmth: the link between women and lapdogs in early Irish literature is suggested as having something to do with the possible palliative effect of the warmth of a small dog on the stomach to relieve period-pains,[52] rather like a hot water-bottle. The association between dogs and mother-goddesses may have been to do with healing; the Mothers did have a curative role. But the animals may also have been present as symbols of protection, just as the Mothers possessed a guardianship role against barrenness, and failure of crops and livestock.

A third possible link between dogs and mother-goddesses was an infernal one: the goddesses were associated with death as well as life, and the connection between dogs and chthonic forces is perhaps indicated by the presence of dogs in deep pits, as occurred at the Iron Age hillfort of Danebury[53] or at the Romano-British temple at Muntham Court.[54] The original link between dogs and death may have arisen from their behaviour as hunters and scavengers but, if their association with the mother-goddesses was chthonic, these Romano-Celtic animals certainly did not represent the horrific savagery of Virgil's hell-hound, Cerberus,[55] or of the canine hunters of human souls which are described in tales of the Welsh Otherworld, Annwn.[56] The Celtic mother-goddesses had a function as protectors of the dead, and it may be in this capacity that the dog appears, as an infernal guardian.

The most important of the dog-goddesses was Nehalennia, a local goddess of the North Sea coast of the Netherlands. Doubt has been expressed recently as to the correct ethnic identity of Nehalennia as a Celtic goddess.[57] Certainly, her locality suggests that she may technically have been a Germanic deity, but the majority of her suppliants were Romano-Celtic and, in any case, the relationship between Celts and Germans west of the Rhine was so strong that it is difficult to distinguish one from the other in cultural terms.[58] Two temples are known to have been dedicated to Nehalennia, both of which have been submerged by the encroachment of the sea: one was at Domburg on the island of Walcheren; the other at Colijnsplaat on the estuary of the East Scheldt river. The Domburg sanctuary was discovered in 1647, when sand-dunes were disturbed by storms and about thirty stone altars to the goddess revealed.

Evidence of the second temple resulted from the activities of a fisherman, who dragged up fragments of altars from the sea-bed: subsequent rescue-operations recovered more than eighty stones dedicated to the goddess.

Nehalennia was clearly an important, powerful and popular divinity; she enjoyed a wealthy cult-following during the second and third centuries AD, being venerated by seafarers, businessmen, traders and Romano-Celtic officials who had reason to brave the hazards of a North Sea voyage and who gave thanks at Nehalennia's sanctuaries for a safe crossing and undamaged merchandise.

Details of Nehalennia's cult have been the subject of many publications,[59] but it is worth examining the imagery associated with her, especially that of her canine companion. Nehalennia's iconography shows her to have possessed three main symbols: a boat or rudder appropriate to a marine deity; fertility emblems such as cornucopiae and baskets of fruit; and a large hound which is almost invariably present. It is this attribute that is the most enigmatic of Nehalennia's emblems. The dog is not a lap-dog but a large, long-legged animal, with big ears and a pointed muzzle. It sits watchfully beside the goddess, turning its head towards her and sometimes touching her with its nose. The dog-image usually balances that of the great fruit-basket on Nehalennia's other side[60] but the dog is present even when the basket is absent. Thus, on the altar dedicated by the ship-owner Vesigonus Martinus at Colijnsplaat, Nehalennia's fruit is replaced by the prow of a boat on which she places her foot, as if in protective command, but the hound remains.[61] Interestingly, on this relief the boat and the dog are depicted the same size, which perhaps reflects a symbolic emphasis of the animal's importance.

One of Nehalennia's roles was clearly that of provider of prosperity; she granted success in whatever activities her devotees were involved, whether administration, trading or sailing. In this capacity, the dog may be a symbol of protection and perhaps also fidelity. Nehalennia guarded those who worshipped at her shrine; she was faithful to them just as her dedicants were faithful in their maintenance of her cult and the upkeep of her temples. The size of the dog is appropriate if it is a protector, and its attitude to the goddess is clearly one of devotion, like that of her suppliants. So Nehalennia's dog may symbolise the mutual support between the goddess and her worshippers. Good faith is particularly important in commerce, and it was predominantly the business community who invoked Nehalennia's protection.

The cult of Nehalennia may have had a more profound significance than merely that of success in trading. Her imagery includes vegetation, and she sometimes holds a pomegranate, the Classical goddess Proserpina's emblem of fertility and rebirth. Even Nehalennia's water-symbolism may not simply be associated with her protection of marine travellers, but may additionally be reflective of a role in which regeneration and healing played a part. It may be no coincidence that Nehalennia's rudder is also Fortuna's symbol, and perhaps a parallel was perceived between sea-travel and the hazards of the journey through life. There may even have been seasonal imagery: the vegetal motifs may reflect the birth of spring and the renewal of sea-travel after the stagnation of winter.

Like the mother-goddesses, Nehalennia may have been a multi-functional deity, associated with physical protection and prosperity but also with the deeper concerns of life, death and rebirth. The goddess was not just a comfortable domestic, peasant's goddess; she was the subject of veneration by the wealthy and cultivated middle classes of Romano-Celtic society, who may have been interested in their fate as humans as well as business people. Nehalennia's dog may have been present in recognition of all these facets of her cult: a guardian in life's success, death and regeneration.

Cattle, Milk and Goddesses

Female divinities associated with both bulls and cows appear in pagan Irish myth. The symbolism of cattle was complex: bulls represented strength and virility, and cows were linked with the fertility of the herd and its milk-yield. In early historical Ireland, cattle were measures of wealth, and we know that women, as well as men, could own herds: Queen Medb of Connacht brought her own cattle with her when she married Ailill; and the focus of the *Táin*, the main tale of the Ulster Cycle, is Medb's desire to acquire the great Brown Bull of Cooley, because she was jealous of the magnificence of Ailill's White-Horned Bull, whom she could not match.[62]

The great Irish goddess, the Morrigán, whose role embraced not only war and destruction but also fertility, was repeatedly associated with cattle. She warned the Donn (the Brown Bull) of his danger from Medb, perching on his shoulder in bird-form. The Morrigán had Otherworld cattle of her own, white with red ears, their colouring betraying their supernatural origins. The goddess guarded her cattle jealously: one of her cows was mated by a bull belonging to a mortal woman Odras and, enraged at such effrontery, the Morrigán transformed her into a pool of water. This violent reaction may have been because of contamination and the mingling of the earthly with the Otherworld. In her various encounters with Cú Chulainn, the Morrigán was often associated with cows. In one episode, she appeared to the champion as a red woman (denoting her Otherworld status), riding in a strange chariot, driving a cow before her. Cú Chulainn challenged her for abducting one of Ulster's animals, and she reviled him, changing to crow-form as she did so (see Chapter 2). The ambivalent relationship between the goddess and the hero is demonstrated by another encounter between them, which contains strong symbolism (see p. 41): when Cú Chulainn spurned the Morrigán's advances, one of the guises in which she attacked him was that of a red Otherworld cow. After the fight, she appeared to him as an old woman milking a triple-teated cow.[63]

Other Insular goddesses were closely associated with cattle. Iuchna was described as possessing three cows on whose heads perched three birds that were transformed men.[64] This is significant because the imagery strongly resembles the iconography of Tarvostrigaranus, the Bull with Three Cranes, who is depicted on a Parisian stone of the earlier first century AD. The image here is of a bull before a willow-tree, two cranes or egrets perched on his back and one on his head.[65] This iconography must relate to a lost Celtic myth associated, perhaps, with shape-shifting. The transformation of humans, specifically women, to cranes, has been mentioned above. In this context, the iconography of a small silvered bronze three-horned bull from Britain may have some relevance. It comes from a fourth-century AD shrine at Maiden Castle (Dorset), and it is

Silver-washed bronze triple-horned bull, the remains of a triad of goddesses on his back; fourth century AD. From a shrine at Maiden Castle, Dorset.

181

remarkable in that it has two – and the remains of a third – female perched on its back.[66]

Boann, divine personification of the River Boyne, and the Irish goddess Brigit (see Chapter 9) both had cow associations. Boann's name means 'She of the White Cow'.[67] Brigit was reared on the milk of an Otherworld cow, a legend which survived the transformation of the pagan goddess to a Christian saint.[68]

Archaeological evidence includes very little in terms of direct associations between cattle and female deities. The Gaulish goddess Damona, venerated at Alesia and elsewhere, was a healer-goddess, but her name 'Great Cow' or 'Divine Cow' suggests that she perhaps originally had another function, one associated with dairy-produce. Indeed, her links with the earth's abundance are manifested in her very fragmentary image at Alesia, which consists of a stone head crowned with ears of corn. What is also interesting about Damona is that she was apparently polyandrous (see Chapter 6). This suggested promiscuity perhaps links the Gaulish goddess with some of the Insular goddesses who were associated with cattle, namely Medb and the Morrígán.

Work on the iconography of some British goddesses is beginning to reveal their possible identity as patrons of milk-yields and dairy-produce.[69] Classical writers comment on the use by the Celts of milk and milk-products: Caesar says that the Germans lived mainly on a diet of milk, cheese and meat.[70] Pliny speaks of cheese-consumption among the Gauls,[71] some of the finest products coming from the area of southern France around Nîmes, which were imported by the Romans. Strabo reports that the Britons used milk but did not make cheese,[72] though this statement is unlikely to have been true generally, and may relate only to a specific region or tribe. There is a group of goddesses depicted in Britain who may be associated with dairy-work: on reliefs at Bath and Gloucester,[73] a divine couple is represented who are normally identified as Mercury and Rosmerta (see Chapter 6). The latter's principal attribute was a stave-bound wooden bucket, and at Gloucester she holds a large ladle-like object over the vessel. A very similar image is present at Corbridge in northern England,[74] where a goddess stirs the contents of a large vat. I have generally interpreted this emblem as a vessel of rebirth, akin to the regenerative cauldron of Irish myth. But Hilda Davidson has made the interesting suggestion[75] that this bucket could be associated with milk-churning, butter-or cheese-making. Another British goddess whom Davidson thinks might also have dairy-symbolism is represented by the small wooden figurine from Winchester.[76] The statuette is of a standing woman, wearing a cloak and a torc; she holds a napkin in one hand and a large key in the other. Davidson's contention is that the figure may represent the divine guardian of the dairy, holding the keys to her domain and a cheese-straining cloth. This interpretation is necessarily speculative, but it may offer some explanation of an otherwise enigmatic image.

Stone relief of a goddess stirring the contents of a vat or bucket, perhaps a butter-churn; Romano-British. From Corbridge, Northumberland.

Epona, the Divine Horsewoman

European iconography and epigraphy of the first four centuries AD present us with evidence for a goddess who was perhaps one of the most popular deities of the Celtic pantheon. There are no surviving remains of her cult prior to the Roman period, but her symbolism shows her to have been native to the Celtic world. She was a horse-goddess whose name Epona comes from the Gaulish *epos*, meaning 'horse'. Her iconography fits closely with her name in that her imagery is always associated with horses.

Epona's importance is demonstrated by the distribution of her cult-objects and by the attention paid to her in the Roman world. The heartlands of her cult were Gaul and the Rhineland, but she was venerated in regions as far apart as Britain, Bulgaria, North Africa and Rome itself where – uniquely for a Celtic goddess – she was honoured with her own official festival in the Roman calendar, celebrated on 18 December. A number of Classical writers allude to Epona's cult and, again, this is rare for a Celtic

Bronze group of Epona with two ponies, one male, one female; Romano-British. The goddess holds a yoke and a sheaf of corn. Unprovenanced, Wiltshire.

divinity: the poet Juvenal mentions her, as do Minucius Felix and Apuleius.[77] This last reference is worth examining: Apuleius is turned into an ass and, while in the stable, he notes a little shrine to Epona, the 'mare-headed mother', standing in a niche of the post supporting the main beam of the building, and decorated with roses. All these Classical references speak of Epona purely as a goddess of stables, but this interpretation of her symbolism demonstrates a superficial, uninformed attitude to the cult. As we shall see, the iconography hints at a far more profound set of beliefs.

Before we leave Graeco-Roman literary observations on Epona, it is worth looking at an obscure Greek text by a writer called Agesilaos, who recounts a curious tale concerning the genesis of Epona. The story is about a misogynist called Phoulouios Stellos, who copulates with a mare, the result of the union being a beautiful baby girl to whom the mare herself gives the name Epona.[78] According to this myth, Epona is very close to being a zoomorphic divinity, as indeed she is described in Apuleius' allusion to her. Markale[79] sees resemblances between this story and an Ulster mythic ritual recorded in the medieval period by Giraldus Cambrensis, in which the Irish sacral king was inaugurated by means of a horse-ceremony.[80] Epona is not mentioned in this myth, but the ritual clearly involves a sacred union between the king and the goddess of sovereignty (see Chapter 4), the personification of territory and fertility symbolised as a mare. We need to see if any of these characteristics can be applied to Epona herself.

In addition to her invocation in many different areas of Celtic Europe Epona, like the mother-goddesses, appealed to a wide social spectrum: she was important to soldiers, both officers and men, serving in the Rhine frontier provinces, especially cavalrymen, but she was equally popular in the small, private house-shrines of Burgundy. Indeed, only one public temple to Epona is recorded in Gaul, at Entrains-sur-Nohain (Nièvre), where one of two inscriptions to the goddess from a ruined sanctuary records its dedication to Epona.[81] The reasons for this wide popularity must lie in the qualities perceived in the goddess herself, and her nature can only properly be understood by examining the symbolism contained within her iconography.

Two main types of image depicting Epona can be distinguished: the first, which is the more common, appears all over Gaul and the Rhineland. This group consists of representations of the goddess seated side-saddle on a mare; a sub-type, occurring particularly in Burgundy, shows a foal asleep beneath its mother, suckling or following her or eating food offered to it by the goddess. Stone carvings at Santenay, Autun and Mellecy exemplify the mare-and-foal imagery.[82] This is overt symbolism of fertility and plenty, and these Burgundian sculptures may also reflect the craft of horse-breeding itself. Many other depictions of Epona repeat the imagery of abundance: she frequently holds loaves of bread or fruit. At Kastel near Bonn and at Dalheim in Luxembourg, Epona is represented with large circular emblems of fruit or bread.[83] The second main group of images depicts Epona standing or seated between two or more ponies or horses. On a British bronze group from Wiltshire, the goddess sits between two ponies, one male, one female, feeding them from a dish of corn.[84] On stone monuments at Beihingen near Stuttgart and Seegraben near Zurich, Epona is at the centre of large groups of horses, which turn respectfully towards her as if in homage.[85]

So far, the iconography of Epona points to two main types of symbolism, fertility and the horse itself. But other images, and also the context in which some depictions have been found, reveal different aspects of her cult. Epona is often accompanied by a dog, which, as we saw earlier, could symbolise healing or death, and both these concepts were relevant to Epona's cult. Such images of Epona occur throughout Gaul, from Medingen in Luxembourg to Rouillac in Aquitaine.[86] That healing was an important aspect of Epona's cult is suggested by her presence at healing spring-sanctuaries such as Luxeuil (Haute Saône) and Allerey (Côte d'Or), where the goddess appears in the guise of a water-nymph.[87]

Epona had a strong link with death: a funerary plaque at Agassac in South-west Gaul depicts the goddess on horseback, accompanied by sea-monsters and celestial symbols,[88] perhaps in reflection of her role as guardian of the dead in their journey over the ocean to the Otherworld, in the same way as dolphins were Classical symbols of the marine journey of the soul to the Isles of the Blessed. According to Irish myth, the Celts, too, believed that access to the Otherworld could be gained by sea. The cemetery of La Horgne-au-Sablon at Metz, the tribal capital of the Mediomatrici, produced several monuments to Epona, including one on which the infernal symbolism is plain: Epona rides her mare, followed by a human whom she is leading, perhaps to the afterlife.[89] The raven which, together with a dog, accompanies the goddess at Altrier, may also reflect her chthonic dimension. At Grand (Vosges) and Gannat (Allier), Epona carries a key, which has been interpreted as both that of the stable and of the entrance to the Otherworld.[90] By contrast, the *mappa* or napkin the goddess bears at Mussig-Vicenz near Strasbourg may represent the beginning rather than the end of life: in Roman sport, the *mappa* was associated with horses, being used as a kind of starter's flag to begin horse-races. If Epona's key could symbolise her concern with life after death, the *mappa* perhaps reflects her protection of the beginning of life. We know that the mother-goddesses (Chapter 5) had just such dualistic symbolism and that their imagery could represent both fertility and the journey of humankind through life to death. Like the mother-goddesses, Epona seems – both from her context and her imagery – to have been associated with life, fecundity, plenty, healing and with guardianship of souls beyond the grave. The link between Epona and the Mothers sometimes seems extremely close. at Thil-Châtel in Burgundy an inscription refers to the goddess as the 'Eponas';[91] and at Hagondange (Moselle), Epona is depicted as a triple image,[92] almost as if she was conflated with the *Deae Matres* themselves.

However diverse Epona's cult seems to have been, one element gives it cohesion,

and that is its horse-symbolism, which is constant and clearly central to her veneration. Horses were important animals in Celtic society, reflective of prestige and
esteemed for their beauty, speed, intelligence and bravery in battle.[93] The ownership
of a horse was the mark of a nobleman: Caesar's *equites* belonged to the highest
stratum of Gaulish society.[94] Celtic cavalry was renowned throughout the known
world, and Gaulish horses were an integral part of the Imperial Roman Army. So it is
no surprise that a horse-deity was so popular among the cavalrymen of the Rhineland
armies: one dedicant was a military riding-instructor.[95] To them, Epona must have
been a divine protectress both of themselves and their horses. The more domestic
aspect of her worship, evidenced particularly among the Burgundian Aedui and
Lingones, was perhaps associated with the perception of Epona as goddess of
horse-breeding.

There is, perhaps, a further dimension to Epona's cult, which serves to link her
military and her domestic popularity and which, furthermore, is appropriate to a
goddess concerned with life, fertility, healing and death. It is possible that Epona was,
in some sense, a goddess of sovereignty, of territory and the tribe. The early Celtic kings
were traditionally selected from the knightly élite of society, a society where the ability
to afford a fighting-horse was a mark of high status. Sovereignty involves the guardianship of tribal boundaries and the keeping of peace within them so that the business
of raising crops and livestock can progress undisturbed. The feminine nature of
Epona's cult is important: she is female and so is her horse. This is surely a deliberate
identification of a spiritual entity in whom the power of fertility was intense. Military
personnel may have venerated her because she represented the protection of land, not
only the territory they were defending but also their own homelands, which were
perhaps far away.

Of all the goddesses associated with animals, Epona above all illustrates the complex
relationship between divinity and sacred beast. She was not herself a horse, although
Classical literary references – in my opinion mistakenly – imply this identification.
However, she was, in a real sense, identified through her equine imagery and the
message of her concerns was conveyed by the constant presence of the animal in her
iconography. The horse could represent many things: prestige and sovereignty, war
and guardianship, prosperity and plenty. The cult of Epona embraced all these roles,
and more besides.

9 From Goddess to Saint

There is evidence of Christianity and of the existence of holy men and women in the Celtic west during the fifth and sixth centuries AD. Indeed, some Britons in the late Roman period were Christians:[1] one of the curses dedicated at the shrine of Sulis at Bath alludes to the victim as either pagan or Christian. But these early followers of the new faith were operating within a society that seems still to have been predominantly pagan.[2] The multiplicity of Celtic gods and goddesses was gradually replaced by one God, but the vacuum left by these multifarious spirits was, to an extent, filled by the numerous saints of the early Church, although pagan beliefs and superstitions may well have co-existed with Christianity at least until the seventh century AD. Some of the early Celtic saints were historical entities, nuns and monks whose lives led to their canonisation. But the genuine historicity of others is questionable and these may, like their pagan predecessors, have been largely the result of mythic tradition.

This final chapter is concerned with the transition from paganism to Christianity, particularly in Ireland and Wales, for it is here that there is substantive evidence for early female saints, whose powers and character show marked resemblances to those which are identifiable in the goddesses of pagan tradition. It is at least possible, therefore, that female saints were deliberately endowed with a kind of pseudo-divine status by their hagiographers or that some of these saints were, in fact, originally goddesses, transmuted into 'historical' holy women by their chroniclers. Whilst many modern hagiographers do not take seriously the notion that saints might represent Christianised pagan deities and whilst there is little direct evidence of the adoption of pagan Celtic divinities as saints, there is nonetheless much in their respective roles that owes something to shared tradition. Indeed, there is evidence, as we shall see below, that some pagan deities and heroes of the early Celtic myths were sanctified and absorbed into the Christian Church by transformation into saints. Like heroes, saints can perhaps be regarded as intermediaries between humans and a remote God. They were perceived as bridging the gulf between the human and divine worlds, super-human but not un-human and able to intercede on behalf of humankind. As we shall see, some saints' Lives (*Vitae*), early chronicles of their birth, lives and spiritual power, make specific reference to the interface of paganism and Christianity. Mention is also made of this transitional world in the vernacular mythic tradition of Ireland and Wales.

Women, Virginity and Christianity

The impact of Christianity upon Celtic women varied within Celtic regions as, indeed, did the status of women generally. Irish and Welsh women appear readily to have accepted the ethics of chastity and Christian values, and by AD 800 there was a strong tradition of holy women who became saints, nuns and abbesses. By contrast, there is no record of early Breton saints.[3] Although Christianity was itself male-dominated and androcentric, its essentially peace-oriented ethos may have attracted Irish women, who perhaps saw the new faith as a means of reducing warfare. Saint Adomnán is the alleged author of a document dating to the seventh century AD, called the *Cáin Adomnán* (the Law of Adomnán) (see also Chapter 1) which is a kind of pro-Christianity propaganda-document. Its apparent purpose was to persuade Irish people, and women in particular, to adopt the Christian faith and abandon the old pagan warrior-society. Adomnán speaks of the adverse condition of women under the old system, their servile status and enforced involvement in battle.[4] Since this text is primarily a piece of image-projection, its factual reliability must be suspect, but certainly the new faith may have offered women an alternative to the status quo. Those who eschewed marriage and male control could choose to adopt celibacy, retire from the secular world and perhaps enjoy considerable power as founders and controllers of monastic establishments. In this early Christian period, virginity meant freedom for women to step outside the bonds of tribal society.[5]

Celtic holy women were virgins but, at the same time, they were symbolic mothers, responsible for the well-being of their people and lands.[6] Indeed, as their model, they looked to the Virgin Mary, herself chaste when she became the Mother of Christ. Mary is presented to us as the essence of womanhood but, paradoxically, her image is that of a virtually asexual being, and one who is wholly subservient to her son. This characterisation has its parallel in Celtic myth: Arianrhod, in the Fourth Branch of the *Mabinogi*, is described as a virgin-mother, whose son, Lleu, attained far higher rank than she enjoyed. With Arianrhod, however, there was ambiguity in her virgin status (see Chapter 3). There is reason to believe that the cult of the Virgin Mary in the early Christian period had strong links with that of the pagan Celtic mother-goddesses. Jean Markale[7] cites a clear example: on the site where Chartres Cathedral was to be built there was a subterranean sanctuary on which stood a statue of a mother-goddess. The shrine was known as 'Our Lady under the Ground'.

Mary was not a Celtic saint but her cult had much in common with that of canonised women in Wales and Ireland and, indeed, with pagan Celtic goddesses. One way in which this manifested itself was in the association between Mary, holy water and healing. Sacred wells with alleged curative powers were dedicated to her all over Wales: Penrhys in Glamorgan and Hafod-y-Llyn in Merioneth are just two examples.[8] Outside the Celtic world, the link between Mary and healing has remained strong up until the present day in many Catholic countries. I recently visited an ancient rock-cut shrine containing a spring dedicated to the Virgin at Mellieha in Malta. This sanctuary predates the large main church on the hill above it. Legend has it that the original statue of Mary by the spring was moved to a 'more respectable place within the main church' but that during the night she always moved back down the forty steps to her old position by the spring.[9] It is not known how old the original shrine is but it may date back at least eight hundred years. The curative power of Mary's spring at Mellieha is believed to be intense: the rock walls of the shrine are lined with modern offerings to Mary the Healer, in prayer or thanksgiving. These take the form of framed baby-clothes, X-rays, plaster-casts from broken limbs, crash-helmets and silver model eyes, hearts and other organs, these last almost identical to the gifts made two thousand years earlier to sanctuaries of pagan healer-goddesses such as Sequana (see Chapter 5).

The Rise of the Celtic Saints

The holy men and women of the early Celtic Christian tradition appear to have had a great deal in common with pagan mythic hero-figures, so much so that Elissa Henken[10] calls the Welsh saints a Christianised form of pagan Celtic folk-hero. Like the gods whom they (at least partially) replaced in the fifth and sixth centuries AD, they were benefactors, purveyors of plenty, law-givers, healers, controllers of the elements and of animals.

The prose Lives of the Welsh saints were mainly compiled in written form in the twelfth and thirteenth centuries. But some of these saints allegedly lived much earlier, some during the fifth and sixth centuries. Whilst many may well have been genuine historical entities, others may indeed belong to the world of Christian myth, sometimes perhaps because, like the gods, they were personifications of springs or other features of the landscape.

The lives of the Welsh saints have certain features in common. They were usually of gentle birth and their conception, birth and early development were often associated with strange circumstances. The birth of a saint may be prophesied and he or she may in some way be marginalised within society, illegitimate or fatherless, or otherwise outside the norm. It is this very abnormality which, at the same time, endowed them with potency and associated them with danger. All these features are also found in the descriptions of pagan mythic heroes. Likewise, the childhoods of both saints and heroes are characterised by abnormal precocity both in physical development and percipience. The lives of many female Welsh saints are distinctive in that it is possible to discern a common pattern: it is an unwelcome sexual encounter which causes them to withdraw from society and take up the celibate life of a holy woman.[11] So whilst the lives of male saints focus on their birth and childhood as well as adulthood, the record

The sacred healing well of Saint Dwynwen on Llanddwyn Island, off the coast of Anglesey, where she is said to have founded a church and convent. Although a virgin, Dwynwen was the patron saint of lovers.

of the female saints is centred upon their response to male sexuality. This can be seen in the lives of Gwenfrewi (Winifride), Dwynwen and Melangell. The same phenomenon is also chronicled in the life of the Irish saint Brigit, although her conception, birth and early life are also important.

A brief examination of two early Welsh female saints demonstrates their close link with a supernatural world which is at least as pagan as it is Christian. Divination, powers of healing and protection of animals were some of the roles of these holy women, just as they were for many goddesses. Healing, often linked with well-water, is particularly stressed: for both goddess and saint the power of healing was based upon the ability to 'see' their way through to the Otherworld and connect with its force.[12]

(*Left*) Drawing of Saint Gwenfrewi (Winifride) holding a model of her church at Holywell, Clwyd; by 'a student of Pugin'; frontispiece to Thomas Meyrick's *Life of Saint Wenefred*, London 1878.

(*Right*) Sketch of crutches and boots offered as votive gifts by Victorian pilgrims to Saint Winifride's sacred healing well at Holywell, Clwyd. From the *Daily Graphic*, 2 October 1894.

Both Dwynwen and Grenfrewi were curative saints: Saint Dwynwen is thought to have died in about AD 545.[13] She was a virgin-hermit who founded a nunnery and a church on Llanddwyn Island off the coast of Anglesey. Her holy well had miraculous therapeutic properties, particularly for animals, but Dwynwen's main role, curiously enough in view of her own celibate state, was as a patron of lovers. The legend of Dwynwen must be viewed with some caution in terms of its authenticity because it was first told in full only as recently as the eighteenth century by the Welsh bard Iolo Morgannwg, whose romantic desire to promote links between modern Wales and remote antiquity caused him to ignore the demands of academic rigour in his recording. The legend of Dwynwen centres around her rejection of the advances of Maelon, a would-be lover, because such a union was outside marriage. After Maelon left her in anger, she prayed that she would be cured of her illicit love for him. God granted Dwynwen certain wishes, including one that should lovers not be steadfast in their affection, they would be cured of their desire; and another that she, Dwynwen, would never wish to be married. The saint's holy well not only had a curative function but was also the focus of Dwynwen's divinatory powers, to whom suppliants came to foretell success or failure in love.[14]

Saint Gwenfrewi (Winifride is the Anglicised version of her name), like Dwynwen, is associated with a holy well, at Holywell near St Asaph in Clwyd. The legend of Winifride has an authentic early pedigree, in that she was the niece of Saint Beuno, a sixth-century abbot. The well itself is documented as early as the eleventh century. Winifride's story has further similarities to that of Dwynwen, in that the focus of her legend is her refusal of the attentions of the young prince Caradoc ap Alyn. In vengeance at his rejection, Caradoc drew his sword and beheaded Winifride. At the point her head touched the ground, a spring gushed out of the dry rock. Saint Beuno restored Winifride to life by replacing her head on her body: only a thin white line round her neck bore witness to her ordeal. Beuno then cursed Caradoc and the earth rose up and swallowed him. His descendants were also blighted so that they barked like dogs until they had made a pilgrimage to the sacred well. Winifride's well is a famous curative shrine which has been visited by pilgrims from all over the world.[15]

Pagan Magic and Christian Miracle

The transition from pagan belief to Christian faith was by no means clear-cut; it is possible to trace features common to them both. This is demonstrable by reference both to Celtic ritual and to documentary sources which specifically allude to the juxtaposition of the two religious systems. In both, the role played by females is crucial.

We have already mentioned manifestations of cult-expression which seem to straddle pagan and Christian practice. The most common are rituals associated with healing and particularly curative wells. The cults of Mary and of several female and male saints are centred on their miraculous therapeutic powers, in which springs and well-water were the instrument of the healing process. Wells were the foci of pre-Christian curative ritual all over pagan Celtic Europe (Chapter 5), and many Romano-Celtic healing-spring sanctuaries belonged to goddesses, such as Sulis of Bath and the Burgundian Sequana. The continuation of the healing-well cult from a pagan to Christian context argues for a basic continuity of tradition, whereby magic and miracle merged in a seamless progression.

A number of early Welsh saints presided over Welsh holy wells, which they may have inherited from pagan spirits. What is frustrating is that comparatively little archaeological investigation has taken place at the sites of such wells,[16] thus making it impossible to assess the antiquity of their sanctity. Winifride was by no means the only saint whose severed head produced a miraculous well. The heads of the female saint Llud and the male saint Decuman, both beheaded in the sixth century AD, caused

(*Right*) Print from a steel engraving dated to 1854, showing the interior of Saint Winifride's church at Holywell, Clwyd.

holy springs to spout from the earth. Many other saints, too, were associated with healing wells: Saint Cadfan's shrine at Tywyn in Gwynedd, established in AD 516, had a reputation for curing rheumatism, and Saint Canna had a holy well the water of which she used to cure intestinal ailments.[17] The magical or miraculous curative properties of such wells came about either as a result of the violent death of a holy man or woman, or to mark miracles performed by saints, or because the holy person bathed in or drank from the water, thus endowing it with sanctity. The saints associated with these wells are very often obscure, there being little known about their lives. The other interesting point is that some holy wells are associated with the production of milk and curds: Saint Winifride's well produced milk for three days after her murder.[18] This particular phenomenon would appear to be associated with perceptions of spring-water as a life-force, perhaps linked with the symbolic maternity of Celtic holy women.

In early Irish myth, certain females appear to span the two worlds of pagan and Christian tradition. Of these, the goddess/saint Brigit is by far the most prominent, and she is discussed separately below. But a comparatively late Irish text, the *Altram Tige dá Medar*, describes an episode in which there is a direct clash between paganism and

Eng & Pub by Newman & Co 48 Watling St London

Interior of St Winifred's Well

Christianity, and thus arguably refers back to the fifth century AD, or even earlier. The story concerns Oenghus and Manannán, two gods of the Tuatha Dé Danann, members of the divine race of Ireland who, according to the Mythological Cycle, inhabited the country before the Celts. In the story the two gods were discussing the existence of a higher divine power, greater than themselves; they agreed that there was such a one, the Almighty God of the Christian faith. The text then chronicles the life of Eithne, a woman whose story epitomises the transition to the new religion. Eithne was insulted by Oenghus' brother and this caused her guardian devil to desert her, its place being taken by a guardian angel. Manannán prophesied that Eithne would now renounce druidry and devilry in favour of the holy Trinity. Eithne became a holy woman, founding a chapel at Brugh ná Bóinne (the site of Oenghus' palace) and, when she died, she became a saint.[19]

Goddess and Saint: the Enigma of Brigit

In the early Christian period, many pagan deities were downgraded to the status of demons, but occasionally the attributes of a particular divinity were reallocated to an appropriate saint. This appears to have occurred in the case of Brigit. Not only is the name shared by a goddess and a saint, but there appears to have been some commonality in function.[20]

Brigit the Goddess

The name Brigit comes from the Celtic word *brig* which is suggestive of power and authority and means 'High One' or 'Exalted One'. So in a sense, like many Celtic god-names, Brigit is a title rather than a true name. The same root gave rise to the name Brigantia, a goddess of the Brigantes (sometimes thought to be the same deity as the Irish Brigit) who had a huge tribal hegemony in north Britain before and during the Roman period. Brigantia's name points to her role as personification and protector of her tribe: at Birrens, an image of the goddess accompanied by a dedicatory inscription, depicts her wearing the mural crown of a tutelary deity. Iconography demonstrates a link between Brigantia and the high Roman goddesses Victory and Minerva.[21] Indeed, Brigit herself is sometimes identified with Minerva, since both Celtic and Roman goddesses were associated with crafts and with healing.[22]

The nature of Brigit and her pagan and Christian identity are extremely complex problems over which there is a great deal of controversy. According to Irish myth, the

(*Right*) Stone relief of the tribal goddess Brigantia from the Roman military site of Birrens, Dumfriesshire. The goddess wears Minerva's symbol of the Gorgon's head on her breast and a mural crown; she carries a spear and the globe of victory.

goddess Brigit was the daughter of the Dagdha, an important member of the Tuatha Dé Danann. She was both a single and a triple goddess, with two eponymous sisters, and she had multifarious roles as patron of poetry, crafts (including smithing, dyeing, weaving and brewing), seers and doctors. As a healer, the goddess particularly protected women in childbirth. Brigit was also a fertility-spirit, whose feast-day of Imbolc on 1 February was one of the great Celtic seasonal festivals. Imbolc celebrated the birth of lambs and the lactation of ewes, and Brigit was active in promoting the welfare of livestock, especially cattle. In the myth of the Battle of Magh Tuiredh, which chronicles the great conflict between the Tuatha Dé Danann and their demon-enemies the Fomorians for the possession of Ireland, Brigit appeared as mediator between the two. Although the daughter of the Dagdha, she was also married to the Fomorian king, Bres. Here Brigit is presented as an ancestor-deity, a mother-goddess whose main concern was the future well-being of Ireland.[23]

Little is known in detail about the goddess Brigit. There is a danger of creating a picture of her pagan role from information we have of Brigit as a saint, because certain elements of her life as a Christian holy woman appear to be pre-Christian in origin. An example of this is the saint's magical association with fire, which has given rise to the deity being identified as a fire-goddess.

Brigit the Saint

We know about Saint Brigit from a number of sources, of which the earliest appears to be the Latin version of her Life, the *Vita Brigitae*, by Cogitosus, which dates to the seventh century AD. The first vernacular Irish Life of Brigit is the *Bethu Brigte*, and in this document the saint is presented as a contemporary of Saint Patrick, who lived in the earlier fifth century AD, but her flowering is generally considered to be from the late fifth to the early sixth century, and her monastery of Kildare is reputed to have been founded in AD 490. Although Brigit is said to have been the founder-abbess of Kildare, there is no firm evidence for the abbess as a historical figure; descriptions of her life are based almost entirely on legend, which gives rise to the suspicion that she may be a mythic figure who underwent a humanisation-process and was thus endowed with a false historicity.[24] The cult of Saint Brigit was not confined to Ireland but was also popular in Scotland, Wales (where she was known as Saint Ffraid), Cornwall, Brittany and the Isle of Man.

This chapter is concerned with the interface of paganism and Christianity and so the primary interest of Saint Brigit here lies in her links with her goddess-namesake and with pre-Christian tradition in general. The accounts of Saint Brigit's birth and childhood show a very direct association with Celtic paganism and the supernatural. She was reared in the household of a druid and, according to some traditions, he was her father. The young girl was made ill by the pagan druid's food and was, instead, fed on the milk of a special white, red-eared cow. This is significant because creatures of this colouring belonged to the Irish mythic tradition of the Otherworld.[25] The druid realised that Brigit's rejection of his food was because he was unclean and she was pure, full of the Holy Spirit, a quality which he recognised and respected. The druid's susceptibility to Christian influence is shown by the vision which he had when the infant Brigit joined his household: three Christian clergy appeared to him in a dream, one proclaiming 'Let Brigit be the name of the girl for you.' So the druid was apparently divinely inspired by a Christian apparition to give the baby the name of a prestigious Celtic goddess. The maternal uncle of this druid was a Christian and it was he who announced the child's holy status.[26]

The life of Saint Brigit is steeped in magic and miraculous happenings, some of which bear a strong resemblance to those surrounding a superhuman, heroic figure of pagan myth. Brigit's association with fire, liminality and prophecy serve to illustrate this connection with pre-Christian tradition. The fire-symbolism is related to a story of the saint's early life, when Brigit's relatives saw a fire rising from the house where the child and her mother were asleep. The fire was shown to be magical: like the burning bush encountered by Moses in the Old Testament, the fire glowed but did not consume the house, and the occupants emerged unharmed. Brigit's monastery at Kildare had an ever-burning fire, like that of the Vestal Virgins of Roman religion. When the Normans arrived at Kildare in the twelfth century, they found a fire constantly alight in the saint's shrine there, a symbol of hearth and home but also of purity. Many saints are associated with fire-imagery, a symbol of the link with the power of God. But some scholars have argued for a connection between Saint Brigit and the pagan goddess Sulis Minerva, whose sacred fire at Bath was recorded by Solinus in the third century AD (see Chapter 5). Certainly both Brigit and Minerva were patrons of crafts. 'Brigit's Crosses' are solar emblems which are still set up in Ireland to protect crops and livestock.[27]

Liminality or boundary-symbolism is traditionally associated with both pagan supernatural beings and Christian saints. Brigit's liminal imagery is intense and manifests itself in various ways. She belonged to both the pagan and Christian worlds; she was born at sunrise, her mother straddling a threshold at the precise time of her birth; one parent, her father Dubthach, was of noble lineage, while her mother, Broicseth, was a slave-woman. Brigit was nourished on the milk of an Otherworld cow, as we have seen, and this increases her symbolism as a being linked to two worlds.[28]

Both the goddess Brigit and the saint of that name were closely associated with prophecy and divination. She was a patron of poet-seers, the Irish learned class of *filidh*, in her capacity both as deity and Christian holy woman. The saint's own childhood was marked with portents and omens, of which the most significant was a prophecy uttered by Brigit as an infant, when she was heard to murmur in her sleep while still too young to speak. The druid was able to interpret her words, which were that the land where she dwelled would belong to her in the future.

Saint Brigit is a paradox, like many goddesses of Irish myth. She remained a virgin but one of her most prominent roles was as a provider of plenty, like a mother-goddess, and she was also a patron of pregnant women. In all these respects, she is analogous to Artemis/Diana of the Graeco-Roman pantheon. The maternal functions were shared by the goddess and the saint. Like many of the early Welsh female holy women, Saint Brigit's virginity is central to her separation from secular life, with all its constraints upon females. She deliberately ruined her beauty and thus her marriageability by blinding herself in one eye. This mutilation gave her freedom to take her vows and promoted her inner beauty of purity, which was so much deeper than that of the body. This paradox is matched by that of her symbolic motherhood. Although virgin, she stimulated fertility and, indeed, was able to cure frigidity in women.[29]

The image of Saint Brigit as a generous provider is indistinguishable from that of the pagan mother-goddesses. Her hospitality symbolism began with her own life-style: her Lives chronicle the annoyance she caused to her family by giving away to the poor precious objects belonging to her father. This 'redistributive generosity' has its roots in a tradition which was well-known in pagan Celtic society, where valuable gifts of weapons and jewellery were circulated between noble families in an obligatory exchange of wealth. Brigit's habit of gift-giving was associated with her miraculous ability to promote fertility and abundance. One manifestation of this is her dairy symbolism. She was a protector of cattle and was reputed to inflict such savage punishments as drowning or scalding upon anyone who dared to steal her cows. In later Christian art, Brigit is frequently represented with a cow by her side. In the Hebrides, she was called the 'Golden-haired Bride of the Kine'. Saint Brigit retained her namesake's pagan spring-festival of Imbolc, a celebration of the lactation of livestock. Examples of her miraculous bounty include the lake of milk that her cows, milked three times a day, could produce; and one churning could fill several baskets with butter. As Abbess of Kildare, Brigit possessed the power to increase the milk-and butter-yield. Her prowess as a provider was not confined to dairy-produce: like her goddess-predecessor, she was patron of the ale-harvest and, at Easter-time, one measure of her malt could make sufficient ale for seventeen of her churches. She could also change water into ale and stone into salt. Her larder was a source of limitless food and never dwindled. These changing-miracles recall Christ's miracles of turning water into wine at the marriage-feast of Cana and the episodes of the loaves and fishes. The strength of Brigit's fertility-imagery is suggested by the medieval carvings of Sheela-na-gigs in Ireland, interpreted by some scholars as grotesque depictions of Brigit with the entrance to her womb wide-open, even though the saint was a virgin.[30] As we saw with some of the Welsh goddesses (see Chapter 3), it may be that it was because Brigit was sexually-intact that her fertile power was so concentrated.

Modern statue dedicated to Saint Brigit at her holy well, Kilaire, Co. Westmeath, Ireland, one of the numerous wells at which the saint is still venerated today.

Like her Welsh holy sisters, Brigit was associated with healing and with sacred wells. At Fouchart in Ireland, a well sacred to the saint is still the focus of cult-practice, involving visiting pilgrims hanging rags by the spring in her honour. It should be stated that the practice of venerating wells in this way is not a specifically Celtic custom: it still exists outside the bounds of modern Celtic regions, for example in Turkey. These cloths are linked with the healing and general well-being of people and animals, particularly cattle, and with increasing milk-production.

So what is the relationship between the goddess and the saint? Clearly the two Brigits have many features in common: both were healers, promoters of fertility and childbirth, patrons of craftsmen, seers and poets. All these shared traditions argue for a pagan origin for the Christian saint,[31] as does the festival of Imbolc which celebrated both Brigits. The shared name or title 'Exalted One' is also significant. We need to consider in what way, if any, the pagan deity became a Christian holy woman and saint. Was the name of the goddess deliberately adopted for the saint in order to enhance the Christian cause in pagan Ireland? Is our knowledge of the goddess derived in part from the Lives of Brigit the saint? When Christianity came to Ireland, the new faith faced not only a strongly stratified society dominated by a warrior-élite but also the powerful religious figure of Brigit. Was she perhaps taken over and modified in order to attract devotees of her cult to a new belief-system? The Lives of saints are themselves an amalgam of myth and folklore. They were compiled partly as a propaganda exercise, to attract revenue to particular monasteries. So it would not be surprising if pagan and Christian tradition were subtly intertwined in the stories of these early religious leaders. Even Brigit's monastery at Kildare is linked with symbolism that is essentially pagan: the name Kildare is derived from *cill-daro*, the 'Church of the Oak', and Brigit's sacred oak-tree was so numinous that no-one could place a weapon near it.[32] Oaks and other trees had special sanctity in pagan Celtic religion and myth.[33] The saint is also alleged to have drawn the boundaries of her monastery by spreading her cloak as far as it would go, the implication being that it was of supernatural size.

Whether or not Saint Brigit ever existed, there is no doubt that she represents the meeting and merging of paganism and Christianity. Thus the great goddess of Ireland was translated into her greatest Christian saint.

Epilogue

The Power of the Divine Female in Early Celtic Religion

This book has set out to present a picture of Celtic religion in which goddesses played a central role. Unlike monotheistic systems, where the gender of the deity is unequivocally male, the polytheistic perception of the Celtic supernatural world allowed for its representation in terms of a rich palimpsest of male and female spirits, where the goddesses were recognised as possessing enormous – and sometimes terrible – powers.

The use of both archaeological and literary evidence for exploring the role of divine females presents us with a number of difficulties. The archaeological data is, in one sense, the more direct but, even if we have both a name and an image of a goddess, we have to build a picture of her cult and her persona by means of such circumstantial evidence as her symbolism and the nature of the offerings made to her. We have to make assumptions about beliefs based upon observation of surviving material evidence, and such an exercise will inevitably present problems of interpretation. The account of divine women given in the literature, especially that of vernacular myth, is even more problematical. As is always the case with mythic stories, it is necessary to strip away some of the legend in order to lay bare perceptions which must have had their origin in a pagan belief-system.

The prominence of female divinities in Celtic religion is, I think, closely linked with the perception of the supernatural as a whole. The Celtic world consisted, essentially, of rural communities and remained so, to a large extent, even after the introduction of urban culture by the Romans. So the close tie with the landscape and natural phenomena was maintained. Most Celtic goddesses and gods were nature-spirits (as, in origin, were most Roman deities), whose roots lay deep in the countryside. Within this framework of religious perception, female spirits found their place alongside and, in some instances, above their male counterparts.

In this book I have attempted to demonstrate the wide-ranging concerns of the Celtic goddesses. They were all, in a sense, protectors, guardians whose functions as deities of land, water, fertility, healing and animals all arose directly from their close link with the natural world. But their concerns also embraced wider, more profound concepts than those resulting from their control of the landscape, though this remained the fundamental source of their power and, indeed, gave rise to their deeper symbolic links with such concepts as warrior-guardianship, sovereignty and human destiny. Much of the power of these goddesses appears to have stemmed, directly or indirectly, from their sexuality. This is clearly indicated in their more obvious roles as spirits of fertility and abundance, but sexual energy was also associated with warfare, sovereignty and healing.

An apparent paradox – which is presented particularly in the early myths – is that both virginity and marriage generated special power in the female. Sexuality played an important role in the stories of Ireland and Wales, where superficially women were passive, powerless individuals. In fact, such women were enablers, catalysts for change, and their relationship with men triggered significant events. Connections between the Otherworld and the human world occurred because of sexual attraction between spirits and mortals. The sexual challenge for a girl between young lovers and older men (suitors or fathers) seems to represent conflict between the old and new orders, which was caused by the female. Interestingly, at the interface of Celtic paganism and Christianity, it was often a sexual encounter which led women to take vows of chastity, adopt the holy life and, later, to become saints.

The Celtic goddesses were by no means tied to the 'female' concerns of procreation and domesticity: they were powerful divine entities, invoked equally by women and men, and their functions embraced the entire religious spectrum: from warfare to healing; from sovereignty to death; from abundance to destiny; from nourishment to the Otherworld. Their potency arose partly from their dualism and ambiguity: they could protect and destroy; cure and curse; they provided nourishment but also predicted and controlled life's end. They could be capricious and vengeful but also gentle and benevolent. Their treatment of humans depended on the respect shown to them. Suppliants who visited their shrines with gifts, prayers and vows, and who accorded them proper reverence, were perhaps granted their desires: a good harvest, a baby, better sight, victory over an enemy. Those who neglected them or committed sacrilege could expect the reverse:

To the goddess Sulis ... whether slave or free, whoever he shall be, you are not to permit him eyes or health unless blindness and childlessness so long as he shall live, unless he return these to the temple.[1]

Notes

Abbreviations used in notes

C.I.L. Corpus Inscriptionum Latinarum 1863–1986 (Berlin)

Espérandieu Espérandieu, E. 1907–66. *Recueil Général des bas-reliefs de la Gaule romaine et pré-romaine* (Paris)

R.I.B. Collingwood, R.G. and Wright, R.P. 1965. *The Roman Inscriptions of Britain* (Oxford)

Prologue

1 *Histories* II, 35 and IV, 48

1 Women in Celtic Society

1 Kraemer 1992
2 Ehrenberg 1989, 22–3; Márkus 1992, 375–88
3 Kelly 1992, 77
4 Keaney 1993; Allason-Jones 1989
5 Megaw and Megaw 1989, 46–7
6 Ibid., 52
7 Ehrenberg 1989, 168–71
8 Megaw and Megaw 1989, 90–2
9 Dent 1985, 85–92
10 *Annales* XII, 35, 40; *Histories* III, 45
11 Ehrenberg 1989, 167
12 *Agricola* XXXI
13 Tacitus *Annales* XIV; *Roman History* LXII, 3–6
14 *Annales* XIV, 34
15 *Agricola* XVI
16 *History of Rome* LXII, 1, 7
17 *De Virtute Mulierum* 6; Pelletier 1984, 11–16
18 V, 28, 32
19 XV, 12
20 *De Bello Gallico* I, 18, 6–7
21 Ibid., V, 19
22 Ibid., V, 14, 4
23 *History of Rome* LXXVI, 12
24 Potter and Johns 1992, 12
25 Op.cit. VI, 19, 3
26 *Geography* IV, 4, 3

27 1989, 11–27
28 Allason-Jones 1989, 21
29 1984, 59–63
30 Márkus 1992, 375–88; Wood 1992, 132–3
31 Davies 1983, 145–66
32 Márkus 1992, 375–88; Davies 1983, 145–66; Melia 1983, 113–128
33 Kelly 1992, 78
34 1989, 172–4

2 Goddesses of War

1 1989, 151–2
2 *Cynegetica* XXIV; Brunaux 1988, 87–97; Green 1992b, 62
3 *Annales* XIV, 30
4 Ammianus Marcellinus *Histories* XV, 12; after Caldicott 1988, 4
5 Green 1992a, 70–2; Wood 1992, 123–5
6 V, 32, 2
7 IV, 4, 3
8 19, 9
9 Ehrenberg 1989, 164
10 *Germania* 18–20
11 e.g. *De Bello Gallico* I, 51, 3
12 IV, 18
13 Tacitus *Annales* XIV, 34
14 Green 1992b, 66–91; Ritchie and Ritchie 1985
15 Melia 1983, 113–28
16 Clark 1991, 1–2, 26–7; Markale 1975, 252–3
17 Markale 1975, 252–3
18 Jones and Jones 1976, 199
19 Markale 1975, 242
20 Caldecott 1988, 130; Kinsella 1969; O'Rahilly 1946, 61
21 Clark 1991, 29–30
22 Tacitus *Annales* XIV, 34
23 Potter and Johns 1992, 43
24 Tacitus *Annales* XIV, 30–5; Dio Cassius *History of Rome* LXII, 1ff.
25 Webster 1978, 15
26 Ibid., 87

27 Ibid., 113–25
28 Op. cit. LXII, 7, 1–3
29 de Vries 1963, 122; Duval 1976, 59
30 Webster 1978, 95
31 Wood 1992, 123–5
32 Hatt 1970, 134; Piggott 1965, 198–9
33 Green 1989, fig. 56
34 Green 1992b, 44–65
35 Abbaye de Daoulais 1987, 132–3; Green 1992b, 87
36 Olmsted 1979, pl. 3e; Diodorus V, 30, 2
37 Megaw 1970, 17
38 Green 1986, 175–89
39 de Vries 1963, 122f.; Duval 1987, 44–50; Green 1992c, 151–63
40 Olmsted 1979, pl. 2
41 Ross 1974, 279
42 Green 1976, 176
43 Green 1992c, 151–63; Linduff 1979, 817–37; Oaks 1986, 77–84
44 Ross 1974, 245–6, fig. 126
45 Green 1986, fig. 40
46 Green 1992a, 104–5
47 Lehner 1918–21, 74ff.
48 Ross 1974, 282, 286, 313
49 Deyts 1976, nos 3, 4; Espérandieu nos 1832, 2347, 2348, 7518
50 Green 1989, 64–5, fig. 26; Deyts 1976, no. 284; Espérandieu no. 2067
51 Green 1989, fig. 28
52 Hatt 1964, no. 101; C.I.L. XIII, 6072
53 Anati 1965; Green 1992b, 60; Hodder 1987, 62–3
54 Caldecott 1988, 242; Lehmann 1989, 1–10; Bhreathnach 1982, 243–60
55 Hennessy 1870–2, 37
56 Mac Cana 1970, 90; Green 1992a, 222–3
57 Ross 1974, 131
58 Green 1992a, 167–8; Mac Cana 1983, 122–31; O'Rahilly 1946, 106–122; Ross 1974, 285
59 Clark 1991, 32–5
60 Clark 1991, 32
61 Ross 1974, 281–3; Hennessy 1870–2, 32–5; Olmsted 1982, 165–72; Kinsella 1969; Stokes 1895, 65
62 Ross 1974, 284
63 Clark 1991, 44–5
64 Green 1992a, 154–5
65 Clark 1991, 50–1

3 The Divine Female in Welsh Myth

1 Jones and Jones 1976
2 Gruffydd 1953, 97, 106; Matthews 1987, 34
3 Jones and Jones 1976, 54
4 Gruffydd 1953, 97
5 *Topographica Hibernica* III
6 Zwicker 1934–6, 64; Markale 1975, 89–90
7 Ford 1987, 29–41
8 1987, 17
9 Gruffydd 1953, 55–60
10 1958, 161
11 Gruffydd 1953, 12
12 Jackson 1961–7, 83–99
13 Mac Cana 1958, 86
14 Jones and Jones 1976, 38
15 Mac Cana 1983; Green 1992a, 62
16 Jones and Jones 1976, 115–16
17 Markale 1975, 36
18 Green 1991a, 1–26
19 Jones and Jones 1976
20 Ford 1987, 29–41; Mac Cana 1958, 8
21 Mac Cana 1958, 151
22 Mac Cana 1958, 154–6
23 Mac Cana 1958, 179
24 Green 1993, 29–36
25 1958, 179
26 Jones and Jones 1976, 35
27 Ibid., 33–4
28 Mac Cana 1958, 98ff.
29 1987, 50
30 Jones and Jones 1976, 31
31 Jones and Jones 1976, 68; Green 1992a, 34
32 Markale 1975, 125–30
33 Gruffydd 1953, 4
34 Matthews 1987, 79
35 Ford 1987, 29–41
36 Green 1992a, 133–4
37 Matthews 1987, 80
38 Markale 1975, 161
39 Jones and Jones 1976, 74
40 Mac Cana 1958, 153
41 Jones and Jones 1976, 55
42 Caldecott 1988, 209–10; Matthews 1987, 77–8
43 Carey 1991, 24–38; Markale 1975, 130–1
44 Green 1993, 34
45 Mac Culloch 1992, 95–6
46 Carey 1991, 24–38
47 Green 1992a, 164–5

48 Green 1992a, 140; Bémont 1981, 65–88; *R.I.B.* 583, 1120–2; Richmond 1943, 206–10; Ross 1974, 276–7
49 Gruffydd 1953, 97ff.
50 Jones and Jones 1976, 95–136
51 Green 1992a, 211–12
52 Jones and Jones 1976, 111
53 Krappe 1927
54 Ford 1987, 29–41; Mac Cana 1958, 38–9
55 Jones and Jones 1976, xxiii
56 Matthews 1987, 114–20, 145; 1991; Rutherford 1987, 85; Markale 1975, 234–5; Henry 1979–80, 114–29
57 Green 1993, 20
58 Carey 1991, 24–38
59 Green 1986, 142–8

4 Sovereignty, Sexuality and the Otherworld in Irish Myth

1 Herbert 1992, 264
2 Green 1989, 9–44
3 Herbert 1992, 264–75; Márkus 1992, 375–88; Lyle 1992, 276–88
4 Herbert 1993
5 1993
6 Clark 1991, 29–34
7 Bhreathnach 1982, 243–60
8 Herbert 1993
9 Green 1992b, 60–5
10 Herbert 1993
11 1992, 118–36
12 O'Cruailaoich 1988, 161
13 Fradenburg 1992, 1–13
14 Binchy 1936; 1970; Wood 1992, 129
15 Watson 1981, 165–180
16 Mac Cana 1955–6, 76–114; 1958–9, 59–65
17 Wood 1992, 118–36
18 Herbert 1992, 264–75
19 Bhreathnach 1982, 243–60
20 Herbert 1992, 264
21 Herbert 1992, 264–75
22 Herbert 1992, 264–75; Wood 1992, 130
23 Condren 1989, 23–43; Hennessy 1870–2, 32–55; de Vries 1963, 136–7; Ross 1967, 219–29; Killeen 1974, 81–6; Mac Cana 1983, 86–9; Clark 1991, 114–15; Herbert 1993
24 Translation in hand-out provided by Herbert in lecture (Herbert 1993)
25 Ibid.
26 Stokes 1895, 31–83; Hennessy 1870–2, 32–55; Olmsted 1982, 165–72; Clark 1991, 33–4; Green 1992a, 154–5; Herbert 1993
27 1992, 264–75
28 1992, 77
29 Márkus 1992, 375–88
30 Lehmann 1989, 1–10
31 Kelly 1992, 81–2
32 Clark 1991, 126–37; Mac Cana 1958–9, 59–65; Hull 1938, 52–61; Green 1992a, 147–9
33 Green 1991b, *passim*; Cross and Slover 1936, 14; Mac Cana 1955–6, 76–114, 356–413; 1958–9, 59–65; Pokorny 1925, 197–202
34 Green 1993, 15–20
35 Mac Cana 1983, 86, 132; Sjoestedt 1949, 24f.; Green 1992a, 30
36 1992, 276–88
37 1974, 279
38 Clark 1991, 115–19
39 Bhreathnach 1982, 243–60
40 Knott 1936; Stokes 1900; 1901; Bhreathnach 1982, 243–60
41 Wagner 1981, 1–28; Herbert 1992, 264–75
42 Murphy 1953, 84; Mac Cana 1981, 143–59; O'Haocha 1989, 308–31; Davidson 1993b, 111–12
43 Márkus 1992, 375–88
44 Mac Cana 1972, 102–42; 1976, 95–115; Sims-Williams 1990, 57–81
45 Green 1993, 29–31
46 Jackson 1961–7, 83–99; Kinsella 1969; Ross 1967, 307; Dillon 1953
47 Mac Cana 1958, 105–7; 1983, 50–4
48 O'Rahilly 1946, 119–20; Mac Cana 1983, 104; Green 1993, 20
49 Mac Cana 1972, 102–42; 1976, 95–115; 1983, 69, 124
50 *Macbeth*, Act I, Scene 3

5 Water-Goddesses, Healers and Mothers

1 Allason-Jones 1989, 156
2 Bradley 1990; Fitzpatrick 1984, 178–90
3 Pelletier 1984, pl. 1
4 Ibid., pl. 40
5 Deyts 1992, 73–84
6 Green 1986, 150–1; Sandars 1984, 148
7 Deyts 1983; 1985; 1992; Green 1989, 40–1, 156–61, figs 16, 69–72

8 Potter and Johns 1992, 107–8
9 *Collectanea rerum memorabilium* 22, 10
10 Cunliffe 1978; 1988 (ed.), 1
11 Cunliffe 1994
12 Allason-Jones 1989, 156ff.
13 1985, 5–6
14 1988, 359–62
15 Walker 1988, 218–358
16 Cunliffe 1988, 359–62
17 Cunliffe 1978
18 Henig 1988, 6–28
19 Green 1991b
20 Ibid., 120–1
21 Gager 1992, 21
22 *Holy Wells of Wales*, 1954
23 Tomlin 1988, 58–277
24 Vitruvius 21
25 Tomlin 1988, no. 41
26 Potter and Johns 1992, 174–7
27 Allason-Jones and Mckay 1985
28 Ibid.
29 Allason-Jones and McKay 1985, 1–12,
      cat. nos 1, 3, 4
30 Green 1989, 42–3, 61–3; Dehn 1941,
      104ff.; Wightman 1970, 220–1, pl. 22;
      Jenkins 1957a, 60–76; Marache 1979, 15;
      Schindler 1977, 33, fig. 92; Szabó 1971, 66;
      Thevenot 1968, 103–4, 110
31 Wightman 1970, 211–23
32 Le Gall 1963, 157–9; Duval 1976, 77, 177;
      Thevenot 1968, 104–7; *C.I.L.* XIII, 5924;
      Green 1992a, 75–6
33 Vallentin 1879–80, 1–36
34 Aebischer 1930, 427–41
35 Deyts 1976, no. 9; 1992, 73–84
36 Wightman 1970, 217; Toussaint 1948,
      207–8
37 Wightman 1970, pl. 21d
38 Deyts 1992, 73–84
39 Green 1989, 191, fig. 84; Deyts 1976,
      no. 222
40 de Vries 1963, 130
41 Clébert 1970, 254
42 Green 1986, 209; *R.I.B.* 105, 106, 151,
      192; Szabó 1971, 65–6; Duval 1976, 87;
      Wightman 1970, 213ff.
43 Allason-Jones and McKay 1985, fig. 12
44 Espérandieu nos. 4786, 4831
45 1989, 77
46 Potter and Johns 1992, 160–4
47 Ibid.
48 Green 1986, 72–102; 1989, 169–205;
      1991c, 100–9; 1993
49 Deyts 1992, 59–72

50 Potter and Johns 1992, 160–4
51 Deyts 1976, no. 5
52 Deyts 1976, nos. 170, 171; 1992, 59–72;
      Green 1989, fig. 84
53 Green 1989, 194
54 von Petrikovits 1987, 241–54
55 Lehner 1918–21, 74ff.
56 Green 1989, fig. 66
57 Ristow 1975, fig. 41
58 Ibid., figs. 41–44
59 Taylor, A.; 1992, 1993, 194–201
60 Green 1986, 80–1; Anon. 1965, 1ff.
61 Rheinisches Landesmuseum Bonn 1973,
      Abb. 67, 70
62 Green 1986, 80; Hassall and Tomlin 1979,
      339–40; Henig 1984, 49–50
63 Potter and Johns 1992, 129
64 Green 1986, 82–3
65 Green 1986, figs 39, 40
66 Brewer 1986, no. 14, pl. 6
67 Le Gall 1963, 174; 1985, 68, fig. 39
68 Deyts 1992, 59–72
69 Megaw and Simpson 1979, 477; Coles
      1990, 315–33
70 Rouvier-Jeanlin 1972; Jenkins 1957, 38–46;
      1978, 149–62; Linckenheld 1929, 40–92
71 *Germania* XL
72 Olmsted 1979, inner plate B
73 *Glory of the Confessors* 76, trans. van Dam
      1988
74 Deyts 1976, no. 134
75 Blanchet 1890; Jenkins 1958, 61; Thevenot
      1951, 1ff.; Green 1989, 39; 1991b, 128
76 1942, 170ff.
77 Bailey 1932, 119; Ferguson 1970, 26
78 Musée de Bretagne 1988; Rouvier-Jeanlin
      1972, no. 207; Green 1984, fig. 1b
79 Allason-Jones 1989, 151–2
80 Deyts 1992, 59–72
81 Green 1991c, 100–9

6 Love, Marriage and Partnership among the Goddesses

1 Markale 1975, 36–7
2 O'Fáolain 1954; Cormier 1976–8, 303–15;
      O'Leary 1987, 27–44; Mac Cana 1983,
      94–7
3 Lehmann 1989, 1–10; Green 1992a, 96–7
4 O'Ráolain 1954; Meyer 1893, 241–7; Meyer
      1897a 462–5; 1897b, 458–62; Lloyd,
      Bergin and Schoepperle 1912, 41–57; Mac
      Cana 1983, 109–12; Campbell 1870–2,
      193–202; Green 1992a, 80–1; 98–9, 108

5 O'Fáolain 1954; Müller 1876–8, 342–60; Le Roux 1966, 132–50
6 Nutt 1906, 325–39; Müller 1876–8, 342–60; Bergin and Best 1938, 137–96; Mac Cana 1983, 90–2
7 Thill 1978, no. 11
8 Wuilleumier 1984, no. 403
9 Thevenot 1968, 125
10 Espérandieu nos 5320, 5341, 5342
11 Wightman 1985, 178
12 Green 1989, fig. 21
13 Green 1989, 56–7
14 Davidson 1993a; Webster 1986
15 Green 1989, fig. 22
16 Salviat 1979, 49
17 Bémont 1969, 23–44
18 Cunliffe and Fulford 1982, no. 39
19 Espérandieu no. 4566
20 Green 1989, 42
21 Espérandieu no. 2039
22 Green 1989, 51
23 Espérandieu no. 2347
24 Espérandieu no. 435
25 Espérandieu no. 5752
26 Green 1989, 75–86
27 Espérandieu no. 3384
28 Espérandieu no. 2065
29 Green 1989, 70
30 Espérandieu no. 2334
31 Espérandieu nos. 1829, 1836, 1837
32 Espérandieu no. 7121
33 Musée Archéologique de Dijon 1973, no. 179, pl. XLVI; Espérandieu no. 7637
34 Espérandieu no. 1319
35 Green 1989, 72
36 Espérandieu no. 2043
37 Deyts 1976, no. 4
38 Ibid., no. 3
39 Espérandieu no. 7518
40 Espérandieu no. 1832
41 Polybius II, 28; Rankin 1987, 68; Ritchie and Ritchie 1985, 29
42 Ross 1967, fig. 138
43 Hatt 1964, no. 101
44 Deyts 1976, no. 284
45 Wightman 1970, 208–23; Thevenot 1968, 60–72
46 Dehn 1941, 104ff.
47 Green 1989, 61–3
48 Le Gall 1963, 157–9
49 Duval 1976, 77, 117
50 Thevenot 1968, 104–7

7 Priestess, Prophetess and Witch

1 *De Bello Gallico* VI, 13–14
2 *Annales* XIV, 30
3 Allason-Jones 1989, 148
4 Op. cit. 148
5 *Annales* XIII, 29
6 Rankin 1987, 253
7 *Numerianus* XIV, 2
8 *Aurelianus* XLIII, 4, 5
9 *Alexander Severus* LX, 6
10 O'Fáolain 1954, 127–8; Markale 1975, 242
11 Mac Cana 1976, 95–115
12 *De Chorographia* III, 6
13 Jones and Jones 1976, xxiii
14 Rees and Rees 1961, 186–204; Green 1992a, 163
15 Strabo IV, IV, 6
16 VII, II, 3
17 Condren 1989, 70
18 Markale 1975, 38
19 Allason-Jones 1989, fig. 56
20 Pelletier 1984, pl. 38; Ross 1986, 84, 147, fig. 37
21 Pelletier 1984, pl. 1
22 Espérandieu nos 4343, 1465
23 Pelletier 1984, 97–113
24 Green 1989, 196
25 Espérandieu no. 7774
26 Green 1989, fig. 85
27 Espérandieu no. 6506
28 *R.I.B.* 1129; Allason-Jones 1989, 80
29 Pelletier 1984, 97–113, pl. 3
30 *C.I.L.* XIII, 3183
31 Pelletier 1984, 110
32 *R.I.B.* 1695
33 Rybová and Soudský 1962; Piggott 1965, 234; 1968, 73–4; Green 1992a, 131–2
34 Keys 1992
35 Collis 1984, 175
36 Kaul 1991, 536–7
37 Olmsted 1979, 120–32; Green 1986, 77
38 Mohen 1991, 105–7; Berthelier-Ajot 1991, 116–17
39 Wiseman and Wiseman 1980, 120
40 1984, 13
41 1993b, 16
42 VII, II, 3
43 Potter and Johns 1992, 21
44 III, 6
45 XV, VIII, 22
46 Pelletier 1984, 26–8
47 *Germania* VIII

48 Ehrenberg 1989, 157
49 *De Bello Gallico* I, 50, 4
50 VII, II, 3
51 VI, 13, 14
52 Stokes 1908, 109–52; Meyer 1907, 112ff.;
     O'Rahilly 1946, 61; Kinsella 1969; Olmsted
     1982, 165–72
53 O'Fáolain 1954, 127–8
54 O'Fáolain 1954; Kinsella 1969,; 1970;
     Rankin 1987, 253
55 Kinsella 1970, 60
56 Ibid., 60–3
57 O'Fáolain 1954, 54
58 Merrifield 1987, 159–83; Henig 1984,
     165–6
59 Stokes 1902, 395–437; Markale 1975, 167
60 1975, 167
61 Lehmann 1989, 1–10
62 Jones and Jones 1976, 198–9, 226–7
63 Meid 1992, 40–4
64 Scullard 1981; Macdonald 1977, 35–9
65 Philpott 1991, 77–89
66 Macdonald 1979, 415–24
67 Goodburn 1975, 336; 1978, 438, 444;
     Wilson 1975, 252
68 Merrifield 1987, 159–83; Green 1986,
     130–1; Philpott 1991, 77–89
69 1936, 109–20
70 Merrifield 1987, 46; Young 1972, 10–31
71 Simco 1984, 56–9; Merrifield 1987, 46
72 Jones 1954, 36–7
73 Matthews 1981
74 1991
75 Green 1986, 216–20
76 O'Shea 1981, 39–42
77 Euripides *Iphigenia in Aulis*, lines 88–92
78 *Annales* XIV, 30
79 *Germania* XL
80 IV, IV, 6
81 VI, 19
82 Wightman 1970, 242
83 Megaw 1970; no. 35
84 XXIII, 24
85 Brewster 1976, 115
86 Glob 1969, 70–100; Coles 1989
87 *Germania* XIX
88 *Germania* VII
89 *Germania* XII

8 Mistress of the Beasts

1 Green 1992b, 3
2 Green 1989, fig. 56; Megaw and Megaw
    1989, 33–4
3 *Cynegetica* XXIV; Brunaux 1988, 87–97
4 Green 1992b, 62
5 Megaw 1970, no. 73
6 Stead 1992
7 Taylor 1992
8 Kaul 1991; Olmsted 1979
9 *Germania* 40
10 Green 1992a, 211–12; Foley 1993
11 Boucher 1976, no. 292
12 Green 1992b, 46; Meniel 1987,
     89–100
13 *Cynegetica* XXIII; Brunaux 1988, 95–7
14 Meniel 1987, 101–43
15 Collis 1984, 163–75; Green 1986, 129
16 Boucher 1976, fig. 291
17 Deyts 1992
18 Kinsella 1969; O'Fáolain 1954; Green
     1992a, 96–7
19 Mac Cana 1983, 104–13; Campbell 1870–2,
     193–202
20 Green 1989, 86–96
21 Dehn 1941, 164ff.; Schindler 1977, Abb. 92;
     Green 1989, figs 17, 24
22 Le Gall 1963
23 Green 1992b, 228
24 Espérandieu no. 1573
25 Espérandieu no. 4831; Wightman 1985,
     178; Bober 1951, 13–51
26 Espérandieu no. 4786
27 Tufi 1983, nos 30, 31, pl. 9
28 von Petrikovits 1987, 242–6; Green 1989,
     fig. 66
29 Guthrie 1954, 246
30 Seltman 1952, 62–77
31 Deyts 1985; Green 1992b, fig. 8.10
32 Espérandieu nos 6000, 4568
33 Green 1992b, 212
34 Espérandieu no. 4219
35 Deyts 1976, nos 50–2
36 Deyts 1985
37 Ross 1967, 279–92; Green 1992a, 68
38 *Expugnatio Hibernica* I, 33
39 Ross 1967, 234–96; An Chraoibhin 1932,
     447ff.
40 O'Rahilly 1946, 271, 279
41 Jones and Jones 1976, 71–2
42 Lambert 1979, 141–69; Nutt 1906,
     325–39; Green 1992b, 174
43 Bergin and Best 1938, 137–96
44 Markale 1975, 115
45 Luzel 1985, 84–92
46 Williams 1930, 45
47 Jones and Jones 1976, 115–16
48 Mac Cana 1958, 105–7; 1983, 50–4

49 Wightman 1970, 217, 223; Jenkins 1956,
   192–200
50 Toynbee 1962, pl. 76; Merrifield 1983,
   167–70
51 Jenkins 1957a, 60–76
52 Cormick 1991, 7–9
53 Cunliffe 1983, 155–71
54 Green 1986, 134
55 *Aeneid* Book VI, line 417
56 Green 1993, 73
57 Davidson 1992
58 Wells 1995, 603–20
59 For example Hondius-Crone 1955; van
   Aartsen 1971; Green 1989, 10–16
60 Green 1989, fig. 2; 1992b, fig. 8.3
61 Green 1989, fig. 3
62 Kinsella 1969
63 Hennessy 1870–2, 32–55; Kinsella 1969;
   Olmsted 1982, 165–72; Stokes 1895, 65
64 Ross 1967, 297–353
65 Duval 1961, 197–9; Green 1989, 181–4
66 Green 1986, 191, fig. 85
67 Gwynn 1913, 28ff.; Stokes 1894, 272–336,
   418–84
68 Bray 1987, 209–15
69 Davidson 1993
70 *De Bello Gallico* VI, 22
71 *Natural History* XI, 97, 240
72 *Geography* IV, 5, 2
73 Green 1986, 97; 1989, 57–8; Toynbee
   1964, 157–8, pl. XLB
74 Webster 1986
75 1993
76 Cunliffe and Fulford 1982, no. 115, pl. 31
77 Juvenal *Satires* VIII; Minucius Felix *Octavianus*
   XXVII, 7; Apuleius *Metamorphoses* III, 27
78 Zwicker 1934–6, no. 64
79 1975, 89–90
80 *Topographica Hibernica* III, 25
81 Magnen & Thevenot 1953, nos 2–3; Oaks
   1986, 77–84
82 Espérandieu nos 7513, 1855, 2128
83 Green 1989, figs 8, 9; Espérandieu no. 5863;
   Thill 1978
84 Johns 1971–2, 37–41
85 Espérandieu no. 5445; German Volume
   no. 404
86 Espérandieu nos 4188, 1380
87 Espérandieu nos 5320, 8235
88 Hatt 1945, no. 23
89 Espérandieu no. 4355
90 Green 1989, 18
91 *C.I.L.* XIII, 5622
92 Magnen and Thevenot 1953, no. 117

93 Green 1992b, 66–91
94 *De Bello Gallico* IV, 13, 15
95 Linduff 1979, 817–37; Magnen and
   Thevenot 1953, no. 32

9 From Goddess to Saint

1 Thomas 1981
2 Lane 1993, pers. comm.
3 Davies 1992, 12–21
4 Condren 1989, 47–64
5 Allchin 1993
6 Wogan-Browne 1992, 14–35
7 1975, 118
8 Jones 1954, 21–57
9 Badger 1838, 286–7
10 1983, 58–74
11 Henken 1983, 59–74; 1991, 1–8
12 Henken 1991, 49–64
13 Bartram 1974, 27
14 Henken 1987, 227–32; Spencer 1991, 35
15 Wales Tourist Board 1993; Edwards and
   Lane 1992, 7–9; Henken 1987, 141–51
16 Edwards and Lane 1992, 7–9
17 Spencer 1991, 17–20
18 Jones 1954, 21–57
19 McCone 1990, 149–51
20 Morris 1989, 47–92; Henken 1987, 161–7
21 Ross 1974, 455–70
22 Davidson 1993b, 46
23 Rankin 1987, 269–70; Davidson 1993b,
   112–13; Bowen 1973–4, 33–47; Bray
   1987, 209–15; 1991, 105–15; McCone
   1990, 161–6; Green 1992a, 50–1; Condren
   1989, 47–64
24 O Cathasáigh 1982, 82ff.; Thomas 1993,
   pers. comm., O'Brien 1992, 130–7;
   Bowen 1973–4, map 1, 33–47; 1977,
   113–14
25 McCone 1990, 182–4; Davidson 1993a
26 Rankin 1987, 255–8
27 Bray 1991, 105–15; Condren 1989, 65–79
28 Bray 1987, 209–15; McCone 1990, 185–6
29 Condren 1989, 65–79
30 Condren 1989, 65–79; Bray 1987, 209–15;
   Davidson 1993b, 112–13; McCone 1990,
   161–6
31 Bray 1987, 209–15
32 Condren 1989, 65–79
33 Green 1992a, 212–14

Epilogue

1 Bath Curse Tablet no. 45: Tomlin 1988, 166

Bibliography

ABBAYE DE DAOULAIS 1986. *Au temps des Celtes, Ve – 1er siècle avant JC*, Musée Departemental Breton de Quimper

AEBISCHER, P. 1930. 'La divinité aquatique Telo et l'hydronomie de la Gaule', *Revue Celtique* 47, 427–41

ALLASON-JONES, L. 1989. *Women in Roman Britain* (British Museum Press, London)

ALLASON-JONES, L. and McKAY, B. 1985. *Coventina's Well* (Trustees of the Clayton Collection, Chester Museum)

ALLCHIN, A.M. 1991. *Praise above All: Discovering the Welsh Tradition* (University of Wales Press, Cardiff)

ALLCHIN, A.M. 1993. 'Places and Poems in Medieval Wales' (Lecture given at Saint Deiniol's Celtic Heritage Summer School, 20 June, 1993)

ANON. undated. *Musée Archéologigue Dijon: Guide* (Dijon)

AN CHRAOIBHIN 1932. 'Cailleach an Teampuill', *Béaloideas* 3, 447ff.

ATKINSON, D. 1916. *The Romano-British Site on Lowbury Hill in Berkshire* (University of Reading)

BADGER, G.P. 1838. *Description of Malta and Gozo* (London)

BARBER, J. and WELSH, G.M. 1992. 'The potential and the reality: the contribution of archaeology to the Green debate', in Macinnes, L. and Wickham-Jones, C.R. (eds), *All Natural Things: Archaeology and the Green Debate* (Oxbow Monograph No. 21, Oxford), 41–51

BARTRAM, P.C. 1974. *Welsh Genealogies: AD 300–1400* Vol. 1 (University of Wales Press, Cardiff)

BEMONT, C. 1968–71. 'Un nouveau monument de Rosmerta', *Etudes Celtiques* 12, 96–100

BEMONT, C. 1969. 'A propos d'un nouveau monument de Rosmerta', *Gallia* 27, 23–44

BERGIN, O. and BEST, R.I. 1938. 'Tochmarc Etáine', *Eriu* 12, 137–96

BERTHELIER-AJOT, N. 1991. 'The Vix settlement and the tomb of the princess', in Kruta, V. *et al.* (eds.), *The Celts* (Thames & Hudson, London), 116–17

BHREATHNACH, M. 1982. 'The Sovereignty Goddess as Goddess of Death?', *Zeitschrift für celtische Philologie* 39, 243–60

BINCHY, D.A. (ed.) 1936. *Studies in Early Irish Law* (Binehy, Dublin)

BINCHY, D.A. 1970. *Celtic and Anglo-Saxon Kingship*. The O'Donnell Lecture 1967–8 (Clarendon Press, Oxford)

BOWEN, E.G. 1973–4. 'The Cult of St Brigit', *Studia Celtica* 8–9, 33–47

BOWEN, E.G. 1977. *Saints, Seaways and Settlements in the Celtic Lands* (University of Wales Press)

BRAY, D.A. 1987. 'The image of Saint Brigit in the early Irish Church', *Etudes Celtiques* 24, 209–15

BREWSTER, T.C.M. 1976. 'Garton Slack', *Current Archaeology* 5, No. 51, 104–16

BRUNAUX, J-L. 1988. *The Celtic Gauls: Gods, Rites and Sanctuaries*, trans. D. Nash (Seaby, London)

CALDECOTT, M. 1988. *Women in Celtic Myth* (Arrow/Hutchinson, London)

CAMPBELL, J.F. 1870–1. 'Fionn's Enchantment', *Revue Celtique* 1, 193–202

CAREY, J. 1991. 'A British Myth of Origins?',*History of Religions* (University of Chicago), 24–38

C.I.L. see Abbrevations p. 205

CLARK, R. 1991. *The Great Queens: Irish Goddesses from the Morrigán to Cathleen Ní Houlihan* (Irish Literary Studies No. 34, Colin Smythe, Gerrards Cross)

CLEBERT, J-P. 1970. *Provence Antique 2: L'époque gallo-romaine* (Laffont, Paris)

COLES, B. 1990. 'Anthropomorphic wooden figurines from Britain and Ireland', *Proceedings of the Prehistoric Society* 56, 315–30

COLES, B. and COLES, J. 1989. *People of the Wetlands: Bogs, Bodies and Lake-Dwellers* (Thames & Hudson, London)

COLIN, J. 1927. *Les Antiquités romaines et germains rhénanie* (Société d'Edition 'Les Belles Lettres', Paris)

COLLIS, J. 1984. *The European Iron Age* (Batsford, London)

CONDREN, M. 1989. *The Serpent and the Goddess: Women, Religion and Power in Celtic Ireland* (Harper & Row, San Francisco)

CORMICK, F. M. C. 1991. 'The Dog in prehistoric and early Christian Ireland', *Archaeology Ireland* 5, No. 4, 7–9

CORMIER, R. 1976–8. 'Remarks on the Tale of Deirdriu and Noisu and the Tristan Legend', *Etudes Celtiques* 15, 303–15

CROSS, T. P. and SLOVER, C.H. 1936. *Ancient Irish Tales* (Barnes & Noble, New York)

CUNLIFFE, B. W. 1969. *Roman Bath* (Society of Antiquaries of London)

CUNLIFFE, B. W. 1978. *The Roman Baths: A Guide to the Baths and Roman Museum* (Bath Archaeological Trust)

CUNLIFFE, B. W. (ed.) 1988. *The Temple of Sulis Minerva at Bath. Vol. 2. The Finds from the Sacred Spring* (Oxford University Committee for Archaeology Monograph No. 16)

CUNLIFFE, B. W. 1994. 'The sacred spring of Sulis Minerva' (Lecture given at the University of Bristol, February 1994)

CUNLIFFE, B. W. and DAVENPORT, P. 1985. *The Temple of Sulis Minerva at Bath. Vol. 1: The Site* (Oxford University Committee for Archaeology Monograph No. 7)

CUNLIFFE, B. W. and FULFORD, M. G. 1982. *Corpus Signorum Imperii Romani. Great Britain Vol. 1, Fasc. 2: Bath and the Rest of Wessex* (British Academy, London/Oxford University Press)

DAM, R. van (trans.) 1988. *Gregory of Tours: 'Glory of the Confessors'* (Liverpool University Press)

DANAHER, K. 1972. *The Year in Ireland: Irish Calendar Customs* (Dublin)

DAVIDSON, H. E. 1992. Review of M.J. Green, *Dictionary of Celtic Myth and Legend*, in *Shadow* 9, 1992, 93

DAVIDSON, H. E. 1993a. 'Milk and the Northern Goddess' (Lecture given at a conference organised by the Katharine Briggs Club entitled *The Concept of the Goddess*, Glasgow University, July 1993)

DAVIDSON, H. E. 1993b. *The Lost Beliefs of Northern Europe* (Routledge, London)

DAVIES, S. 1993. *The Four Branches of the Mabinogi* (Gomer Press, Llandysul)

DAVIES, W. 1983. 'Celtic Women in the Early Middle Ages', in Cameron, A. and Kuhrt, A. (eds.), *Images of Women in Antiquity* (Croom Helm, London), 145–66

DAVIES, W. 1992. 'The Myth of the Celtic Church', in Edwards, N. and Lane, A (eds.), *The Early Church in Wales and the West* (Oxbow Monograph 16), 12–21

DEHN, W. 1941. 'Ein Quelheiligtum des Apollo und der Sirona bei Hochscheid', *Germania* 25, 104ff.

DENT, J. 1985. 'Three Cart Burials from Wetwang, Yorkshire', *Antiquity* 59, 85–92

DEYTS, S. 1976. *Sculptures gallo-romaines mythologigues et religieuses: Dijon – Musée Archéologique* (Editions des Musées Nationaux, Paris)

DEYTS, S. 1983. *Les Bois Sculptés des Sources de la Seine* (XlII Supplément à Gallia, Paris)

DEYTS, S. 1985. *Le Sanctuaire des Sources de la Seine* (Musée Archéologique Dijon)

DEYTS, S. 1992. *Images des Dieux de la Gaule* (Editions Errance, Paris)

DILLON, M. 1953. *Serglige Con Culainn* (Dublin)

DOAN, J.E. 1983. 'A structural approach to Celtic Saints' Lives', in Ford, P.K. (ed.), *Celtic Folklore and Christianity* (University of California, Los Angeles), 16–28

DOBLE, G.H. 1971. *Lives of the Welsh Saints* (University of Wales Press)

DONLEY, B. 1987. *Arianrhod: A Welsh Myth Retold* (Stone Circle Press, Oakland, California)

DUVAL, P-M. 1976. *Les Dieux de la Gaule* (Paris)

EDWARDS, N. and LANE, A. 1992. 'The Archaeology of the Early Church in Wales: an Introduction', in Edwards, N. and Lane, A. (eds.), *The Early Church in Wales and the West* (Oxbow Monograph No.16), 1–12

EHRENBERG, M. 1989. *Women in Prehistory* (British Museum Press, London)

ESPERANDIEU, E. 1907–66. *Recueil Général des Bas-Reliefs de la Gaule Romaine et Pré-Romaine* (Leroux, Paris)

EVANS, J.W. 1986. 'The Early Church in Denbighshire', *Transactions of the Denbighshire Historical Society* 35, 61–81

FOLEY, L-A. 1983. *Ceremonial, prestige and religious regalia in Iron Age and Roman Britain* (unpublished M.Litt. dissertation, University of Oxford, 1993)

FRADENBURG, L.O. 1992. 'Introduction: Re-Thinking Queenship', in Fradenburg, L.O. (ed.) *Women and Sovereignty* (Cosmos: Yearbook of the Traditional Cosmology Society 7, Edinburgh University Press), 1–13

GAGER, J.G. (ed.) 1992. *Curse Tablets and Binding Spells from the Ancient World* (Oxford University Press)

GLOB, P.V. 1969. *The Bog People* (Faber & Faber, London)

GOODBURN, R. 1976. 'Roman Britain in 1975', *Britannia* 7, 291–377

GOODBURN, R. 1978. 'Roman Britain in 1977', *Britannia* 9, 404–72

GOODCHILD, R.G. 1938. 'A priest's sceptre from the Romano-Celtic temple at Farley Heath, Surrey', *Antiquaries Journal* 18, 391ff.

GREEN, M.J. 1976. *A Corpus of Religious Material from the Civilian Areas of Roman Britain* (British Archaeological Reports, Oxford, (BS) No. 24)

GREEN, M.J. 1978. *Small Cult-Objects from Military Areas of Roman Britain* (British Archaeological Reports, Oxford, (BS) No. 52)

GREEN, M.J. 1989. *Symbol and Image in Celtic Religious Art* (Routledge, London)

GREEN, M.J. 1991a. *Women and Goddesses in the Celtic World* (British Association for the Study of Religions Occasional Paper No. 1)

GREEN, M.J. 1991b. *The Sun-Gods of Ancient Europe* (Batsford, London)

GREEN, M.J. 1991c. 'Triplism and Plurality: Intensity and Symbolism in Celtic Religious Expression', in Jennings, D., Skeates, R. and Thoms, J. (eds.), *Sacred and Profane* (Oxford University Committee for Archaeology Monograph No. 32), 100–9

GREEN, M.J. 1992a. *Dictionary of Celtic Myth and Legend* (Thames & Hudson, London)

GREEN, M.J. 1992b. *Animals in Celtic Life and Myth* (Routledge, London)

GREEN, M.J. 1992c. 'The Pipeclay figurines', in Taylor, A. *A Roman Lead Coffin with pipeclay figurines from Arrington* (Cambridgeshire County Council)

GREEN, M.J. 1992d. 'The Iconography of Celtic Coins', in Mays, M. (ed.) *Celtic Coinage: Britain and Beyond* (11th Oxford Symposium on Coinage and monetary History: British Archaeological Reports, Oxford (BS) No. 222, 151–63

GREEN, M.J. 1993. *Celtic Myths* (British Museum Press, London)

GREEN, M.J. 1995. 'The Horse in Celtic Religion', in Davies, S. and Hughes, N. (eds), *The Celtic Horse* (University of Wales Press, Cardiff, in press)

GRUFFYDD, W. J. 1912. 'Mabon ab Modron', *Revue Celtique* 33, 452–61

GRUFFYDD, W. J. 1953. *Rhiannon: An Enquiry into the Origins of the First and Third Branches of the Mabinogi* (University of Wales Press, Cardiff)

GUTHRIE, W. K. C. 1954. *The Greeks and their Gods* (Methuen, London)

GWYNN, E. 1913. *The Metrical Dindshenchas* (Dublin)

HATT, J. J. 1945. *Les Monuments Funéraires Gallo-Romains du Comminges et du Couserans* (Annales du Midi, Toulouse)

HATT, J. J. 1964. *Sculptures antiques Régionales Strasbourg* (Musée Archéologique de Strasbourg/Paris)

HATT, J. J. 1989. *Mythes et Dieux de la Gaule* (Picard, Paris)

HENIG, M. 1984. *Religion in Roman Britain* (Batsford, London)

HENIG, M. 1988. 'The Small Objects', in Cunliffe. 1988 (ed.), 5–56

HENKEN, E. R. 1983. 'The Saint as Folk Hero: Biographical Patterning in Welsh Hagiography', in Ford, P. K. (ed.), *Celtic Folklore and Christianity* (University of California, Los Angeles), 58–74

HENKEN, E. R. 1987. *Traditions of the Welsh Saints* (Boydell & Brewer, Cambridge)

HENKEN, E. R. 1991. *The Welsh Saints. A Study in Patterned Lives* (D.S. Brewer, Cambridge)

HENNESSEY, W. M. 1970–72. 'The ancient Irish Goddess of War', *Revue Celtique* 1, 32–55

HENRY, P.L. 1979–80. 'The Caldron of Poesy', *Studia Celtica* 14/15, 114–28

HERBERT, M. 1992. 'Goddess and King: The Sacred Marriage in Early Ireland', in Fradenburg (ed.), 264–75

HERBERT, M. 1993. 'Representations of the Goddess in Early Irish Literature' (Lecture given at a conference organised by the Katharine Briggs Club, entitled *The Concept of the Goddess*, Glasgow University, July 1993)

HULL, E. 1905. *Early Christian Ireland* (Gill, Dublin)

HULL, V. 1938. 'Aided Meidbe: the Violent Death of Medb', *Speculum* 13, 52–61

JACKSON, K. H. 1961–7. 'Some popular motifs in early Welsh tradition', *Etudes Celtiques* 11, 83–99

JENKINS, F. 1956. 'Nameless or Nehalennia', *Archaeologia Cantiana* 70, 192–200

JENKINS, F. 1957a. 'The role of the dog in Romano-Gaulish religion', *Collection Latomus* 16, 60–76

JENKINS, F. 1957b 'The Cult of the Dea Nutrix in Kent', *Archaeologia Cantiana* 71, 38–46

JENKINS, F. 1958. 'The Cult of the 'Pseudo-Venus' in Kent', *Archaeologia Cantiana* 72, 60–76

JENKINS, F. 1978. 'Some interesting types of clay statuettes of the Roman period found in London', in Bird, J. *et al.* (eds), *Collectanea Londinensia* (London and Middlesex Archaeological Society), 149–62

JOFFROY, R. 1979. *Musée des Antiquités Saint-Germain-en-Laye: Guide* (Paris)

JOHNS, C. M. 1971–72. 'A Roman bronze statuette of Epona', *British Museum Quarterly* 36 (1–2), 37–41

JONES, F. 1954. *The Holy Wells of Wales* (University of Wales Press, Cardiff)

JONES, G. and Jones, T. (trans.) 1976. *The Mabinogion* (Dent, London)

KAUL, F. 1991. 'The Dejbjerg Carts', in Kruta, V. *et al.* (eds), *The Celts* (Thames & Hudson, London), 536–7

KEANEY, R. M. 1993. *Celtic women in the Roman World* (unpublished M. A. thesis, HISAR, University of Wales College of Cardiff)

KELLY, P. 1992. 'The *Táin* as Literature', in Mallory, J. P. (ed.), *Aspects of the Táin* (Universities Press, Belfast), 69–102

KEYS, D. 1992 pers. comm. from the Archaeological Correspondent for *The Independent*, October 9, 1992

KILLEEN, J.F. 1974. 'The debility of the Ulstermen – a suggestion', *Zeitschrift für celtische Philologie* 33, 81–6

KINSELLA, T. 1969. *The Táin* (Dolmen, Dublin)

KINSELLA, T. 1970. *The Táin* (Dolmen, Dublin)

KNOTT, E. 1936. *Togail Bruidne Da Derga* (Dublin)

KRAEMER, R.S. 1992. *Her Share of the Blessings* (Oxford)

LANE, A. 1993. pers. comm. November 11, 1993

LE GALL, J. 1963. *Alésia* (Fayard, Paris)

LEHMANN, R.P.M. 1989. 'Death and Vengeance in the Ulster Cycle', *Zeitschrift für celtische Philologie* 43, 1–10

LEHNER, H. 1918–21. 'Der Tempelbezirk der Matronae Vacallinehae bei Pesch', *Bonner Jahrbücher* 125–6, 74ff.

LE ROUX, F. 1966. 'La Rêve d'Oenghus', *Ogam* 18, 132–50

LETHBRIDGE, T.C. 1936. 'Further Excavations in the Early Iron Age and Romano-British Cemetery at Guilden Morden', *Cambridge Antiquarian Communications* 36, 109–20

LINCKENHELD, E. 1929, 'Sucellus et Nantosuelta', *Revue de l'histoire des religions* 99, 40–92

LINDUFF, K. 1979. 'Epona: a Celt among the Romans', *Collection Latomus* 38, fasc. 4, 817–37

LLOYD, J.H., Bergin, O.J. and SCHOEPPERLE, G. 1912, 'The Reproach of Diarmaid', *Revue Celtique* 33, 41–57

LUZEL, F.M. 1985. *Celtic Folk-Tales from Armorica*, trans. by D. Bryce (Llannerch Enterprises, Lampeter)

LYLE, E. 1992. 'A line of queens as the pivot of a cosmology', in Fradenburg (ed.), 276–88

MAC CANA, P. 1955–6. 'Aspects of the theme of King and Goddess', *Etudes Celtiques* 7, 76–114, 356–413

MAC CANA, P. 1958–9. 'Aspects of the Theme of King and Goddess', *Etudes Celtiques* 8, 59–65

MAC CANA, P. 1958. *Branwen, Daughter of Llyr: A study of the Irish affinities and of the composition of the Second Branch of the Mabinogi* (University of Wales Press, Cardiff)

MAC CANA, P. 1972. 'Mongán mac Fiachna and "Immram Brain"', *Eriu* 23, 102–42

MAC CANA, P. 1976. 'The sinless Otherworld of Immram Brain', *Eriu* 27, 95–115

MAC CANA, P. 1981. 'Mythology in Early Irish Literature', in O'Driscoll (ed.), *The Celtic Consciousness* (Canongate, Edinburgh/Dolman Press, London), 143–55

MAC CANA, P. 1983. *Celtic Mythology* (Newnes, London)

MACALISTER, R.A.S. 1949. *The Archaeology of Ireland* (Methuen, London)

MACDONALD, J. 1977. 'Pagan religions and burial practices in Roman Britain', in Reece, R. (ed.), *Burial in the Roman World* (CBA Research Report No. 22, London), 35–9

MARACHE, R. 1979. *Les Romains en Bretagne* (Ouest France)

MARKALE, J. 1975. *Women of the Celts* (Cremonesi, London)

MARKUS, G. 1992. 'Celtic Feminism', *New Blackfriars* 73, No. 862, 375–88

MATTHEWS, C.L. 1981. 'A Romano-British Inhumation Cemetery at Dunstable', *Bedfordshire Archaeology Journal* 15, *passim*

MATTHEWS, C. 1987. *Mabon and the Mysteries of Britain: An Exploration of the Mabinogion* (Arkana, London/New York)

MEGAW, R. and MEGAW, V. 1989. *Celtic Art from its beginnings to the book of Kells* (Thames & Hudson, London)

MEID, W. 1992. *Gaulish Inscriptions* (Archaeolingua Alapítvány, Budapest)

MENIEL, P. 1987. *Chasse et elèvage chez les Gaulois (450–2 av. J.C.)* (Errance, Paris)

MERRIFIELD, R. 1987. *The Archaeology of Religion and Magic* (Batsford, London)

MEYER, K. 1893. 'Two tales about Finn', *Revue Celtique* 14, 241–7

MEYER, K. 1897a. 'The death of Finn MacCumall', *Zeitschrift für celtische Philologie* 1, 462–5

MEYER, K. 1897b. 'Finn and Gráinne', *Zeitschrift für celtische Philologie* 1, 458–62

MEYER, K. 1907. 'The death of Conla', *Eriu* 1, 112ff.

MOHEN, J-P. 1991. 'The Princely tombs of Burgundy', in Kruta, V. *et al.* (eds.), *The Celts* (Thames & Hudson, London), 102–7

MORRIS, R. 1989. *Churches in the Landscape* (Dent, London)

MULLER, E. 1876–8. 'Two Irish Tales', *Revue Celtique* 3, 342–60

MURPHY, G. 1953. 'The Lament of the Old Woman of Beare', *Proceedings of the Royal Irish Academy* 55, 84

MUSEE ARCHEOLOGIQUE DE METZ. 1981. *La civilisation gallo-romaine dans la cité des Médiomatriques* (Musée Archéologiqe, Metz)

MUSEE ARCHEOLOGIQUE DE SAINTES. 1984. *Saintes à la recherche de ses dieux* (Société Archéologique et d'histoire de la Charente-Maritime)

MCCONE, K. 1982. 'Brigid in the seventh century – a saint with three lives', *Perítía* 1, 107–45

MCCONE, K. 1990. *Pagan Past and Christian Present in Early Irish literature* (An Sagart, Maynooth)

NUTT, A. 1906. 'Tochmarc Etaine', *Revue Celtique* 27, 325–39

OAKS, L. S. 1986. 'The goddess Epona: concepts of sovereignty in a changing landscape', in Henig, M. and King, A. (eds), *Pagan Gods and Shrines of the Roman Empire* (Oxford University Committee for Archaeology Monograph No. 8), 77–84

O'BRIEN, E. 1992. 'Pagan and Christian Burial in Ireland during the first millennium AD: Continuity and Change', in Edwards, N. and Lane, A. (eds), 130–7

O'CATHASAIGH, D. 1982. 'The Cult of Brigid: a Study of Pagan-Christian Syncretism in Ireland', in Preston, J. J. (ed.), *Mother Worship: Theme and Variations* (Chapel Hill), 75–94

O'CRUALAOICH, G. 1988. 'Continuity and Adaptation in Legends of Cailleach Bhearra', *Béaloideas* 56, 153–78

O'FAOLAIN, E. 1954. *Irish Sagas and Folk-Tales* (Oxford University Press)

O'HAOCHA, D. 1989. 'The Lament of the Old Woman of Beare', in O'Corrain, D., Breatnach, L. and McCone, K. (eds) *Sages, Saints and Storytellers: Celtic Studies in honour of Professor James Carney* (An Sagart, Maynooth), 308–31

O'LEARY, P. 1987. 'The honour of women in early Irish literature', *Eriu* 38, 27–44

OLMSTED, G. S. 1982. 'Morrigan's warning to Donn Cuailnge', *Etudes Celtiques* 19, 165–72

O'RAHILLY, T. F. 1946. *Early Irish History and Mythology* (Dublin)

O'RIAIN, P. 1978. 'Traces of Lug in early Irish hagiographical tradition', *Zeitschrift für celtische Philologie* 36, 138–55

O'SHEA, J. 1981. 'Social configurations and the archaeological study of mortuary practices', in Chapman, R., Kinnes, I. and Randsborg, K. (eds) *The Archaeology of Death* (Cambridge University Press), 39–52

PELLETIER, A. 1974. *Vienne gallo-romaine au Bas-Empire 275–468 av. J-C* (Lyon)

PELLETIER, A. 1984. *La Femme dans la société gallo-romaine* (Picard, Paris)

PETRIKOVITS, H. von. 1987. 'Matronen und Verwandte Gottheiten', *Ergebnisse eines Kolloquiums veranstaltet von der Göttinger Akademiekommission für die Altertumskunde Mittel – und Nordeuropas* (Köln/Bonn, Beihafte der Bonner Jahrbücher, Band 44), 241–54

PHILPOTT, R. 1991. *Burial Practices in Roman Britain: a survey of grave treatment and furnishing AD 43–410* (British Archaeological Reports (BS), No. 219

POKORNY, J. 1925. 'Der Namen Eriu', *Zeitschrift für celtische Philologie* 15, 197–202

POTTER, T. W. and JOHNS, C. 1992. *Roman Britain* (British Museum Press)

RANKIN, H. D. 1987. *Celts and the Classical World* (Croom Helm, London/Sydney)

RAUDVERE, C. 1993, 'Goddess or Female Demon', Lecture given at a conference organised by the Katharine Briggs Club entitled *The Concept of the Goddess* (Glasgow University, July, 1993)

RHEINISCHES LANDESMUSEUM BONN. 1973. *Wir Entdecken die Römer* (Bonn)

R.I.B. see Abbreviations on p. 205

RISTOW, G. 1975. *Religionen und ihre Denkmäler in Köln* (Römisch-Germanisches Museum der Stadt Köln)

RITCHIE, W. F. and RITCHIE, J.N. G. 1985. *Celtic Warriors* (Shire Archaeology, Princes Risborough, No. 41)

ROLLESTON, T. W. 1985. *Myths and Legends of the Celtic Race* (Constable, London)

ROSS, A. 1967. *Pagan Celtic Britain* (Routledge, London)

ROSS, A. 1974. *Pagan Celtic Britain* (Cardinal, London)

ROUVIER-JEANLIN, M. 1972. *Les figurines gallo-romaines en terre cuite au Musée des Antiquités Nationales* (XXIVe supplément à *Gallia*, Paris)

RUTHERFORD, W. 1987. *Celtic Mythology* (Aquarian Press)

SHARPE, R. 1982. 'Vitae S. Brigitae; the oldest texts', *Perítia* 1, 81–106

SCHINDLER, R. 1977. *Führer durch des Landesmuseum Trier* (Trier, Rheinisches Landesmuseums)

SCULLARD, H. H. 1981. *Festivals and Ceremonies of the Roman Republic* (Thames & Hudson, London)

SELTMAN, C. 1952. *The Twelve Olympians* (Pan, London)

SIMCO, A. 1984. 'The Roman Period', in Bedfordshire County Council *Survey of Bedfordshire*

SIMS-WILLIAMS, P. 1990. 'Some Celtic Otherworld terms', in Matonis, A.T. E. and Melia, D. F. (eds.), *Celtic Language, Celtic Culture. A Festschift for Eric P. Hamp* (van Nuys, CA), 57–81

SJOESTEDT, M-L. 1949. *Dieux et héros des Celtes* (Paris)

SPENCER, R. 1991. *A Guide to the Saints of Wales and the West Country* (Llannerch Enterprises, Lampeter)

STEAD, I. M., BOURKE, J. B. and BROTHWELL, D. 1986. *Lindow Man: The Body in the Bog* (British Museum Press, London)

STEAD, I. M. 1991, 'The Snettisham Treasure: excavations in 1990', *Antiquity* 65, No. 248, 447–64

STEVENS, C. E. 1966. 'The Social and Economic aspects of rural settlement', in Thomas, C. *Rural Settlement in Roman Britain* (CBA Research Report No. 7), 108ff.

STEWART, R. J. 1990. *Celtic Gods Celtic Goddesses* (Blandford, London)

STOKES, W. 1894. 'The prose tales in the Rennes *Dindshenchas*', *Revue Celtique* 15, 272–336, 418–84

STOKES, W. 1895. 'The Rennes *Dindshenchas*', *Revue Celtique* 16, 31–83, 274

STOKES, W. 1900. 'Bruiden Da Choca', *Revue Celtique* 21, 149–65

STOKES, W. 1901. 'The Destruction of Dá Derga's Hostel', *Revue Celtique* 22, 9, 165, 282, 390

STOKES, W. 1902. 'The Death of Muirchetach mac Erca', *Revue Celtique* 23, 395–437

STOKES, W. 1908. 'The training of Cúchulainn', *Revue Celtique* 29, 109–52

SZABO, M. 1971. *The Celtic Heritage in Hungary* (Corvina, Budapest)

TAYLOR, A. 1992. *A Roman Lead Coffin with Pipeclay figurines from Arrington* (Cambridgeshire County Council)

TAYLOR, A. 1993. 'A Roman lead coffin with pipeclay figurines from Arrington, Cambridgeshire', *Britannia* 24, 194–201

TAYLOR, T. 1992. 'The Eastern Origins of the Gundestrup Cauldron', *Scientific American* No. 266 (3), March 1992, 66–71

THEVENOT, E. 1968. *Divinités et sanctuaires de la Gaule* (Fayard, Paris)

THOMAS, C. 1981. *Christianity in Roman Britain to AD 500* (Batsford, London)

THOMAS, C. 1993. pers. comm. 29 January 1993

TOMLIN, R. S. O. 1988. 'The Curse Tablets', in Cunliffe, B. W. (ed.), 1988, 58–277

TOUSSAINT, M. 1948. *Metz à l'époque gallo-romaine* (Imprimerie Paul Even, Metz)

TUFI, S. R. 1983. *Corpus Signorum Imperii Romani: Great Britain. Vol. 1, Fasc. 3: Yorkshire* (British Academy, London/Oxford University Press)

VALLENTIN, F. 1879–80. 'Les dieux de la cité des Allobroges, d'après les monuments épigraphiques' *Revue Celtique* 4, 1–36

VENDRYES, J. 1924. 'Imbolc', *Revue Celtique* 41, 241–4

VESLY, L. de. 1909. *Les fana ou petits temples gallo-romains de la région Normande* (Rouen)

VRIES, J. de. 1963. *La religion des Celtes* (Payot, Paris)

WAGNER, H. 1981. 'Origins of Pagan Irish Religion', *Zeitschrift für celtische Philologie* 38, 1–28

WALKER, D. R. 1988. 'The Roman Coins', in Cunliffe, B. W. (ed.), 1988, 281–358

WATSON, A. 1981. 'The King, the Poet and the Sacred Tree', *Etudes Celtiques* 18, 165–180

WEBSTER, G. 1978. *Boudica* (Batsford, London)

WEBSTER, G. 1986. *The British Celts and their Gods under Rome* (Batsford, London)

WELLS, C. 1995. 'Celts and Germans in the Rhineland', in Green, M. J. (ed.), *The Celtic World* (Routledge, 1995); 603–20

WIGHTMAN, E. M. 1970. *Roman Trier and the Treveri* (Hart-Davis, London)

WIGHTMAN, E. M. 1985. *Gallia Belgica* (Batsford, London)

WILSON, D. R. 1975. 'Roman Britain in 1974', *Britannia* 6, 220–83

WISEMAN, A. and WISEMAN, T. P. 1980. *The Battle for Gaul* (Chatto & Windus, London)

WOGAN-BROWNE, J. 1992. 'Queens, Virgins and Mothers: Hagiographic Representations of the Abbess and her Powers in Twelfth and Thirteenth Century Britain', in Fradenburg, L. O. (ed.), 1992, 14–35

WOOD, J. 1992. 'Celtic Goddesses: Myth and Mythology', in Larrington, C. (ed.), *The Feminist Companion to Mythology* (Pandora Press/Harper Collins, London) 118–36

YOUNG, C. J. 1972. 'Excavations at the Churchill hospital 1971: Interim Report', *Oxoniensia* 37, 1972, 10–31

ZWICKER, J. 1934–6. *Fontes Historiae Religionis Celticae* (Walter de Gruyter, Berlin)

Index